KILLING THE
COMPETITION

KILLING THE COMPETITION

ECONOMIC INEQUALITY AND HOMICIDE

MARTIN DALY

Transaction Publishers
New Brunswick (U.S.A.) and London (U.K.)

Library of Congress Catalog Number: 2016017681
ISBN: 978-1-4128-6325-4 (hardcover); 978-1-4128-6336-0 (paper)
eBook: 978-1-4128-6357-5
Printed in the United States of America

Library of Congress Cataloging-in-Publication Data

Names: Daly, Martin, 1944- author.
Title: Killing the competition : economic inequality and homicide / Martin Daly.
Description: New Brunswick : Transaction Publishers, [2016] | Includes bibliographical references and index.
Identifiers: LCCN 2016017681 (print) | LCCN 2016022608 (ebook) | ISBN 9781412863254 (hardcover) | ISBN 9781412863360 (pbk.) | ISBN 9781412863575 (eBook)
Subjects: LCSH: Homicide--Economic aspects. | Income distribution--Social aspects. | Crime--Sociological aspects.
Classification: LCC HV6515 .D353 2016 (print) | LCC HV6515 (ebook) | DDC 364.2/5--dc23
LC record available at https://lccn.loc.gov/2016017681

Contents

Preface

Income inequality is a correlate of homicidal violence, and I believe that the evidence strongly favors the hypothesis that the relationship is causal. Not everyone agrees with me on this point, however, and my primary agenda in this book is to refute the counterarguments. I think we have sufficient evidence that the inequality of wealth and income that now prevails in the developed world has toxic effects, including effects on violence, to justify political action to reduce it.

I have been studying homicide for more than thirty-five years, but I began my research career in animal behavior, and the Darwinian world view that I acquired studying other species continues to inform my understanding of all living things, including human beings. Any evolutionist would anticipate that whenever desired goods are distributed relatively inequitably, dangerous competition and violence will be relatively prevalent. Analysts whose thinking is not informed by Darwinism, however, often miss this point and misinterpret self-interested aggression as pathology. Two secondary aims of this book are thus to introduce an evolution-minded perspective into discussions of human violence, and to counter the simplistic notion that because violence is distasteful, it must be pathological.

Many people have contributed to the writing of this book, above all my late wife Margo Wilson, who decided in 1978 that we should study homicide; all my research on the subject was done in collaboration with her until her death in 2009. Margo and I probably would have abandoned homicide research were it not for substantial early support from the Harry Frank Guggenheim Foundation and its high-spirited research directors Lionel Tiger and Robin Fox. Subsequently, our research was supported for many years by the Natural Sciences & Engineering Research Council of Canada and by the Social Sciences & Humanities Research Council of Canada.

Despite our strange backgrounds in animal behavior, many sociologically trained homicide researchers welcomed us into their community, especially Becky and Dick Block, and Russell and Rebecca Dobash. My education in economics began when Rob Boyd and Herb Gintis invited Margo and me to join the Preferences Network, sponsored by the John D. and Catherine T. MacArthur Foundation, at whose meetings we learned a great deal about how economists approach risk and sex differences, especially from Catherine Eckel, and a great deal about economic inequality, especially from Sam Bowles.

This book was written mainly during a three-year stint in 2012–15 as a Research Professor of Anthropology at the University of Missouri, Columbia, which was made possible primarily by Mark Flinn and Brian Foster. My education in anthropology began when Margo and I spent a sabbatical year at Harvard University in 1985–86 under Irven DeVore's generous sponsorship, and was furthered during another sabbatical year at the University of New Mexico in 1994–95, where Jane Lancaster was an equally generous host. My primary academic affiliation is still in psychology, and I am now back in the Department of Psychology, Neuroscience & Behaviour at McMaster University, which has been my main home since 1978, and which is far and away the most collegial university department that I have ever seen.

Four people deserve special thanks for providing a steady stream of useful links and references, encouragement and critical discussion, while I was writing this book. They are Danny Krupp, Karthik Panchanathan, Gretchen Perry, and Adam Sparks. I have also benefited from collegial input from Pat Barclay, Sam Bowles, Napoleon Chagnon, Dov Cohen, Helena Cronin, Maurice Cusson, Angus Deaton, Robin Dunbar, John Fox, Willem Frankenhuis, Daniel Hicks, Joan Hamory Hicks, Sarah Hrdy, Arjun Jayadev, Ichiro Kawachi, Bruce Kennedy, Rob Lynch, Michelle Mahnke, Sandeep Mishra, Paulo Nadanovsky, Richard Nisbett, Michael Norton, Marc Ouimet, Josephine Pemberton, Kate Pickett, Steven Pinker, Aubrey Sheiham, Mary Shenk, Seth Stahlheber, Shawn Vasdev, and Richard Wilkinson.

Finally, I could not have written this book without the unflagging support of my wonderful wife Gretchen Perry.

Martin Daly
Hamilton, Ontario, Canada
September, 2015

1

Why Homicide?

Crimes as serious as murder should have
strong emotions behind them.
—George Orwell, *Decline of the English Murder*, 1946

Inequality, Competition, and Homicide

Homicides are intensely interesting. When there's a murder, anyone who has even a remote connection to the case craves details. People want to know exactly what happened, and why. This morbid fascination is healthy and normal. The natural habitat of the human mind is a social universe of personal acquaintances, gossip, and hearsay. In such a social universe, it has always been important to gather all the information you can about who is dangerous, and in what situations. Lethality is a big deal.

As fascinating as the stories behind individual murder cases may be, homicides become even more interesting when we study their statistical properties dispassionately. When they are appropriately aggregated and summarized, the statistics of homicide provide us with a sort of "window" on human passions. What are the sources of interpersonal conflict that can induce someone to kill? The most important is apparently inequality: the degree to which the things that men desire are equitably or inequitably distributed.

Decades of research have shown that if you want to predict the homicide rate of a nation, or a state, or a city, the best single piece of information to help you make that prediction is the level of *income inequality*. Unfortunately, the criminologists who have confirmed this result again and again remain befuddled about what to make of it. One reason for their befuddlement is that, like many other social scientists, most criminologists believe that violence itself is a form of pathology. This is a mistake. Although some killers are indeed insane, violence itself is an organized, evolved capability of normal human beings,

1

pursuing their interests in a world in which people's interests conflict. The misunderstanding of violence as pathology has blinded analysts to a simple, intuitively appealing interpretation of the facts before them. A local homicide rate is a manifestation of the local level of competition for scarce resources, and economic inequality is a major determinant of the severity of that competition. One of my aims in this book is to lay out the case that this straightforward interpretation is correct.

To make this argument, I will have to familiarize readers with some little-known facts. First, it is not just killers who are overwhelmingly male, but their victims, as well. More specifically, in developed countries with stable governments and judicial systems, both those who kill and those whom they kill are primarily young, disadvantaged men. Second, the contexts in which these men kill one another are *competitive* contexts: sexual rivalries, turf wars, robberies, and, above all else, contests over the limited social resources of dominance, respect, and "face." Third, these competitive killings make up not only the majority of *all* homicides, but *the most variable component* of the overall homicide rate as well. Together, these facts imply that if you wish to know why homicide rates are so variable, you should be looking at those aspects of society that determine the intensity of local competition and thereby affect men's readiness to resort to dangerous tactics in their struggles with rivals.

In short, I will argue that the observed association between inequality and lethal violence is one of *cause and effect*. This cannot simply be assumed. In areas of science in which controlled experiments are impossible, it is a truism that correlation doesn't necessarily imply causation. Life expectancy and the consumption of sugary soft drinks have both been increasing for decades, for example, and life expectancy furthermore tends to be low in those backwaters that sugary soft drinks have yet to reach. But it would be loony to infer that soda-pop extends lives! Other correlates of modernization presumably explain the association. In principle, the robust association that I will show you between economic inequality and the homicide rate may also turn out to be meaningless in this way. However, unlike the soda-pop example, there is a straightforward and highly plausible causal chain leading from economic inequality to homicide. When desired goods are more unequally distributed, there is more to be gained from being one of the winners and there is a higher likelihood of utter failure, raising the incentives for the competitors to resort to extreme tactics, including potentially dangerous tactics. An elevated homicide rate is just one predictable consequence of this escalated competition.[1]

I find this causal interpretation of the association between income inequality and homicide rates compelling, but not everyone agrees. Skeptics who doubt that inequality plays a direct role in causing violence have put forward three challenges. The first is a claim that the low levels of lethal violence in egalitarian nations like Japan and the Nordic countries are due to the simple fact that very few of their citizens live in poverty. In other words, the *relative* disadvantage of inequality is itself supposedly harmless, but happens to be associated with a high incidence of *absolute* destitution, which is the real culprit. The second challenge resides in the fact that some small-scale societies studied by anthropologists are supposedly egalitarian and yet have very high homicide rates. The third challenge is that occasional episodes in which inequality and homicide are seen to be moving in opposite directions—such as in the United States during the 1990s, when inequality was rising and the homicide rate was falling—imply that the usual association between the two cannot be causal. One of this book's major aims is to confront each of these challenges and demonstrate that they do not, in fact, undermine the hypothesis that links inequality to homicide through its effects on competition. Those who have advanced the first and second of these three challenges have simply got their facts wrong, and the third challenge withers when we recognize that any genuine effects of inequality must of necessity be "lagged" effects of *past* inequality.

Can well-chosen policies reduce violence? One pessimistic line of thought in the social sciences attributes violence to the existence of cultures in which the local norms reinforce and "valorize" violence, and further maintains that such *cultures of violence* are highly resistant to change. The relatively high rate of homicide in the southern United States, for example, is manifestly associated with a "culture of honor," in which being willing and able to use violence is admired as a manly virtue, and many writers accept that this culture has perpetuated itself generation after generation for no other reason than that children are socialized to adopt the relevant values and that anyone who forsakes them suffers social costs. Another aim of this book is to refute this view. The glorification of violence in certain value systems is utilitarian and self-defensive,

---

[1] The evidence that inequality exerts an influence on competitiveness and risk-taking is mostly correlational, but a few experimental efforts to assess whether the link is causal indicate that it is; see Mishra, Barclay, and Lalumière (2014) and Mishra, Son Hing, and Lalumière (2015).

but it is not immutable. People are not the passive recipients of cultural indoctrination that this pessimistic theory would have them be. Attitudes, values, and behavior can all change quickly when incentives change, and rates of homicide soar and plummet with surprising rapidity. Moreover, economic inequality plays a clear role in the persistence of "southern violence" in the United States, and the alleged "inertia" of the local culture provides no justification for despair and inaction.

If I am successful in persuading you that inequality almost certainly has harmful effects, including that of exacerbating lethal violence, you might nevertheless question the wisdom of policies aimed at reducing it. A relentless message to which we have all been exposed is that economic inequality is a necessary evil if we are to maintain the rising tide of productivity and innovation that supposedly raises all our boats. Leveling policies such as a progressive income tax would kill the goose that lays the golden eggs, or so the story goes. In this book's concluding chapters, I will make the case that this is mere propaganda on behalf of the privileged. What the science of economics actually indicates is that even if we cared not at all about suffering and injustice, but wished *only* to maximize productivity and growth, the economic inequality that now prevails in the rich countries is counterproductive and needs to be reduced.

The case against economic inequality as an important cause of lethal violence is strong. It has also been indicted by many researchers for its damaging health consequences. Economic inequality reinforces inequality of opportunity and other injustices, and economists now agree that it even damages the economy itself, by creating waste and inefficiency. No redeeming benefits to society have been identified. Economic inequality persists because of the disproportionate power that is wielded by a minority who are its beneficiaries and the disinformation that they cynically disseminate. Political action aimed at reducing it is overdue.

Getting Hooked on Homicide Research

When my late wife Margo Wilson and I began doing homicide research in 1978, it wasn't because we were specifically interested in murder, nor even in human affairs. Our area of expertise was the behavior of other animal species. I was primarily interested in how ecological variables, such as the way that food resources are distributed in space, might help explain the diversity of animal social systems, and the particular animals that I studied were desert rodents: kangaroo rats in California and gerbils in the Algerian Sahara. As for Margo, most of her previous research had been concerned with the ways in which castration and hormone replacement therapy affect the behavior of monkeys.

We were teaching at the University of California, Riverside, where, in collaboration with a few colleagues from the psychology, biology, and mathematics departments, we had organized a weekly seminar for the graduate students in the area of "sociobiology." One day, our topic was why animals sometimes kill infants of their own species. Harvard primatologist Sarah Hrdy and other researchers had recently proposed that in certain animals, such as the langur monkeys that Hrdy had studied in India, infanticide might be a normal response to a particular situation, namely that in which a new male establishes a mating relationship with a female partner who is still burdened with dependent young sired by her previous partner. The proposed utility of this horrific behavior—the reason why Hrdy thought it could have contributed to the reproductive success of the killers and thus have evolved by Darwinian selection—was that by disposing of his prede-cessor's baby, the male monkey stops the mother from expending her time and energy raising the progeny of a rival male, and redirects her efforts toward reproducing with the killer and rearing *his* young instead.

The discussion was lively. Hrdy's "sexually selected infanticide" hypothesis is now well established, but in those days, it was contro-versial. Some class members recoiled from the very suggestion that anything as repugnant as infanticide could possibly be a normal behav-ior that had been actively favored by the evolutionary process. Other students countered—correctly, in my view—that their classmates were guilty of a version of the "naturalistic fallacy": the naïve assumption that anything that is "natural" must be nice, and that anything we find dis-tasteful must be pathological. What could not be denied was that Hrdy's hypothesis had pinpointed a recurrent feature of the circumstances in which infanticide had been observed or inferred in her monkeys, in lions, and in a few other species of animals.[2]

It was in the context of this discussion that one of the students in the class, Suzanne Weghorst, raised a question: Are human stepchildren disproportionately mistreated in reality, as they are in folklore? (Think of Cinderella. Think of Snow White.) No one in the room knew the answer, and so, in a pre-internet world, we suggested that Suzanne

---

[2] See Hrdy (1974) for her initial proposal of the sexually selected infanticide hypothesis, and Hrdy (1979) for an early review. For reviews of the history of the controversy and the evidence on sexually selected infanticide, see Ebensperger (1998), van Schaik and Janson (2000), and Palombit (2012).

should go to the university library, look up the relevant research literature, and report back to the class. A week later, what she had to report was a surprise: No relevant research could be found. Child abuse had been a topic of intense investigation since 1962, when Colorado pediatrician Henry Kempe and his collaborators announced the discovery of a "battered child syndrome." But somehow, no-one had thought to ask whether children who are living with stepparents are abused at higher rates than other children. If we wanted to know the answer, we would have to do the research ourselves. And so we did.[3]

Margo, Suzanne, and I were soon able to demonstrate that stepchildren are indeed heavily overrepresented in child abuse case files. In 1976, there were laws obliging health care professionals and others to report suspected cases of child abuse in jurisdictions comprising about half of the population of the United States, and within those jurisdictions, we found that one of every 160 children under three years of age who dwelt with a birth parent and a stepparent had been a victim of physical abuse that had been validated by some sort of follow-up investigation subsequent to the initial report. The corresponding incidence of validated abuse for same-age children living with both birth parents was much less than one in a thousand. However, we realized immediately that this statistical fact could, in principle, be an "artifact": an illusion arising from biases in the detection of abuse rather than a reflection of a genuine elevation of the rate at which stepchildren are actually mistreated.[4]

To see how this might be so, imagine that you live next door to a family in which you have noticed that one small child keeps showing up with bruises. Is it not possible that you would be just a little bit more suspicious if you happened to know that the mother's partner was a new boyfriend and not the child's father? And is it not possible that your likelihood of contacting child welfare authorities would therefore be just that little bit greater? Okay, maybe not you, but *some* people might react in this way, and for that reason, we placed special emphasis on the fact that the contrast between rates of abuse at the hands of stepparents *versus* birth parents got larger when we made our criterion of "child abuse" more and more stringent, and that the greatest difference was seen in the relatively rare cases of *fatal* abuse. If biased detection were an important source of apparent differences in abuse risk, then

---

[3] Kempe et al. (1962) coined the phrase "battered child syndrome" and launched the field of child abuse research.

[4] For the initial demonstration that stepchildren are overrepresented as child abuse victims, see Wilson, Daly, and Weghorst (1980).

that bias, and hence the overrepresentation of stepparents, should have shrunk or disappeared when we confined our attention to those least ambiguous lethal cases. However, what we actually observed was precisely the opposite. Surely biased detection could not explain away a *hundred-fold* difference in a toddler's probability of being beaten to death by a co-residing stepfather *versus* a genetic father![5]

Inspired by these dramatic results—and perhaps also by discovering that research on human violence attracts a larger audience than research on squirrel monkeys or kangaroo rats—Margo had a further brainwave: Killings might provide a good "assay" of conflict in *any* relationship category. Because homicides are more reliably recorded than nonlethal manifestations of antagonism, she reasoned, they may be especially revealing of both the circumstances that inflame conflicts of interest and the circumstances that alleviate them.

We could think of many questions and hypotheses, derived from our interest in social evolution, which looked as though they might usefully be addressed by analyses of homicide data. Is infidelity a uniquely potent source of intimate partner conflict, as common experience and certain theories might suggest? Was the father of psychoanalysis, Sigmund Freud, correct in his belief that antagonism between parents and their children is a manifestation of sexual rivalry, pitting son against father and daughter against mother? Or would the facts instead support evolutionary biologist Robert Trivers's theoretical explanation of parent–offspring conflict, in which the child's sex is immaterial and there is no reason to expect the antagonism to be confined to same-sex pairs? Asking volunteer research participants to rate and describe their personal relationships would never settle questions such as these. Maybe looking at who kills whom, and under what circumstances, would be more enlightening.[6]

---

[5] Regarding differential risk of lethal abuse, see Wilson et al. (1980) and Daly and Wilson (1988a). Daly and Wilson (1998, 2008) reviewed the evidence that stepparents discriminate against stepchildren more broadly, and the controversies that this finding has engendered, as well as explaining why it is not plausible that sexually selected infanticide is a human adaptation and the elevated rates of abuse, including lethal abuse, in stepfamilies must instead be understood as an ugly, nonadaptive byproduct of evolved parental preferences.

[6] For evidence that male sexual jealousy and suspicions of infidelity are indeed uniquely potent motives for lethal wife assault, see Daly, Wilson, and Weghorst (1982), Daly and Wilson (1988b), and Wilson and Daly (1996). Freud's infamous Oedipal theory (especially Freud, 1925) attributed parent-offspring conflict to sexual rivalry; although no actual evidence *ever* supported it (see, e.g., Daly & Wilson, 1990a), Oedipal theory refuses to die. Trivers (1974) laid out the modern evolutionary theory of parent–offspring conflict, which implies no same-sex contingency when children are young; at least as regards parental violence, the data support Trivers, not Freud (Wilson, Daly, and Weghorst 1983; Daly and Wilson 1990).

Once we had begun assembling some high-quality datasets and assessing patterns of differential risk, we were hooked on homicide research. There was so much to discover! No researcher before us had ever asked whether the probability that a woman would be murdered by her romantic partner might vary as a function of her age or the couple's age disparity. Nobody had previously asked if the correlated attributes of being young and being unmarried had distinct effects on the likelihood that a new mother would kill her baby. Nobody had determined the age trajectory of a child's risk of being slain by its mother *versus* its father. We found striking, interpretable answers to these and many other such questions.[7]

Our results were novel because our "epidemiological" style of investigation was novel. Our approach was to combine the homicide data with information about the entire population that we extracted from the census or from surveys, in order to describe patterns of homicide risk—how sex, age, marital status, and other such variables were related to one's chances of becoming a killer or a murder victim—and to assess how these demographic patterns differed among the various sorts of relationships between killers and their victims. This just wasn't the sort of question that previous research on homicide had addressed. With the exception of some psychiatric studies of "abnormal" killers, criminological research on homicide was dominated by sociologists, who were primarily interested in explaining differences over time and between jurisdictions in the gross *per capita* rates at which homicide occurs, and they tackled that question by seeking other societal-level variables that seemed to be related to homicide rates and that might therefore be inferred to have a causal impact on homicide's frequency. This approach to the issue of variation in homicide rates across time and space is important, and it will be a major focus of this book. But Margo and I initially had other interests.

Coincidentally, just as we were getting immersed in homicide research, epidemiologists themselves joined the fray, after US Surgeon General Everett Koop gave the Atlanta-based Centers for Disease Control (CDC) a mandate to study violence as a public health problem. We hadn't thought of our own research in quite those terms,

---

[7] Wilson, Johnson, and Daly (1995) report patterns of spousal homicide in relation to age and age disparity. Daly and Wilson (1988b) show that maternal youth and unwed status are distinct risk factors for infanticide. Wilson and Daly (1994) report and interpret the distinct victim's age trajectories of child murder by mothers *versus* fathers.

but the approach taken by the *CDC* researchers was essentially the same as ours. Margo flew to Atlanta to describe some of our findings about spouse-killing in Canada, showing them, for example, that the younger a wife, the greater her chance of being slain by her husband; that common-law unions looked very different, with the highest homicide rates occurring in middle age; and that a big difference in the partners' ages was a distinct risk factor. Two of the CDC researchers in the audience, Jim Mercy and Linda Saltzman, were inspired to see whether similar patterns existed in the United States, and indeed they did. Our evolutionary overview must have seemed strange to our new epidemiologist colleagues, but that hardly mattered. We were all intrigued to discover striking demographic patterns of homicide risk, and in that, we were all very much on the same page.[8]

What Counts as a "Homicide"?

Australia, Japan, and several other countries publish official statistics in which the reported number of "homicides" includes incidents of "attempted murder" in which no-one actually died! There is an undeniable logic to this practice. Why, after all, should a particular assault be included or excluded on the basis of the proximity of an emergency room or the skills of its surgeons? But the problem with including "attempted murders" in your data is that there are no clear, consensual criteria for deciding whether a nonfatal assault makes the cut. Once you start including nonfatal assaults in your data, you can therefore be sure that suitable cases will be less consistently detected and recorded than if you had stuck to dead bodies, and that comparisons across time and place will be less reliable. It is better, in general, to stick with actual killings. But which ones?

The first *Global Study on Homicide* was produced by the United Nations Office on Drugs and Crime (UNODC) in 2011, followed by another in 2013. The body counts that inform these reports come mainly from the World Health Organization (WHO), which collects detailed cause of death reports from all its member countries. Because police and justice system reporting practices vary widely, "crime" data from the International Criminal Police Organization (Interpol) do not have the same degree of consistency and reliability, and the WHO cause

---

[8] These and other demographic patterns of homicide risk in Canada were reported by Daly and Wilson (1988b). Mercy and Saltzman (1989) were inspired by Margo's visit to replicate the results using US data.

of death data are generally recognized as the most suitable homicide data for international comparisons.[9]

The UNODC asserts that its reports are concerned only with killings that are *unlawful* and *intentional*. However, both of these criteria are problematic, and the data on which the United Nations relies don't actually comply very well with either of them.

Consider first the restriction to "intentional" killings. The UNODC justifies this supposed provisio on the grounds that it excludes "those deaths caused when the perpetrator was reckless or negligent but did not intend to take a human life (non-intentional homicide)." Read literally, this would rule out not only accidents, but also even deliberate, violent assaults if they were not *intended* to "take a human life," and that would make a UNODC "homicide" synonymous with what Anglo-American law calls a *murder* (a fatal act of interpersonal aggression with lethal intent), while excluding *manslaughters* (fatal acts of interpersonal aggression that were *not* intended to kill). But in this regard, the UNODC definition is simply a misstatement. The WHO cause of death guidelines that coroners and others follow define "homicides" as deaths resulting from "injuries inflicted by another person with intent *to injure or kill*" (emphasis added), and thus include manslaughters after all. (Note that this still leaves the killer's "intent" a part of the definition. Since intentions are invisible, there will always be some ambiguity, and no available definition of "homicide" fully disposes of this problem.)

Now consider the "unlawful" qualifier. The aim here is to distinguish *criminal* homicides from both legal executions and acts of war. Whether these distinctions can be drawn in a principled, defensible way is debatable, as is the question of how consistently they are now being applied. A codicil to the WHO cause of death guidelines explicitly removes killings in the course of "legal intervention" to a separate category that is not included in the usual "homicide" counts; in practice, this seems to be applied only—and even then, inconsistently—to killings by police officers while on duty. A complication is that many additional killings may also be deemed lawful, and exactly what is decriminalized varies wildly among jurisdictions. Killing in self-defense is "justifiable" almost everywhere, but defending property, punishing blasphemy, and avenging

---

[9] The UN's *Global Study on Homicide* can be downloaded from http://www.unodc.org/gsh/. The World Health Organization's cause of death codes can be downloaded from http://www.who.int/classifications/icd/en/.

anything from adultery to an insult directed at a female relative all justify homicide in some of the countries reporting to the WHO, but not in others. In fact, the cause of death coding guidelines would seem to make these cases *homicides* nonetheless, and thus the "unlawful" criterion is another that is not literally adhered to.

At first glance, warfare seems like an entirely different kettle of fish: violence that is not simply legitimized but positively enjoined by governments, and that has nothing to do with the personal, conflictual agendas of the individual combatants. However, warfare is an intrinsically fuzzy category: Individual acts of vengeful violence grade insensibly into lethal feuding between lineages, which in turn elides into the sort of chronic raiding and infrequent pitched battles that characterize many small-scale, nonstate societies. Moreover, the polities that legitimize an armed conflict between groups may themselves be of debatable legitimacy, and essentially similar conflicts may be characterized as wars here and as illegal gang activity there. The UNODC acknowledges this fuzzy boundedness, as follows:

> Intentional homicides are estimates of unlawful homicides purposely inflicted as a result of domestic disputes, interpersonal violence, violent conflicts over land resources, intergang violence over turf or control, and predatory violence and killing by armed groups. Intentional homicide does not include all intentional killing; the difference is usually in the organization of the killing. Individuals or small groups usually commit homicide, whereas killing in armed conflict is usually committed by fairly cohesive groups of up to several hundred members and is thus usually excluded.[10]

The caveats and ambiguities that I have been discussing are important, but at the end of the day, we *can* compare homicide rates with a reasonable degree of confidence. If our interest is in the differences between demographic groups, or between the cities or states of a modern country—both of which will be important kinds of comparisons in the next few chapters—we have little reason to fear that inconsistent criteria for attributing a death to homicide will undermine our analyses. Comparability is also very good for international comparisons among modern, developed countries. Some caution is warranted when we cast our net more broadly still, especially since the question of whether a

---

[10] Quote downloaded from http://data.worldbank.org/indicator/VC.IHR.PSRC.P5 on April 5, 2015.

major conflict causing many deaths represents a civil war or homicidal gang activity is sometimes contested. But the WHO and the United Nations are sensitive to these issues of comparability and have taken pains to ensure that differential coding practices are not the source of spurious differences in estimated homicide rates. When the *Global Study on Homicide* tells us that *per capita* rates of homicide in Southern Africa and Central America in 2012 were more than one hundred times greater than those in Western Europe, these immense differences are real.

What Homicide Rates Can Tell Us

I got hooked on homicide research because the statistics of lethal violence offer a revealing window on broader social phenomena: things like the substance of the particular conflicts that are characteristic of particular social relationships, and the differential intensity of competition in different societies. Of course, conflict and competition aren't usually lethal, and it may therefore sound peculiar to suggest that events as extreme as homicides provide a good lens through which to view conflict in general. But if you would prefer to investigate everyday, low-level social conflict instead, you'll run into some obstacles.

Social scientists who want to investigate interpersonal conflict often distribute questionnaires to large samples of people, and the results are sometimes enlightening. However, there are many pitfalls facing survey research of this sort. One big problem is that if you ask people about their aspirations or preferences, they may distort the truth to put themselves in a more favorable light. The people who conduct surveys know this, of course, but they have no fully satisfactory remedies. And there is another problem that is subtler than deception, and not nearly as widely recognized: Even the most sincere and helpful respondents have surprisingly little conscious access to the mental processes underlying their own decisions. Ask people how and why they chose their present careers or their spouses or their favorite foods, and they'll usually give you a coherent, confident story. But a great deal of psychological research has now shown that these explanations of past action are just that—stories—and often *post hoc* stories at that: explanations that the respondent patched together only after the question was asked.[11]

---

[11] The classic study of people's surprisingly limited introspective access to the workings of their own minds is Nisbett and Wilson (1977); see also Wegner (2002). One appealing hypothesis is that a primary function of our conscious stream of thought is to interpret our own actions and construct socially acceptable *post hoc* accounts of our motives for public consumption; see, for example, Gazzaniga (2011).

At first glance, asking people what they have actually done, rather than why they did it, sounds like it would solve these problems. But of course what respondents say about what they have done won't necessarily be true either, partly because of faulty memory and partly because of bald-faced lying. Both forgetting and lying probably play some role, for example, in the fact that sex researchers routinely find that the average man reports having had sex with more partners of the opposite sex than does the average woman. Yet another complication is that the people who are willing to fill out a questionnaire or talk to a telephone interviewer are never a representative sample of humankind. In sum, there are many reasons why responses to surveys provide a systematically distorted reflection of what people think and do, and many reasons why this may be an especially big problem when you ask questions about sensitive matters like sex and violence.[12]

Crime statistics provide a less self-serving and seemingly more direct window on human behavior. Unfortunately, most crime statistics have serious shortcomings, too. If you ask a random sample of people whether they have been assaulted or robbed, for example, you'll get much higher estimates of assault and robbery rates than those derived from police reports, suggesting that a large fraction of crime remains unreported and hence unrecorded. Moreover, there can be little doubt that those assaults and robberies that do get reported to the police differ in various ways from those that don't, rather than constituting a representative subset. If you therefore decide to privilege the victimization surveys over the police reports, all the problems with survey research that I just discussed rear their ugly heads again. Criminologists agree, however, that the one crime for which the records are most nearly complete and least biased is homicide. Dead bodies are usually found, and the circumstances surrounding suspicious deaths are usually investigated. Even homicide data aren't perfect, of course, but at least in developed, democratic nations, there's no reason to believe that they're badly out of whack, and they're the best that we've got.

Killing is obviously an extreme way to resolve conflicts, and it's often counterproductive as well. It is therefore easy to dismiss killers as aberrant and to jump to the conclusion that they can't tell us anything of

---

[12] Regarding discrepancies between women's and men's reports of numbers of sexual partners, see, for example, Wiederman (1997). For analyses and discussion of when self-report data are relatively likely to be trustworthy and when they are not, see Stone et al. (2000).

interest about normal human motives and behavior. But jumping to that conclusion is a mistake. Although brain disorders play a causal role in some homicides, most killers have no identifiable psychopathology, and even those who are in some way "abnormal" typically exhibit extreme versions of the same social passions that motivate "normal" homicides.

Consider, for example, male sexual jealousy and possessiveness. Some jealous men who have killed their wives are manifestly delusional, pointing indignantly to zany "evidence" of their wives' infidelity such as a supposedly tell-tale rearrangement of the cushions on a sofa. However, there are many other jealous husbands who have killed partners they suspected of infidelity and who exhibit no signs of psychopathology. According to common law in the English-speaking world, killing in reaction to a revelation of adultery is the act of a "reasonable man." I mention this legal tradition not to suggest that this is a defensible conception of what is "reasonable," but to draw your attention to the interesting fact that the common law reflects a folk understanding of human passions that grants revelations of infidelity a special status. And the evidence on wife-killings confirms that folk understanding: Suspicion or knowledge of female infidelity is indeed an exceptionally potent provocation, regardless of whether the killer is mad or sane.[13]

More generally, the considerations that intensify or soften conflict in a specific type of relationship, such as that between partners in a marriage, have predictable, systematic effects on the rates of homicide in that relationship. These patterns then differ among the various sorts of everyday social relationship—rivals *versus* romantic partners *versus* parents and their children—because the substance of their characteristic conflicts differs. In other words, homicide rates provide a sort of "assay" of the conflicts characterizing particular kinds and subsets of interpersonal relationships.[14]

Many things about homicide are consistent across times and places. For example, men kill other men vastly more often than women kill other women, everywhere. A small child is very much more likely to be beaten to death in anger by a father figure if that father is actually an

---

[13] Regarding delusional (also called "morbid") jealousy, see, for example, Mowat (1966), and King-ham and Gordon (2004). For the "reasonable man" doctrine of Anglo-American common law, see Edwards (1954). Regarding the statistical prevalence of male sexual jealousy as a motivator in wife-killings, see references in this chapter's footnote 5.

[14] For a fuller exposition of the idea that homicides "assay" relationship-specific determinants and patterns of conflict, see Daly and Wilson (1988b).

unrelated stepfather or mother's boyfriend than if the child still resides with his birth father. And the risk that a woman will be stalked and slain by her husband if she leaves him is especially severe if she is still young and fertile. These and other statistical regularities in the epidemiology and demography of lethal violence support the view that the underlying passions are components of a cross-culturally universal human nature. Tempting though it may be to marvel at the strange customs and beliefs of exotic people in faraway lands, human beings throughout the world have a huge amount in common with one another.[15]

A central tenet of my argument in this book will be that differences in homicide rates between and within nations cannot be adequately explained by invoking differences in local beliefs, values, and customary practices. The variability can be better understood if we think of homicide rates as the aggregate consequences of the ways in which essentially similar human beings respond to different social and economic incentive structures. I am not denying that people are affected by the cultures within which they were reared and within which they operate, nor that cultures differ in many potentially relevant ways, including differences in such crucial considerations as whether a man's willingness to resort to violence is admired or abhorred. There is no question that cultural differences are real and influential. It does not follow, however, that the sources of those cultural differences are arbitrary or functionless, nor, most importantly, that they are immaterial.

In some areas of the social sciences, culture is conceived of as an extrinsic determinant of how people think and act. Where homicide rates are high, a "culture of violence" is blamed. We'll scrutinize this claim in Chapter 7, but for now, I'll just declare my own view that this sort of *cultural determinism* is simplistic and wrong-headed. People are not just passive, helpless recipients of whatever the local norms and values happen to be. We do, of course, internalize an enormous

---

[15] For the generality of certain homicide risk patterns across different kinds of society, see Daly and Wilson (1988b). When I speak of a "cross-culturally universal human nature," I am not downplaying either individual differences or the role of "nurture." From a comparative zoological perspective, "human nature" includes such attributes as trichromatic color vision, skeletal adaptations for bipedalism, some metabolic innovations that may reflect a very long history of cooking our food, and very much more, arguably including many psychological attributes that are components of our capacity for culture. (Human language capability should be an uncontroversial example.) For a richly contentful and eloquent defense of the view that such a complex shared human nature exists, cross-cultural variability notwithstanding, see Brown (1991).

amount of cultural information, including seemingly arbitrary norms, but individuals also filter and reject a great deal that isn't working for them, and by so doing, they shape their cultural milieus no less than those cultural milieus shape them. And few things show the instability of culture more clearly than the volatility of homicide rates.

Why So Variable?

Much of what Margo Wilson and I discovered about patterns of killing and being killed appeared in a 1988 book that we entitled simply *Homicide*. It contained many novel findings, and it influenced a lot of subsequent research. We were pleased with its reception, and I'm still proud of it. But it had one big gap. In a final chapter on "cultural variation" in homicide rates, we said less than we could and should have done about the issue of greatest interest to most other homicide researchers: why homicide rates are so variable.

We had, even then, the germ of a plausible answer. In earlier chapters, we had presented evidence that a very large majority of killers are men and that most of their victims are men, too; that victims and their killers are usually acquainted, often strangers, and only very rarely blood relatives; and that the prototypical homicide is the dénouement of an escalated contest over honor or "face." We had also argued, in contrast to a prevalent criminological characterization of such cases as "trivial" in substance, that these are meaningful contests over an important scarce resource, namely social status, and that in developed countries, these dangerous confrontations are entered into mainly by men who have little to lose. In our final chapter, we reviewed various lines of evidence indicating that the particular kind of homicide whose incidence varies the most between countries and over time is that involving unrelated male rivals, and we continued as follows:

> Why should homicides involving young men constitute an especially variable component of the overall homicide rate? One possible reason is that these are the cases most responsive to varying economic circumstances and other cues that disadvantaged young men use to predict their prospects and modulate their risk-proneness.[16]

We went on to discuss a popular theory that differences in violence between subgroups within modern western nations are caused by

---

[16] Quoted from Daly and Wilson (1988b, 286).

differences in the attitudes toward violence that prevail in different "subcultures." We weren't buying it:

> If we think we can explain why poor young men behave violently in terms of the 'transmission' of 'values' within a 'subculture,' then we are unlikely to seek more utilitarian explanations. In fact, poor young men have *good reason* to escalate their tactics of social competition and become violent. Among the many social structural variables that criminologists have attempted to correlate with homicide rates, one of the more promising is *income inequality*: It is not simply poverty that seems to be associated with high rates of violent crime so much as the within-society variance in material welfare. Such an association is highly compatible with our view of homicides—especially those male–male nonrelative cases that constitute the most variable component in national rates—as manifestations of an escalated social competition more rational than it may first appear.[17]

A quarter century of subsequent research has shown that we were barking up the right tree. Income inequality is the single best predictor of the variability in homicide rates both between and within nations, and the reason why is evidently that greater inequality implies more intense social competition, especially among young men. However, the relationship between inequality and lethal violence is not widely appreciated, partly but not solely because the proposition that income inequality has destructive effects of *any* sort is fiercely opposed by inequality's beneficiaries. A large part of the remainder of this book must therefore consist of an examination and dissection of the counter-arguments.

But I'm getting ahead of myself. In the 1980s, criminologists began to pay serious attention to income inequality, and after the 1988 publication of our book, we began to do so, too.

---

[17] Quoted from Daly and Wilson (1988b, 287–8).

2

Homicide and Economic Inequality

*Unlike totalitarian times, when the future, though wretched, was
certain, today it is very unclear. The single (if ubiquitous) familiar
danger represented by totalitarian oppression seems to have
been replaced by an entire spectrum of new and unfamiliar or
long-forgotten dangers: from the danger of national conflicts to the
danger of losing social-welfare protection to the danger of the new
totalitarianism of consumption, commerce, and money.*
—Václav Havel, President of the Czech Republic, in a speech
opening Austria's Salzburg Festival, July 26, 1990[1]

An Eventful Year

When I first became interested in the problem of explaining the variability in gross homicide rates more than twenty years ago, the most recent
available data were for the year 1990. That had been a momentous year
on the world stage. It was the year in which the ban on anti-apartheid
organizations was lifted in South Africa, Nelson Mandela was released
from prison, and the transition to democratic majority rule began. The
Soviet Union was then on the brink of collapse, and the countries it
had dominated were breaking free. In Germany, a euphoric citizenry
was literally tearing down the Berlin Wall; by October, the country was
fully and officially reunited. In Czechoslovakia, more than 96 percent
of eligible voters cast ballots in a June election that legitimized the
presidency of the dissident playwright Václav Havel. In Poland, the
leader of the Solidarity trade union federation, Lech Wałęsa, also won
his country's presidency handily, although it took him a second run-off
election to do so.

---

[1] downloaded June 20, 2014 from http://www.vaclavhavel.cz/showtrans.php?cat=projevy&
val=302_aj_projevy.html&typ=HTML

Significant elections were held in many other countries in 1990, too, but their outcomes weren't always such clear and inspiring reflections of the popular will. In Burma, the first multi-party election in thirty years produced a landslide victory for Aung San Suu Kyi's National League for Democracy; the military dictatorship responded by putting her under house arrest and hanging on to power. In Pakistan, Benazir Bhutto was removed from office in an election which, according to a ruling by the country's Supreme Court more than twenty years later, was rigged. And in Nicaragua, a weary populace bowed to a decade of US-sponsored terrorism by electing the coalition that the US government favored.

Millions of human lives were lost in 1990, of course, many in tragic circumstances. In June, a magnitude 7.4 earthquake near the south coast of the Caspian Sea killed at least forty thousand Iranians. Hundreds of thousands of Somalis and North Koreans starved to death. Wars that had begun many years earlier continued to extinguish lives in Angola, Afghanistan, El Salvador, Ethiopia, Sudan, and elsewhere, and two significant new wars were launched. In August, Iraq invaded Kuwait, sparking the first Gulf War. In October, exiled Tutsis invaded their native Rwanda from Uganda, an event that precipitated years of civil war and a horrific genocide.

The year 1990 also happens to be the first year for which anyone ever made a serious effort to compare the world-wide death toll imposed by wars to the mortality that results from the autonomous acts of personal violence that we call "homicides." Remarkably, the latter evidently killed an even larger number of people in 1990 than did all of the various wars. Researchers from the US Centers for Disease Control (CDC) and the World Health Organization (WHO) have estimated that more than a million people died violent deaths at the hands of others in that year: 502,000 died by acts of war and 563,000 were homicide victims.[2]

The United States of America, whose population in 1990 was just a little bit shy of 250 million, had almost exactly its expected proportionate share of the world's homicides: According to the CDC/WHO study, the US rate reached 100 homicides per million persons per annum for the first time that year, which was just a little below the overall world rate of 105. Although Brazil, Colombia, South Africa, and several other countries had even higher homicide rates, the US death toll was

---

[2] For the CDC/WHO study of violent deaths in 1990, see Reza, Mercy, and Krug (2001).

unique among the rich countries. The authors of the CDC/WHO study aggregated the data for "established market economies excluding the United States" and reported that their overall homicide rate was just 10 deaths per million persons per annum.

Why is it that the citizens of the United States were killing one another in the late twentieth century at a rate ten times higher than their counterparts in Europe or Japan? There is never a single, simple answer to such a question, but in this case, research has pinpointed one factor that can shoulder a surprisingly large share of the explanatory burden. What best explains American exceptionalism in this domain is apparently not that country's lingering racism, not its "cowboy" culture, not even the insidious influence of its gun lobby. The primary culprit appears to be the exceptional magnitude of the gap between the haves and the have-nots.

Inequality and Violence

It is widely known that different countries have very different homicide rates, but the sheer magnitude of those differences might nevertheless surprise you. According to the *United Nations Demographic Yearbook*, the Japanese homicide rate in 1990 was 6 victims per million persons per annum. Most of Western Europe had similar or slightly higher rates, in the range of 5 to 15. The U.N. estimate for the United States was a whopping 98 (slightly below the 100 estimated in the CDC/WHO study described above). And in the developing world, especially where the rule of law was fragile, rates were sometimes very much higher than that. In Colombia in 1990, there were an estimated 744 homicides per million persons per annum.[3]

Social scientists have tried hard to elucidate why this variability exists. Their main approach to the question has been to look for other phenomena that exhibit some association with the murder rate. Many things that vary across nation states have been found to have some statistical association with homicide, including the proportion of the population who are young adults, the divorce rate, female labor force participation, and various measures of economic development,

---

[3] The homicide rates for Japan, the United States, and Colombia that I quote here are based on cause of death data reported in the *United Nations Demographic Yearbooks*. Homicide rates are customarily reported on a *per 100,000 persons per annum* basis, but for purposes of exposition, because the lowest such national values fall below 1.0, I prefer to present them on a *per million persons per annum* basis, and will do so throughout this book.

including average income and unemployment. The most successful of these predictors of the homicide rate have turned out to be measures of how the nation's riches are distributed. Murder rates tend to be highest where income inequality is high, and are low where income is relatively equitably distributed.[4]

We have already noted that the homicide rate is higher in the United States than in other rich ("developed") nations. Well, inequality in the citizenry's access to resources and hence in the quality of people's lives is higher in the United States, too. A currently popular way of illustrating the magnitude of inequality is to contrast the top 1 percent with everyone else. A recent analysis of income survey data from the year 2005 provides a good example. In that year, the average household income of the top 1 percent of US earners was 20.9 *times* greater than the average household income of the remaining 99 percent. Echoing what we just saw in a cross-national comparison of homicide rates, this ratio of the average income of "the 1%" divided by the average income of "the 99%" was even higher in certain developing economies than in the United States, but the US value topped the table for developed countries. Britain ranked second, with the top 1 percent receiving 16.5 times as much, on average, as the remaining 99 percent. The most equitable developed country was the Netherlands, where the average household income of the top 1 percent was "only" 5.6 times higher than that of everyone else. In 1990, income inequality was not yet as extreme as it has become in the twenty-first century, but the United States already led the way.[5]

For many years, international comparisons of income inequality have been hampered by a lack of data that are strictly comparable from one place to another. If you want to compute an index of inequality, you need to know the distribution of incomes, and the available survey data won't always give you what you need. The problem isn't simply that some people earn their living through illegal means or hide income from the tax man, although these are important sources of error. An even bigger problem is that until very recently, different countries didn't

[4] For cross-national studies demonstrating that homicide rates are correlated with various social and economic indicators, especially income inequality, see Gartner (1990), LaFree (1999), Fajnzylber, Lederman and Loayza (2002), Messner et al. (2002), Jacobs and Richardson (2008), Nadanovsky and Cunha Cruz (2009), and Ouimet (2012).
[5] Atkinson, Piketty, and Saez (2011) summarize trends in top income shares in selected countries over the past century. The relative income shares of the 1% and the 99% in 2005 quoted here are based on data in their Table 6.

even summarize their income distributions and compute inequality in a consistent way. The most common approach has been to estimate income inequality among "households," but some countries have compared across individual earners instead. In the official data of some countries, but not others, the distribution of household income has been computed by formulas that adjust for the number of people residing in each home. Most countries have included households with no income in their calculations, but a few have excluded them. It wasn't until the mid-1990s that serious efforts were made to produce comparable data that would permit valid international comparisons, and the problems haven't all been solved yet. A particularly thorny problem is deciding how to compare the income distributions of populations who live under different sociopolitical systems that deliver different benefits in areas such as health care, education, and unemployment insurance. If the government provides universal access to quality health care in a given country, for example, the income distribution there is in effect more equitable than in another country in which the wage distribution looks similar but people have to buy medical services.

These problems still impede international comparisons, although many researchers have been working hard to assemble more comparable data. But if we narrow our focus and make comparisons among more homogeneous units, such as the fifty US states, most of these difficulties are reduced or abolished. So that is where we began when my collaborators and I turned our attention to these issues in the 1990s.[6]

The high homicide rate that characterizes the United States as a whole does not prevail throughout the country. Indeed, the variability among the states, although not as striking as that among nations, is surprisingly large: There is more than a *ten-fold difference* in rates between the least and the most murderous states. And as in cross-national comparisons, so too across the states: Income inequality is the best predictor of this variability that has yet been discovered. Figure 2.1 shows how closely homicide rates tracked income inequality in the United States in 1990. Each data point represents one of the fifty states. In the upper right corner of the figure, long before Hurricane Katrina devastated New Orleans, Louisiana held the dubious distinction of having both the highest homicide rate in the country and the most extreme income

---

[6] Regarding the limited cross-national comparability of income surveys and inequality estimates, see especially Atkinson and Brandolini (2009). For an exemplary effort to create a more consistent, standardized international data base, see Babones and Alvarez-Rivadulla (2007).

inequality. Mississippi ranked second on both measures. Overall, the correlation between homicide and income inequality was 0.725, indicating that slightly over half of the variability in homicide rates could be predicted from—and hence, perhaps, "explained" by—income inequality.[7]

In addition to having ranked first and second among the United States on both income inequality and homicide, Louisiana and Mississippi also happen to have been two of the poorest states. This raises the question of whether inequality is really the culprit here. Might it simply be prosperity, not equality, that has the effect of reducing the rate of lethal violence?

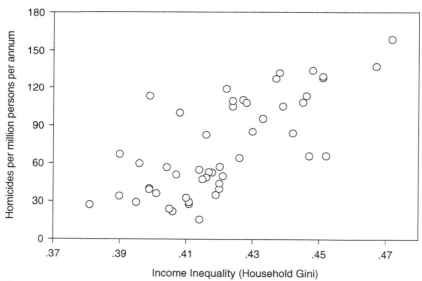

Figure 2.1. Homicide rates in the fifty US states in 1990, as a function of the state-specific Gini coefficient of income inequality, computed from the distribution of total pre-tax household income.

---

[7] Figure 2.1 is from Daly, Wilson, and Vasdev (2001).The Gini coefficient, the most widely used index of income inequality, equals zero when all incomes are identical, and approaches 1.0 when income is monopolized by a single recipient. Here and elsewhere, when I quantify a correlation, I am referring to a Pearson product–moment correlation coefficient (r). This statistic ranges from –1.0, when two variables are perfectly, linearly, and negatively related, through zero when they are utterly unrelated, to +1.0 when the relationship is perfect, linear, and positive. If r were equal to –1.0 or +1.0, then a particular Gini value would allow you to specify the corresponding homicide rate exactly; if r were equal to 0, then a particular Gini value wouldn't help you predict the homicide rate at all.

The specific issue at hand is an example of a more ubiquitous problem that bedevils the social sciences. Our goal is to figure out what causes what, but everything that seems like it might be relevant tends to be correlated with everything else. People with relatively low incomes, for example, also tend to have relatively little education, poor nutrition, and limited access to the justice system. Do these correlated factors have distinct effects on the probability that someone will commit a crime? That's not an easy question to answer. In the experimental sciences, you can manipulate each candidate causal variable, one at a time, while preventing other potential influences from varying. In large parts of the social sciences, by contrast, it is seldom either ethical or feasible to conduct a controlled experiment. We therefore use clever but fallible quantitative methods to "isolate" the effects of each variable of interest, while the effects of other variables (so-called "confounds") are supposedly "held constant" by statistical legerdemain.[8]

So back to the matter at hand. First, is it indeed the case that low income and inequality are correlated ("confounded") with one another across states, such that genuine effects of one of these variables could be erroneously attributed to the other? The short answer is "yes": The poor US states tend to have more unequal income distributions than the wealthier ones. In 1990, the cross-state correlation between the average (median) household income and the Gini coefficient of income inequality was −0.568. This is not as strong a relationship as the one between income inequality and homicide, but it's still substantial and "statistically significant" (which means that such a strong relationship would be very unlikely to appear by chance if there were no genuine underlying association between the two). But what, then, about the correlation between median household income and homicide? That turns out to be just −0.167, a value no greater than what we might expect to occur by chance when the two variables have no causal connections at all. The following graph (figure 2.2) shows the weak

---

[8] The simplest form of this "statistical legerdemain" is "partial correlation." In figure 2.1, for example, we can compute an equation for the line that best represents how the homicide rate increases as inequality increases. Because the relationship is imperfect, most data points will lie either above or below that "regression" line, and we can therefore proceed by assessing what *other* variables might predict *how far* off the line the various data points fall. Conceptually similar methods can be brought to bear on the problem of multiple predictors of an outcome variable such as homicide. These methods require the analyst to make specific assumptions about how the variables of which we possess only a sample are really distributed and interrelated, and those assumptions may be wrong.

relationship between the median household income of a given state and its homicide rate; the data points are scattered all over the place.[9]

These results are exactly what we should expect if it is inequality itself that raises the risk of lethal violence, so they support the hypothesis that that is indeed the case. But they don't prove it, and the fact that the most unequal states are also the poorest remains a nagging concern. Even though average income has no apparent relationship to the homicide rate, one might still be able to make a case that "absolute deprivation" (poverty) is the real risk factor, not "relative deprivation" (inequality). In fact, a few criminologists have tried to make precisely that case, and I will dissect their arguments in detail in Chapter 4. For the present, the relevant point is that although the Gini index is specifically a measure of how the income "pie" is *distributed*, regardless of the size of that pie, we must nevertheless consider the possibility that the Gini's apparent

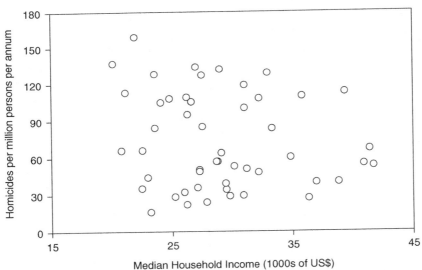

Figure 2.2. Homicide rates in the fifty US states in 1990, as a function of state-specific median household income.

[9] Figure 2.2 is again from Daly, Wilson, and Vasdev (2001). If there were no genuine underlying relationship between average income and Gini, a correlation coefficient with a magnitude (positive or negative) of 0.568 or greater would be expected only about one in sixty thousand times; hence, we say p = 0.000017. However, if there were no genuine relationship between average income and homicide, a correlation coefficient (positive or negative) as large as 0.167 would be expected on almost one of eight occasions (p = 0.123), which is not generally deemed "statistically significant."

relevance here derives from the fact that inequality happens to be high where many people live in poverty.

Two different sorts of evidence in the 1990 data speak against this "absolute deprivation" hypothesis. First, consider the fact that if two states have the *same* level of inequality, then the one with the higher average income will have a lower proportion of its populace living below some designated poverty line. It follows that the state with higher income should have less homicide if variability in the homicide rate is really driven by the proportion living in poverty. We can test this by using the sort of statistical legerdemain that I described above to hold inequality constant. If poverty is the real causal factor, then we should find that the weak negative association between average income and homicide becomes stronger and statistically significant: higher average income, less killing. But when we do the analysis, what we actually find is precisely the opposite: When Gini is "held constant," median income actually becomes a statistically significant *positive* predictor of the homicide rate. In other words, when the effects of inequality, if any, are removed by statistical methods, higher average incomes are associated with more killing, not less! This is very hard to reconcile with the hypothesis that "absolute deprivation" (poverty) is what really matters and that "relative deprivation" (inequality) is unimportant.[10]

Canada and the United States

The second line of evidence against the idea that homicide rates are affected by the "absolute" deprivation of poverty, but not by the "relative" deprivation of inequality, arises when we look beyond the fifty US states. More than thirty years ago, University of Maryland sociologist David Jacobs concluded that, regardless of whether one is analyzing across nations, states, or cities, the correlation between inequality and average income is "always negative" such that "the poorer the area, the more one can expect unequal income distributions." And yet when you think about it, there's no obvious reason why this should *always* be true. In principle, everyone *could* be on a more or less equal footing and yet impoverished in one jurisdiction, whereas the entire populace could be sitting securely above the poverty line and yet have highly unequal

---

[10] The partial correlation between median household income and homicide with Gini "held constant" (or "partialled out") is 0.431, p < 0.002. Moreover, when it is income that is "held constant" instead, the partial correlation between the Gini and homicide actually increases to 0.776, which provides further support for the conclusion that inequality is a more crucial determinant of the homicide rate than is absolute income.

incomes somewhere else. These considerations set us to thinking. Could we find an instance in which Jacobs's generalization was contradicted, and if so, could we use it to conduct a better test of the hypothesis that inequality is one of the causes of lethal violence?[11]

It turned out that we didn't have to look far. Our home and native land, Canada, provided the necessary contrast to the United States. Canada consists of ten provinces (in addition to three thinly populated territories), and in 1990, the most equitable provinces (Newfoundland, Prince Edward Island) were also the ones with the lowest average income and the highest poverty rates. Conversely, the wealthiest provinces (British Columbia, Ontario, Alberta) were at or near the top in income inequality. In the United States, as we have already seen, the correlation between income inequality and median household income was negative at r = −0.568. In Canada, this relationship was reversed: the correlation was a positive 0.508, contradicting Jacobs's generalization.

What, then, about homicide? Canada has a very much lower homicide rate than the United States, and this has been true for as long as data have been available. In 1990, according to the *United Nations Demographic Yearbook*, the Canadian homicide rate was 21 killings per million persons per annum, less than a quarter of that in the United States. Nevertheless, inequality proved to be a positive predictor of homicide rates in Canada no less than in the United States. In fact, the relationship was slightly stronger in Canada. The relatively equitable provinces had scarcely any homicides at all, despite their substantial levels of poverty. Murders occurred mainly in the wealthier but inequitable provinces. This result, too, is hard to reconcile with the proposition that absolute deprivation matters whereas relative deprivation does not.[12]

The big surprise emerged when we combined the 1990 data for Canada with the data for the United States. In figure 2.3, the fifty open (white) circles are the US data that you've already seen, and the ten filled (black) circles represent the Canadian provinces. The data for both countries fall roughly along the same trajectory. The "worst" Canadian provinces, in terms of inequality and homicide, were indiscriminable from the "best" states.[13]

---

[11] The mistaken assertion that the correlation between inequality and average income is "always negative" is from Jacobs (1981, 14).
[12] The correlation between income inequality and the homicide rate across the ten Canadian provinces in 1990 was 0.803. See Daly, Wilson, and Vasdev (2001).
[13] Figure 2.3 is again from Daly, Wilson, and Vasdev (2001).

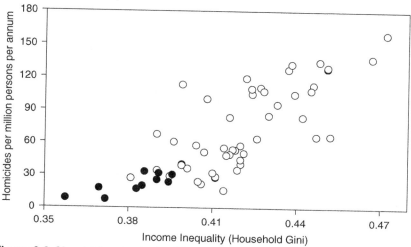

Figure 2.3. Homicide rates in the fifty US states (open circles) in 1990, and the ten provinces of Canada (filled circles) averaged over 1988–1992, as a function of state- and province-specific income inequality (the Gini coefficient for total pre-tax household income).

This was truly unexpected. When we Canadians try to characterize our national identity, we do so largely in terms of contrasts with our mighty neighbor to the south, and we tend to pay a lot of attention to the violence in US society. A few standard explanations for the large national contrast in this domain get trotted out repeatedly. The trouble with the Americans is their legacy of slavery. And their addiction to guns. And the fact that their military prowess reinforces a Rambo mentality. And that their settlers pushed west in advance of any police force and therefore had to become their own enforcers, whereas the *Royal Canadian Mounted Police* preceded our settlers.

These proposed explanations all sound plausible, and I had always been inclined to believe that there's probably some truth to all of them. Well, maybe there is and maybe there isn't, but what the 1990 data appeared to be telling us is that the large and much-discussed difference in homicide rates between these two neighbors could be accounted for *entirely* by the effects of state- and province-level income inequality! This didn't look like it was just another story. Astonishingly, what the data seemed to be saying is that this might be the *whole* story.

3

Competition and Violence

*[Natural] selection has nothing to do with what is necessary or
unnecessary, or what is adequate or inadequate, for
continued survival. It deals only with an immediate
better-vs.-worse within a system of alternative, and
therefore competing, entities.*
—George C. Williams, *Adaptation and
Natural Selection*, 1966

Natural Selection

Two years after Charles Darwin returned to England from a long voyage around the world on *H.M.S. Beagle*, and fully twenty years before his theory of evolution by natural selection was made public at a meeting of the Linnaean Society in London, he "happened to read for amusement" a book that provoked a sort of epiphany. In an autobiography that he wrote for his children many years later, Darwin reconstructed his state of mind on that October day in 1838.

For more than a year, Darwin had been collecting copious information on the detailed effects of selective breeding of domestic plants and animals. He was, as his notebooks confirm, already well aware that "Selection was the key-stone of man's success in making useful races of animals and plants. But how selection could be applied to organisms living in a state of nature remained for some time a mystery to me."[1]

The book that helped Darwin see the light was *An Essay on the Principle of Population* by the Reverend Robert Malthus. Its prose was vivid, its thesis simple and compelling:

> Through the animal and vegetable kingdoms nature has scattered the seeds of life abroad with the most profuse and liberal hand; but

---

[1] Darwin's 1876 autobiography is reprinted in Glick and Kohn (1996), where the sentences quoted appear on page 310.

has been comparatively sparing in the room and the nourishment necessary to rear them. The germs of existence contained in this earth, if they could freely develop themselves, would fill millions of worlds in the course of a few thousand years.

In other words, rather than reproducing only enough to replace the parental generation, plants and animals launch many more seeds and babies into the world than mere replacement would require, and Malthus recognized that if every infant were to survive and eventually reproduce in its turn, populations would grow "geometrically," like compound interest. Obviously, such population growth cannot be sustained indefinitely in a finite world. It must somehow be "checked." And so, he concluded, if disease and other sources of mortality don't stop population growth first, then famine will.[2]

Reading Malthus, the twenty-nine-year-old Darwin suddenly grasped what had been eluding him: "it at once struck me that under these circumstances favourable variations would tend to be preserved and unfavourable ones to be destroyed. . . . Here then I had at last got a theory by which to work. . . ." And work he did, building "one long argument" that natural selection is the agent responsible for the adaptive attributes of living creatures, an argument that he at last synopsized and published only after another British naturalist, Alfred Russel Wallace, derived essentially the same insight from his own reading of Malthus and his own rich experience, and sent Darwin an essay on the subject.[3]

What Darwin and Wallace were the first naturalists to fully grasp can be summarized as follows. Those individuals who survive and reproduce are likely to differ, statistically, from those who do not, with the result that each generation consists of the progeny of a select subset of the parental generation. This "natural selection" of those who will reproduce and those who will not can make populations evolve over generations, such that the creatures in question become better and better adapted to the various challenges that they confront. Darwin chose to call this mindless, automatic process *natural selection* in order

---

[2] Malthus's *Essay on the Principle of Population* was first published in 1798. The quotation here is from Chapter 1 of the sixth edition (1826), which is the one that Darwin owned, as excerpted by Glick and Kohn (1996, 325).

[3] The story of how Darwin and Wallace independently discovered natural selection and were jointly credited for it in 1858, before the *Origin* appeared in 1859, has been told many times. A rich account is that by Desmond and Moore (1991).

to highlight an essential similarity with the *literal* selection exercised by animal breeders and horticulturalists who decide which individuals should be kept as breeding stock. In both cases, only a "selected" (non-random) subset of a population gets the opportunity to reproduce, and over generations, the entire population evolves accordingly, regardless of whether there is any actual agent doing the selecting.

The theory stands on three premises. The first is that the variability in the traits of individuals affects their prospects for survival and reproduction. The second is that this variability is to some degree "heritable," which simply means that young tend to resemble their parents more, on average, than they resemble a random member of the parental generation. The third is Malthus's observation: Young are produced in such numbers that not everyone could possibly survive and reproduce, with the result that competition with other members of one's own species for the limited resources required for survival and reproduction is ubiquitous. Each of these three propositions is undeniably true.

Put these three uncontroversial premises together, and the theory of evolution by natural selection follows as an inescapable, logical deduction. When differential survival and reproduction are nonrandomly related to differences in the attributes of individuals *and* those differences in attributes are heritable, systematic change over generations of the sort that we now call "evolution" can ensue.[4]

Malthus's imagery also helped Darwin appreciate that natural selection is a competitive process. All the exquisitely functional attributes of plants and animals must necessarily have been forged in the crucible of reproductive competition. Why? Because the only criterion by which traits will proliferate under natural selection is if they somehow help those who possess them to reproduce at higher rates than conspecific (same-species) rivals who happen to have alternative traits. Every one of our evolved attributes—every organized, functional anatomical, physiological, or psychological attribute that can be said to be a component of "human nature" (or of the human nature of just one sex)—can thus be interpreted as a means to the end of reproducing

---

[4] I say that evolution *can* ensue, not that it *will* ensue, because even if individual differences are both heritable and consequential, selection is often "stabilizing" rather than "directional": When a trait's central tendency is *already* optimal (usually as a result of past selection), ongoing natural selection will tend to "stabilize" it; that is, selection against suboptimal variants will *prevent* the trait from evolving ("drifting") away from the optimum.

more successfully than other people. I will henceforth refer to such attributes as "adaptations."[5]

A brief *caveat* is required. When I say that natural selection is a "competitive process," or even that all evolved adaptations are "functionally competitive," I am not suggesting that every adaptation must be competitive in any direct sense. Some animals rarely or never confront the competition aggressively. Ecologists refer to the situation in which rivals ignore one another and focus their efforts on finding and consuming scarce resources as quickly as possible as a "scramble competition," which they contrast with confrontational "contest competition." Moreover, although natural selection favors such anti-predator adaptations as fleetness of foot, it would be perverse to say that out-running a predator constitutes an act of competition against other potential prey.

What justifies the word "competition" here is that in each case, there's a prize at stake, namely one's eventual share of the parentage of the next generation, and there are winners and losers. Natural selection is chronically in action, weeding out the less successful types. And although reproductive competition is often indirect and subtle, it can also be blatant. Selection clearly can, and frequently does, favor vanquishing rivals in combat, incapacitating them, and usurping the resources that they've collected. In any complexly social species in which individuals have abilities to assess how their rivals are doing and to adjust their own efforts accordingly, we can expect to see a rich variety of tactics of direct competition.[6]

Violent Adaptations

At first blush, it may seem implausible that violence could be interpreted as an adaptation like vision or fleetness of foot. Violence is a source of immeasurable pain and injustice. Merely witnessing an act of violence can be nauseating, and most people sensibly steer wide of violence-prone individuals "like the plague." It is therefore only a short

---

[5] This use of the word "adaptation" is standard in evolutionary biology. Unfortunately, the same word is also used to refer to the *process* of becoming better matched to one's environment, whether evolutionarily or as a result of processes in individual development such as learning. To avoid confusion, note that when a writer refers to *an* adaptation, the meaning is almost certainly the functional attribute itself and not the process.

[6] For "scramble" *versus* "contest" competition, see, for example, Anazawa (2011) and references therein. Regarding adaptations for contest competition, including assessment of opponents, see Hardy and Briffa (2013).

mental leap to the metaphorical characterization of violence itself as "sick." But such a pejorative dismissal of violence as pathology is wrong.

The erroneous value-laden interpretation of violence as pathological is pervasive not only in popular discourse but even in the writings of psychiatrists and social scientists. A recent popular science book entitled *The Anatomy of Violence* provides a striking example. Its author, University of Pennsylvania criminologist Adrian Raine, describes in some detail the brain abnormalities that have been found in some notorious perpetrators of certain, predominantly violent, crimes, and then jumps to a breathtakingly general conclusion: "criminals [have] broken brains . . . that are physically different from those of the rest of us." Not "some criminals," mind you, nor even "violent criminals." Just "criminals." Raine's relentless message is that those who commit crimes are sick, and that we can and should intervene to "cure" them.[7]

Adrian Raine is a distinguished researcher who has made valuable contributions in areas ranging from longitudinal studies of the childhood antecedents of adult criminality to high-tech imaging of the brains of wife-beaters and sex offenders. He has been a tireless champion of the view that criminology must move beyond its sociological origins and become more "biological." It is therefore ironic that he seems not to have grasped a basic implication of Darwin's theory: Minds have been "designed" by selection to promote self-interest, and we have no reason to anticipate that their healthy functioning will always be socially benign. Like other animals, human beings have evolved to be effective competitors, both by promoting their own fortunes and by undermining the fortunes of their rivals.[8]

People often sound positively righteous when they denounce violent behavior as "sick," and it's easy to see why. Deploring violence in this particular way functions as a cheap-talk advertisement of one's commitment to non-violence; it can even make the speaker sound generous

---

[7] For the "broken brains" quote, see page 180 in Raine (2013).

[8] You needn't be a Darwinian to be skeptical of Raine's message. A prominent mainstream criminological alternative to his view that crime is pathological is "rational choice theory" (e.g., Cornish and Clarke 1986). Its proponents argue that normal people may be motivated to rob, exploit, and harm others when the perceived benefits exceed the perceived costs, and that criminalizing these actions is how society alters incentive structures to reduce crime's profitability. Rather than counter this perspective with evidence or arguments, Raine virtually ignores it. His sole citation of rational choice theorists takes the form of a brief, dismissive caricature (175) in which he claims that the theory's advocates invoke it only as special pleading to explain white-collar, but not blue-collar, crime; this is simply untrue.

and politically progressive: "I'm not blaming these poor benighted souls for their dastardly deeds. They're sick, and they need therapy, not condemnation!" Appealing as this stance may seem, however, it is an impediment to both analysis and remedial action. Violence cannot be explained away as mere pathology.

To understand why not, consider what the word "pathology" actually refers to and implies. A pathology exists when an anatomical, physiological, or psychological mechanism or process is "broken," such that its effectiveness in achieving the purposes for which it evolved is compromised. Certain pathologies, such as bone fractures and aneurysms, are quite literally breakages. Other failures of function are induced by such things as parasitic worms, bacteria and viruses, which are collectively referred to as "pathogens": life forms that engender pathology. The harms that pathogens cause are unsurprising once we realize that they have themselves been targets of natural selection, and that the sole criterion of their evolutionary success has been how effectively they can exploit host tissues to reproduce and disperse, regardless of their effects on host well-being. Finally, a third major category of pathology includes degenerative conditions like osteoarthritis, arteriosclerosis, and various cancers, which (when they are not induced by pathogens) may be consequences of accumulated toxins and genetic mutations, or even simple wear and tear, and which typically increase in prevalence with age.[9]

Each of these three sources of pathology is relevant to certain particular instances of violent behavior, but none of the three can even begin to explain the *existence* of violence or its typical features. As regards the first source of pathology, literal breakage, there is no question that damage to particular brain structures can lead to pathologies *of* violence, but these are predicated upon the prior existence of neural organization *for* the generation of adaptively organized violence. Damage to the midbrain structure known as the amygdala, for example, can induce rage and attacks, precisely because one function of an intact amygdala is to *regulate* anger and attack behavior. As regards the second source of pathology, the story is the same: In those unusual cases

---

[9] For an evolutionary perspective on adaptation *versus* pathology and a taxonomy of pathologies, see Nesse and Williams (1994). For discussion of the vexing question of whether antisocial behavior reflects adaptation or pathology, see Wakefield (1992) and Krupp et al. (2013). Regarding senescent decline (i.e., age-related diminution of function for intrinsic reasons other than the effects of pathogens), see Rose (1991) and Kirkwood and Austad (2000).

in which violence is induced by a pathogen, such as the snapping and biting behavior of animals infected with rabies, it is the normal regulation of violent capacities that has been disrupted. Finally, although degenerative pathologies sometimes entail irritability and aggression, violence is obviously not itself a phenomenon indicative of age-related decay. Quite the contrary, in fact: In the human case, the most violent demographic class is young adult males, and it is no accident that they are also the most physically formidable demographic class.[10]

But if violence is not a disease, what sort of positive evidence justifies interpreting it as an instance of complex adaptation instead? In one of the most influential biological books of the twentieth century, *Adaptation and Natural Selection*, the late George C. Williams argued persuasively that criteria of "good design" provide our only sound basis for concluding that some aspect of an organism has been shaped by selection to achieve a particular function. The vertebrate eye provides a classic example. Why are we sure that the eye is an evolved adaptation? Because of the uncanny match between its putative function, vision, and its attributes. There's a transparent cornea that allows light to reach internal photoreceptors, a pupillary opening that responds to brightness, a lens that changes shape in such a way as to permit objects at varying distances to come into focus, many levels of neural machinery that transduce light energy and process it, and much, much more. It is no more plausible that all these elements evolved for a purpose other than vision, or for no purpose at all, and that they just happen to be thrown together in a way that incidentally permits vision, than that a tornado sweeping through a junkyard should incidentally assemble a Boeing 747 from the materials therein.[11]

The case that violence is an evolved adaptation, rather than the detritus of a junkyard tornado, may not be so transparent as the case for the vertebrate eye, but it too is compelling. The first essential point in making that case is to recognize that violent behavior typically

---

[10] Regarding brain mechanisms organized for the production of violent action, see Nelson and Trainor (2007). Regarding the violent capabilities and proclivities of young men, see Wilson, Daly, and Pound (2010).

[11] The classic work on evolutionary adaptation and how to recognize it is Williams (1966); a popular exposition is Dawkins (1986). The "junkyard tornado" quip is borrowed from astronomer Fred Hoyle. Ironically, Hoyle imagined that he was debunking the possibility that cellular life could have evolved on earth and that he was thereby supporting its extraterrestrial origin; his imagery has been gleefully co-opted by anti-evolutionists. But see Dawkins (1996) for why Hoyle's *reductio ad absurdum* makes better sense as an argument *for* Darwinian "gradualism."

promotes its perpetrators' interests. Its primary elicitors are threats to Darwinian fitness, and its effects are typically to counter those threats. Animals—present company included—behave violently primarily in response to the usurpation of essential resources by rivals and/or in order *to* usurp resources *from* rivals, and they direct their violence primarily against those rivals. Those who initiate violence typically have something to gain: Overt aggression occurs where territories are limited or food is scarce, when one's offspring are under threat, and in the context of mating competition.[12]

In addition to this contextual appropriateness of violent aggression, the motivational state of angry readiness to attack prepares potential aggressors both to inflict harm and to tolerate possible damage to themselves. Effective attack postures are the most obvious components of this mobilization, but beneath the skin, there are adaptive shifts in blood circulation and clotting potential, pain sensitivity, and the availability of energy to the muscles, all of which prepare the angry individual both to be a more effective attacker and to be more resistant to the damage that a counterattack may inflict.[13]

Animals possess anatomical structures that serve solely or primarily as weapons. These are often characteristic only of the particular life stages in which aggressive competition is required, and are often peculiar to the more competitive sex, which is usually but not always the male. Especially telling is the widespread phenomenon of seasonal shutdown: In various species, once all the fertile females are pregnant and there are no further perquisites of dominance, testicles regress, weapons such as antlers are literally cast aside, and males who had recently raged at the sight of one another forage quietly side-by-side. A good deal of mammalian neuroanatomy and neurochemistry is dedicated to aggression, and the structure and function of the relevant brain areas also differ systematically between the sexes and across the seasons.[14]

---

[12] For reviews of theory and research on contest competition in animals, see Hardy and Briffa (2013).

[13] On physiological mobilization for aggressive action and its contingent controls, see, for example, Huntingford (1992). Sell (2011) reviews the natural history of human anger, arguing that displays of anger communicate genuine threat, but are nevertheless best interpreted as modulated "negotiation tactics" rather than as manifestations of being "out of control".

[14] On the neuroscience of aggression and violence, see, for example, Nelson and Trainor (2007); Trainor and Nelson (2012) provide further detail on the diversity of evolved neuroendocrine regulatory mechanisms. Siegel and Victoroff (2009) focus on the neuroscientific basis of aggression and pathologies thereof in our own species.

The obvious conclusion is that both violent capability and the inclination to aggress have been significant targets of Darwinian selection. This should surprise no-one. Aggressors sometimes reap large gains, but the costs of bad decisions in aggressive competition can be disastrous. If there are *any* domains of social action in which there's a premium on good decision-making, potentially violent confrontation is surely one!

The Variable Intensity of Competition

Comparisons across species provide further testimony to the potency of selection in shaping the anatomy and psychology of aggressive behavior. Sex differences in both weaponry and action are much more dramatic in some animals than in other related species, and the reasons for this diversity are now reasonably well understood. Consider the following examples.

In herd-living antelopes such as kudus and elands, and in herd-living primates such as Hamadryas baboons, some males monopolize "harems" while others never get to breed at all. In such a "winner-take-all" society, male competition is fierce, and even a casual human observer can easily see that the males are much bigger and more heavily armed than the females. Meanwhile, in related species, the ecology of feeding and predation is such that the females won't gather together into tight groups that males can defend from rivals, and most males therefore stick with a single mate. No one male in such a situation is likely to father many more young than a single female can bear, and a much larger percentage of adult males will become fathers than is the case in their harem-forming relatives. In other words, reproductive success in these latter species is relatively equitable, and their mating systems are more nearly monogamous than in the harem species. In these animals, the males tend not to be nearly so specialized for combat, and a casual human observer may have trouble even telling the sexes apart. Examples of these more peaceable species include pair-forming antelopes such as klipspringers and dikdiks, and pair-forming primates such as owl monkeys and gibbons.[15]

If only a few males reproduce successfully and those few winners win big, the competition to become one of the winners is obviously going to be intense. Selection then favors whatever it takes to win, which often means size and weaponry. If you knew nothing else about

---

[15] On the association between a species' characteristic degree of sexual dimorphism in body size and weaponry, on the one hand, and the extent to which its mating system is polygamous, on the other, see, for example, Alexander et al. (1979) and Lindenfors et al. (2007).

a newly encountered animal's way of life, but could see that the males have powerful musculature and fearsome horns or claws or teeth that distinguish them from the females, you could safely bet that the mating system is highly *polygynous*, which means that a breeding male mates with multiple females. You would also be wise to bet that males aspiring to join the select ranks of the breeders will be willing to fight tooth and nail for that privilege. Natural selection has no reward for avoiding injury and enjoying a long life if those outcomes can be achieved only by avoiding contest competition and never breeding. Like the young male killed in battle, the long-lived noncombatant will be nobody's ancestor and his genes will eventually die with him. At least the male who risked his life fighting for dominance gave himself a chance.

Think of it like this. In any sexually reproducing species, the males are engaged in a "zero-sum" contest for shares of the paternity of future generations: For one male to gain a percentage point, some other male or males must incur an equivalent off-setting loss. Meanwhile, the females are engaged in a distinct, parallel contest over maternity. Each individual is in competition with others of its own sex to divide up that sex's half of the species' total genetic posterity, and the male and female "pies" that are to be divided are thus identical in size.

On the basis of what I've said so far, the situations facing females and males sound identical. However, the two parallel single-sex competitions need not be equally intense, and they seldom are. Males commonly have both a higher ceiling on their potential number of offspring than females, and a greater probability of dying without having produced any young at all. When this is so, and when the sexes are equally numerous, then males and females necessarily have the same *mean* (average) number of offspring, but the males have a higher *variance* (a statistical index of variability). This variance can be thought of as an index of the intensity of competition. When everyone gets the same prize regardless of performance, the outcome variance is zero, and there is no real competition. A winner-take-all contest, by contrast, has the highest possible payoff variance, and the competition is maximally intense.

The red deer (*Cervus elaphus*)—the handsome beast that is called an "elk" in North America—is a highly polygynous animal. The sexes differ greatly in size and weaponry, and successful stags (males) defend "harems." A healthy hind (female) can bear only one calf in any one year, but a successful stag might sire a dozen. Figure 3.1 portrays an evidence-based projection of the eventual lifetime breeding success of a hundred newborn males and a hundred females on the Isle of Rum, just off the coast of Scotland. As is the case in most wild animals—and as the Reverend Malthus anticipated more than two hundred years ago—many newborns of both sexes leave no descendants. Note, however, how much more likely total reproductive failure is for the males: Only 22 percent of newborn males will ever sire a calf, whereas 44 percent of the females will eventually give birth to at least one. Note, too, that the most successful stag will sire thirty-three young in his career, whereas the most fecund hind will bear only thirteen.

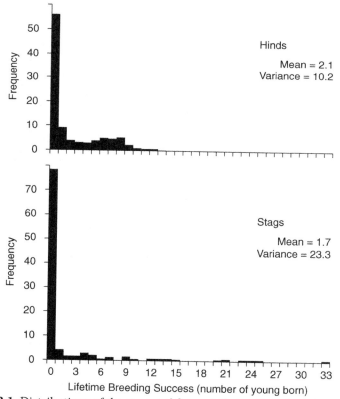

Figure 3.1. Distributions of the expected future Lifetime Breeding Success (LBS), at birth, for a cohort of 100 red deer (*Cervus elaphus*) females (hinds) and 100 males (stags), based on the LBS attained by deer born between 1983 and 1989 on the Isle of Rum, Scotland.[16]

---

[16] The data for figure 3.1 were generously provided by Professor Josephine Pemberton, University of Edinburgh. Estimates required different assumptions for hinds and stags. Hinds seldom dispersed far, and very few bred on the study area although born off it, so I included all female

Why is it specifically the male sex that has the higher ceiling on maximal reproductive potential and the greater fitness variance, and not the female? The simple answer is that one stag can inseminate many hinds in a single season, whereas a hind can gestate and nurse only one youngster. More generally, in any species in which females put more time and energy into the production of each offspring than their male counterparts, males have the potential to reproduce at shorter intervals and higher rates than is possible for any female.

This asymmetry is common, but it is not a universal feature of animal reproduction. There are several species of birds, for example, in which these familiar sex roles are switched: The females fight with one another over the males, who provide most of the parental care. However, there are no mammals in which sex roles are reversed in this way. Once our distant ancestors had become committed to a reproductive strategy in which young completed much of their development inside their mother's body and continued to feed on her milk after they were born, that avenue was apparently shut off.[17]

There is, of course, considerable diversity even within the mammals, and the patterning of that diversity is intelligible. The extent to which males have higher fitness variance, grow larger, die younger, and otherwise differ from females varies greatly even among closely

---

records. For males, by contrast, I excluded presumed emigrants, and I assumed that immigrants and emigrants had identical success. The sex difference in mean LBS is due mainly to a biased sex ratio at birth (127 males for every 100 females in the birth cohorts of 1983–89), such that more males than females divided up equivalent sex-specific "pies" of parenthood; regarding year-to-year variation in the sex ratio at birth, see Kruuk et al. (1999).

The reproductive maxima portrayed in figure 3.1 (33 young for a stag; 13 for a hind) have both been surpassed by animals born in subsequent cohorts, but I cut off the figure at the 1989 birth cohort because some of the deer born in each subsequent year were still alive and their final LBS tallies were therefore still to be determined at the time of writing. The new record for a stag is 48, and for a hind 14.

[17] Bateman (1948) was the first biologist to recognize that males have greater variance in reproductive attainment than females where (and because) females invest more in each offspring; Trivers (1972) generalized the argument, and showed that where males provide more "parental investment" (PI) than females, sex roles in courtship and aggressive competition are also reversed. Clutton-Brock and Vincent (1991) proposed that the sex difference in potential rates of reproduction is a more basic issue than the difference in PI, but since differences in PI are almost always the source of differences in potential reproductive rate, the basic explanation is little changed. Following Kokko and Jennions (2008), it is now fashionable to criticize Trivers for portraying sex differences in PI as a prior cause of other sex differences while ignoring the fact that each sex's parental efforts are themselves evolutionarily labile and may respond to, as well as cause, mating competition. But regardless of the evolutionary trajectory leading to contemporary sex differences in PI, it remains true that the sex that invests more (usually females) is a limiting and contested resource from the perspective of the sex that invests less (usually males).

related species, and these aspects of sexual differentiation are strongly correlated with one another. Most notably, wherever pairs remain together and care for their young cooperatively—as foxes and beavers and some monkeys do, for example—all of these sex differences tend to be diminished or abolished. Biparental care of this sort is rather rare in mammals, however, presumably at least partly because it is difficult for males to have reliable cues of paternity, with the result that fathers are vulnerable to *cuckoldry*—unwitting investment in young sired by rivals—and paternal investment is therefore evolutionarily unstable. Nevertheless, there are mammals in which females and males care for the young together and mateships can persist for years, and *Homo sapiens* is, of course, one such species. What, then, of reproductive competition in human beings?

Homo Sapiens: A Somewhat Polygamous Animal

Human attributes obviously didn't evolve in the context of a mating system exactly like the red deer's. One sign that our ancestral mating system was different is the fact that men and women aren't nearly as different in their average body size and their anatomical weaponry as stags and hinds. Another is the fact that pair formation and at least a modicum of paternal participation in child care are characteristic of virtually every human society, including the hunter-gatherers whose ecological circumstances are most similar to those of evolving *Homo*. Men and women marry, and raise families together. Stags and hinds do not.

But if humans cannot be described as extreme polygynists, neither can we be said to be as monogamous in our behavior as owl monkeys or gibbons. Women and men also differ more in body size and musculature than do the females and males of these monogamous primate species, which provides a further indication that we didn't evolve as perfect monogamists. In terms of "sexual dimorphism"— the sex differences in gross size and in various anatomical dimensions — *Homo sapiens* is an in-between sort of primate species, suggesting that the same may be true with respect to the degree to which females and males differ in the intensity of reproductive competition. And human behavior bears this out.

Anthropologists have documented the practices of hundreds of traditional societies that function without written laws or governmental controls, and it is almost everywhere the case that a minority of men—specifically those who are recognized by their peers as the most successful —may have more than one wife. A result is that men have a higher maximum number of children than women, a higher reproductive variance, and a higher probability of dying childless. As we saw in red deer, although not necessarily to the same degree, reproductive competition among human males is therefore more intense than reproductive competition among human females.

About ten to twelve thousand years ago, people began to domesticate plants and animals, and soon, once agriculturalists were able to mass-produce food, new levels of inequality in wealth and in access to fertile women emerged. Cross-cultural variability in inequality and competition is a topic to which I'll return in subsequent chapters. Here my point is simply that hunter-gatherers, who subsist on the wild foods that they can gather or catch, rather than on domesticated crops, tend to be relatively egalitarian compared to some more "modern" societies in which high-ranking men often monopolize large numbers of wives and concubines. And because it is hunter-gatherers who arguably provide our best approximation of the conditions that prevailed during the lion's share of human evolution, I'll use data from a well-studied hunter-gatherer population, namely the Dobe !Kung San of Botswana's Kalahari Desert, to illustrate the magnitude of reproductive competition in our own species.

Hunting and gathering societies have been observed and studied on every continent (except, of course, Antarctica), but their traditional ways of life are rapidly disappearing as they are enticed and/or coerced into residency in settled communities and into participation in modern economies. The various San groups of the Kalahari—the so-called "Bushmen"—are no exception. However, the Dobe !Kung persevered with their ancestral practices through the mid-twentieth century, and they were carefully studied by anthropologists, medical scientists, and others.

For present purposes, the most noteworthy of the scientists who have documented the lives of the Dobe !Kung is University of Toronto demographer Nancy Howell. Figure 3.2 portrays her estimates of the eventual lifetime reproductive success of an average cohort of 100 newborn boys and 100 newborn girls living the traditional hunter-gatherer life. The format is identical to that of figure 3.1, and that's not a coincidence: I deliberately organized the red deer information in such a way as to parallel Howell's data.[18]

---

[18] The demographic data used here are from Howell (1979); see also Howell (2010).

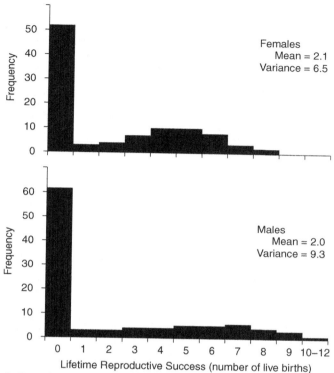

Figure 3.2. Distributions of the expected future lifetime reproductive success (LRS), at birth, for a cohort of 100 newborn girls and 100 newborn boys, based on data collected by Howell (1979) among the Dobe! Kung, living as hunter-gatherers in Botswana's Kalahari Desert in the 1960s.

In some ways, the human data in figure 3.2 are reminiscent of the red deer data in figure 3.1, but there are important differences. Like stags in comparison to hinds, the !Kung males had a higher maximum number of progeny than their female counterparts, a greater chance of dying childless, and a higher variance in reproductive success. But these sex differences are not nearly as dramatic in the human case. A newborn !Kung girl had a 48 percent chance of eventually becoming a mother, and a newborn boy a 38 percent chance of becoming a father; this is not a trivial difference, but it's much smaller than the two-to-one difference (44 percent *vs.* 22 percent) that we saw in the deer. Similarly, with respect to both the maximum number of young and the variance therein, the values for male deer were more than twice as high as the corresponding female values, whereas in Howell's human data, the male values are less than 1.5 times as high as the female values.

If every marriage were monogamous, indissoluble, and untroubled by adultery, then every woman who gave birth to a given number of children would have a corresponding male partner who sired exactly that same number, and the female and male distributions in a portrayal like that of figure 3.2 would thus be identical. Clearly, things didn't work quite like that among the Dobe !Kung, and they don't work quite like that in any other human population either. In the case of the !Kung, the reason for the sex differences is clear: A few men got more than a monogamist's share of the fitness pie by monopolizing much or all of the reproductive careers of more than one woman, sometimes sequentially, sometimes simultaneously. And to varying degrees, that happens in virtually every human society.[19]

Figure 3.2 suggests that human reproduction "in a state of nature" exhibits patterns of variability among females and males similar to that of a mildly polygynous animal species. According to Howell's data and estimates, at any single slice-in-time census, about 5 percent of !Kung men would have had two wives simultaneously, and a somewhat larger percentage of women, but fewer than 10 percent, would have been sharing a husband with a co-wife.[20]

In this and other regards, the !Kung seem to have been somewhat more monogamous and egalitarian than most hunter-gatherers. According to a recent review of the available data by Cambridge University anthropologist Frank Marlowe, the average prevalence of polygamous marriage in "warm-climate, non-equestrian" hunter-gatherers was approximately twice as high as what Howell observed in the Dobe !Kung. Sex differences in maximum numbers of children and in reproductive variance are also much larger in many populations, including other hunter-gatherers, than in the Dobe !Kung. Using Howell's data to envision what ancestral human marital and reproductive competition may have been like is therefore a "conservative" choice in the following

---

[19] Even if monogamous marriage were obligatory and extramarital conception were vanishingly rare, the fact that men have longer potential reproductive careers than women would enable a few serial monogamists to reproduce like bigamists. But in fact, in the !Kung and in other traditional nonstate societies, monogamy is *not* obligatory and the most successful men are simultaneous polygamists.

[20] The reason why the percentage of !Kung women married to bigamists was a little less than twice the percentage of men who were bigamists is that adult women outnumbered men, as a result of greater male mortality throughout the lifespan.

sense: We are more likely to have underestimated the ancestral variance in male reproduction and the level of effective polygamy than to have overestimated these things.[21]

The cross-cultural prevalence of polygynous marriage is testimony to its deep history. In almost every known hunter-gatherer society, it was legitimate and normal for a highly successful man to take a second wife. And in the few exceptions, the absence of polygyny was apparently attributable not to societal prohibitions, but to harsh environments in which no man was able to support more than one wife. In a recent analysis, combining information on the degree to which different hunter-gatherer groups have diverged from one another genetically with information on the distribution of polygamy across the same societies, University of Missouri anthropologist Rob Walker and his colleagues used statistical techniques designed for reconstructing evolutionary trees to generate an educated guess about the marital practices of the earliest modern humans. Their conclusion was that an ancestral social system in which marriages were arranged by kin and in which some men had multiple wives is "at least 50,000 years" old.[22]

Reproductive Competition and Warfare

If the idea that human marriage practices are not fundamentally monogamous surprises you, that's probably because you are accustomed to a world in which polygamy is almost everywhere outlawed. But this prohibition is a cultural innovation that is nowhere more than a few centuries old. Its novelty and the current predominance of legislated monogamy raise an interesting question: Why have laws against polygamy, which curtail one of the most cherished perquisites of power, been so successful in recent history? I think the most compelling answer is one proposed by University of Michigan evolutionary biologist Richard Alexander, who attributes the ascendancy of "socially imposed monogamy" to the utility of distributing local marital and reproductive opportunities more equitably when you are threatened by hostile, expansionist neighbors. A society in which only monogamous marriage is deemed legitimate is likely to be more cooperative, solidary,

---

[21] For the prevalence of polygynous marriage among warm-climate, non-equestrian hunter-gatherers, see Marlowe (2010, 272).

[22] See Walker et al. (2011) for the "phylogenetic" reconstruction of early human marriage practices. They estimate that a "low level" of polygyny prevailed among ancestral hunter-gatherers, with "low level" defined as a situation in which fewer than 20% of married men have multiple wives.

and militarily effective than a rival polity in which the elites keep harems and a large underclass of men is consigned to bachelorhood. When you're trying to rally the foot soldiers, "A chicken in every pot and a wife in every bed" is likely to be a more effective slogan than "You take care of the fighting while I take care of the women."[23]

If we define "war" broadly, such that it includes institutionalized feuding between patrilineages under weak governments and recurrent violent raids on neighboring bands or villages, then warfare is ancient, ubiquitous, and undoubtedly a part of the explanation for our evolved capacity for lethal violence. To citizens of modern nation states, the illegitimate murder of an ingroup member may seem to be an entirely different matter than the legitimate killing of an enemy in war. In practice, however, the line between the two is blurry and to some degree arbitrary.[24]

The chronic state of war that cast a shadow over many nonstate societies, and that lingers in parts of lowland Amazonia and highland New Guinea, was overwhelmingly a matter of conflicts between factions within the same ethno-linguistic group. Individual warriors might join a raid or battle hoping to kill a particular, personally known individual; conversely, they would sometimes stay home because of marital or other ties to particular men on the other side. However, the fact that larger coalitions tend to defeat smaller coalitions creates a pressure for ever larger alliances, and as the technology of warfare has advanced, the more formidable coalitions have repeatedly annihilated less cohesive groups. As coalitions became larger, with boundaries increasingly likely to match ethno-linguistic boundaries, it became easier to draw a distinction between "us" and "them." But this distinction, in and of itself, could not put an end to rivalries within groups. Men compete with their allies, even their close kinsmen, for status, influence, wealth, and women, and history tells us that these competitions could be lethal.[25]

For centuries, even as clans with their own military capabilities were coalescing into nascent kingdoms, the killing of a within-group rival continued to be treated as a personal matter, to be settled by

---

[23] Alexander (1987) lays out the argument that monogamous marriage has spread because it facilitates large-scale cooperation and military success. See also Betzig (1986) and Sanderson (2001).

[24] For evidence of the high prevalence of warfare in prehistory and in small-scale nonstate societies, see Keeley (1996), Otterbein (2004), and Gat (2006).

[25] Regarding individual initiative in small-scale warfare, see, for example, Macfarlan et al. (2014) and references therein.

compensatory payments from the killer to the victim's kin, or by blood revenge. But for obvious reasons, leaders have always disliked wasteful squabbles among their underlings, and when they have had the power to do so, kings have proclaimed that all within-group slayings (and much else) were crimes against themselves and hence against the state. In our own Anglo-American history, this central authority over the entitlement to kill is still not quite a millennium old. It was decreed by William the Conqueror, and it is only since William that we have a basis for classifying some killings as criminal homicides.[26]

Homicide as Contest Competition

In 1995, one of my students, Nuala Kehr, conducted a survey to see how much her fellow McMaster University students knew about homicide in Canada. We wanted to know whether any misperceptions that the students might hold were systematically biased, and whether particular beliefs might be associated with particular attitudes. For each question about factual matters, we asked each participant to provide his or her "best guess," and to then rate "how sure you are that your answer is roughly correct" on a scale ranging from "not at all confident (pure guess)" to "absolutely confident."

As we anticipated, the 194 students' responses were biased in a number of ways. One of our questions was about trends "over the last twenty years." The students were given five options: Had Canada's homicide rate "increased substantially," "increased somewhat," "stayed about the same," "decreased somewhat," or "decreased substantially"? The overall trend was a little bumpy, but the correct answer was clearly that homicide in Canada had "decreased somewhat" over the preceding twenty years (figure 3.3). This was hardly a secret. The fact that the 1994 rate had hit a new low had been a prominent story, both in print media and on television news, in the weeks before we conducted our survey. Nevertheless, fully 90 percent of the students picked one of the first two options, guessing that homicide in Canada had been on the rise.[27]

Despite the ready availability of information to the contrary, we had anticipated that the students' beliefs might be distorted in this way.

---

[26] Regarding the historical conversion of homicide from a "tort" to a "crime," see Daly and Wilson (1988b), Chapter 10.

[27] For the survey of McMaster students' beliefs about homicides, see Kehr et al. (1997). More or less regardless of the particular question, men were more confident of their answers, although no more accurate, than women.

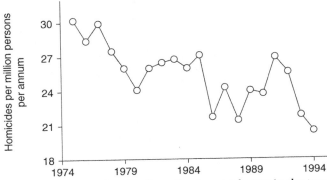

Figure 3.3. Downward trend in the Canadian homicide rate in the twenty years (1975–94) prior to a 1995 survey of students' beliefs about homicide in Canada. (Data courtesy of Statistics Canada.)

False belief in a "rising tide of violence" is a hardy perennial and a significant impediment to informed action, a point to which we'll return. We couldn't decide whether we should be alarmed or amused, however, by a more surprising additional finding: Those students who chose the option "increased substantially," and were thus as wrong as they could possibly be, were far and away the most confident that they were right!

Another major misperception among the McMaster students concerned which sex is more likely to be killed. Before you picked up this book, I'm sure you would have guessed correctly that a randomly selected *killer* is much more likely to be a man than a woman. Everyone seems to know that. But if you had to bet on the sex of a randomly selected homicide victim, would you have again picked a male? If not, you should have. Except in a handful of countries where overall homicide rates are exceptionally low, men constitute the majority of both killers *and* victims. In Canada, at the time of our survey, slain men outnumbered slain women by more than two to one. Nevertheless, the majority of the women who answered our survey, and almost half the men, believed that women are killed at higher rates than men. And the average confidence rating of those who got it wrong was exactly the same as the average confidence rating of those who got it right.

The FBI amasses data on all known homicide cases in the United States, and their numbers show that men outnumber women as homicide victims in that country by an even wider margin than in Canada. In the thirty three years from 1980 through 2012, US homicide victims included 431,128 adult men and 122,482 adult women. Is this excess of male victims typical of homicide more broadly? Yes, it is. According to the *Global Study on Homicide 2013*, released by the United Nations Office on Drugs & Crime, 79 percent of the world's homicide victims are male and 21 percent female. Worldwide homicide rates—computed by aggregating the data for the most recent available year, usually 2012, for each country—were 97 deaths per million men and boys per year, and 27 deaths per million women and girls.[28]

We can't determine the proportions of the killers who are male *versus* female with the same precision, because many cases are left unsolved. However, there can be little doubt that men constitute an even larger proportion of those who kill than of their victims. One relevant bit of evidence from the same U.N. study is that 95 percent of those who were *convicted* of a homicide, anywhere in the world in the most recent available year, were men.

So if there's one thing that we know for sure about homicides, it is that they are predominantly the dénouements of interactions between men. And I believe that we are justified in saying something more than just that: Homicides are predominantly the resolutions of interactions between men who are competing over scarce, valued resources. Explaining why I feel justified in saying this requires an excursion into the ethnography of homicides in a modern urban environment.

In 1980, when Margo Wilson persuaded me that we should be studying homicide, we were living in Hamilton, Ontario, 70 km west of Toronto. Apart from Toronto, the closest big city with a population in excess of a million people was Detroit, Michigan, which the press had recently crowned the "murder capital" of the United States. In the late 1970s, there had been more homicides in Detroit each year than in all of Canada, and a single police force was responsible for investigating them. Margo therefore suggested that we should contact the Detroit police and request access to their files. The man who was apparently in charge of managing police force operations was the Deputy Chief, Dr. James Bannon, so we wrote him a letter.

We were absurdly lucky. From out of the blue, a letter from a couple of Canadian academics had arrived on Deputy Chief Bannon's desk,

---

[28] The "FBI" is the *Federal Bureau of Investigation* of the United States. For FBI homicide data, see Puzzanchera et al. (2014). I define "adults" as persons over 17 years of age; for victims of all ages, the US totals are 480,212 males and 144,738 females. The UN's *Global study of homicide 2013* is available at http://www.unodc.org/documents/gsh/pdfs/2014_GLOBAL_HOMICIDE_BOOK_web.pdf.

asking if we could stick our noses into the police department's investigative files to pursue an agenda that was purely intellectual! How many busy managers of urban police forces in the United States would have replied at all, much less have invited us down for a chat? Very few, I suspect, but Dr. Bannon, whose title reflected a Ph.D. in sociology from Detroit's Wayne State University, did just that. When we entered his office, we saw two tall, framed, all-black oil paintings on the wall behind a desk on which a brass nameplate announced:

Dr. James Bannon. Take two aspirins and call me in the morning.

The affable Deputy Chief of Police didn't need to be convinced that basic research using the information in his department's files could be of value; he had published analyses of assault data drawn from those files himself, and after a brief discussion of our aims and interests, he took us to meet Robert Hislop, the head of the homicide unit.

Our ambition was to amass detailed information on an unbiased sample of homicide cases, by examining *all* the case files for some delimited period of time. When we explained this to Inspector Hislop, he immediately recalled that a graduate student from Wayne State had done a similar project a few years earlier. As research for her PhD thesis on "the social realities of participating in homicides," the student, Marie Wilt, had made extensive notes and had recorded a number of variables for every one of the 690 homicides that had occurred in Detroit in 1972, Since completing that project, Dr. Wilt (subsequently Wilt Swanson) had become a public health researcher, and she had never published her homicide work. When we contacted her, she generously handed over several boxes of her original notes and coding efforts. This gave us a huge leg up on our own project, so we, too, elected to focus on the 1972 cases, adding codes for some additional variables from the police investigative files, and updating information on the cases that had been solved or adjudicated only after Wilt had last visited the files.

What we were initially interested in was lethal conflicts between spouses and other family members. But we could hardly ignore the much larger number of homicides in which the victim and killer were unrelated. Unlike the family homicides, the antagonists in these non-familial cases were overwhelmingly male. In 1972, there had been a total of 385 solved Detroit homicides in which killers and victims were related neither by blood nor by marriage. Men constituted 91 percent of the offenders in those 385 cases, and 89 percent of the victims.

Circumstantial evidence indicated that killer and victim were unrelated men in the great majority of the 178 unsolved cases, too.[29]

The Detroit killers and their victims were similar in other ways, as well. The age distributions of both parties reached sharp peaks among men in their twenties and then declined steadily with age. Forty-three percent of the identified adult male offenders were unemployed, and so were 41 percent of adult male victims, both numbers being far in excess of the 11 percent unemployment rate for same-age Detroit men. They were also similar in that 73 percent of the offenders and 69 percent of the victims were unmarried, compared to 43 percent of all same-age men in the city. Almost exactly half of the killers and half of their victims had been born in Michigan and the other half in some other state; in both cases, that other state was more often Mississippi than anywhere else. The similarities were uncanny. Rather than there being a population of criminal offenders who preyed upon some other component of the populace, it looked like killers and their victims had been plucked from the same pool.

And that wasn't actually very surprising if you read the case files. Some of these Detroit homicide cases had occurred in the context of robberies and other crimes, but the majority had not. Instead, they seemed mainly to involve what we called "retaliations for previous verbal or physical abuse" or "escalated showing-off disputes." The latter usually occurred in public places, such as bars; the former typically entailed waylaying and shooting someone who had recently humiliated the shooter in the presence of mutual acquaintances. A great many of the case descriptions read as if it might have been a bit of a crapshoot which of the two parties was going to end up dead.

Of course, quite a lot of homicides do in fact occur in the context of robberies. And what could be more transparently competitive than a robbery, in which one party has something that the other wants, and takes it for himself? Many additional homicides take place in the context of business rivalries, especially if the business happens to be an illegal one such as the drug trade or one of the other illicit businesses run by gangs who compete for turf. Legal business rivalries spawn the occasional homicide, too, but illegal business tends to be more lethal,

---

[29] Wilson and Daly (1985) provide more details on these Detroit homicides. Regarding the cases in which killers and their victims were romantic partners or relatives, see Daly and Wilson (1982) and Daly, Wilson, and Weghorst (1982). Marie Wilt's prior analyses of these same 1972 Detroit cases can be found in Wilt (1974).

presumably because rivals can't use the law to deter and punish usurpation, enforce contracts, and settle disputes, and must be prepared to defend their own interests by all means necessary. Their situation is much like that faced by the citizens of "primitive" societies with no central authority, no police, and no third-party justice, and homicide is frequent in those societies, too; we'll come back to this in Chapter 10.

For present purposes, the crucial point is that homicides committed in a context of other criminal activities are overwhelmingly clear and unequivocal manifestations of *competition*: They arise from contests over some sort of resource in which one party's gain is experienced by the other as a loss. And what I now wish to argue is that the same goes for the so-called "social conflict" homicides that are not associated with any other crime: the ambushes in retaliation for a humiliation, the escalated showing-off disputes in bars, the angry confrontations that ensue when a man makes advances to another man's girlfriend.

In 1958, the prolific and influential American criminologist Marvin Wolfgang (1924–98) published a pioneering study of homicides, based on police investigative files in the city of Philadelphia. Wolfgang's study was one of the first to seek generalizations by tabulating information on all the cases, instead of just dwelling on some particularly juicy ones, and subsequent researchers, including Margo and me, followed his lead in that regard. Wolfgang divided the Philadelphia killings into twelve main "motive" categories, of which one turned out to be far and away the most frequent. His label for that most prevalent conflict typology was an "altercation of relatively trivial origin: insult, curse, jostling, etc."[30]

Ten years later, amid public alarm about political assassinations in the United States, President Lyndon Johnson established a *National Commission on the Causes and Prevention of Violence*. Seven task forces were constituted to study the issue, and in 1969, they produced a 13-volume report. Having amassed data from many post-Wolfgang studies of homicide, its authors reaffirmed that "altercations appeared to be the primary motivating forces" in US homicides, and that the "ostensible reasons for disagreements are usually trivial." The word "ostensible" hinted at the possibility of nontrivial issues beneath the surface, but unfortunately, the report's authors didn't follow through. Instead, they approvingly quoted a Dallas homicide detective to the

---

[30] See Wolfgang (1958).

effect that "Murders result from little ol' arguments over nothing at all," and continued from there with a string of lurid accounts of petty cases, inviting readers to shake their heads in amazement: "Believe it or not, here's the police summary of another killing . . ."[31]

This derisive mockery could only impede understanding of these altercations. Calling the precipitating circumstances "trivial" encourages us to dismiss the antagonists as men whose limited reasoning abilities and lack of impulse control suffice to explain their fate. But in reality, the motives of men who face off in potentially lethal confrontations warrant sober consideration. An outsider may disparage their disputes as "trivial," but the protagonists themselves have good reason to see things very differently. Detailed accounts of these sad episodes make it abundantly clear that the triggers of lethal altercations are almost always *status challenges*. To ignore acts of disrespect by your rivals is to imperil your reputation and relinquish your entitlement to your limited material possessions and social capital. In other words, the limited resources over which men in these dangerous disputes are competing are the intangible but crucial resources of "face," status, and respect, and they are limited because their social value is a matter of where one stands relative to others.[32]

Does Male Competition Drive the Variability in Homicide Rates?

The ubiquitous sex difference in the intensity of reproductive competition provides a satisfying explanation for the cross-culturally universal fact that it is overwhelmingly men, not women, who kill one another in response to disrespect, as well as in business rivalries and even in robberies. Arguably, a basic reason why men are readier to resort to dangerous tactics than women is the same as the reason why red deer stags compete more dangerously than hinds: Male fitness is more variable than female fitness, and has been so throughout the species' evolutionary history. But that's only part of the story. Lethal outcomes of men's competitive struggles are daily occurrences in certain social milieus, such as that of downtown Detroit in 1972, and are virtually

---

[31] The quoted US government report is Mulvihill et al. (1969).
[32] Wolfgang (1958), Luckenbill (1977), Daly and Wilson (1988b), and many other homicide studies provide numerous illustrations of the central role of "dissing" (public shows of disrespect) in lethal altercations. Many ethnographic studies also document the centrality of maintaining respect, by violent means if necessary, in the lives of the urban poor; two particularly fine examples are Lewis (1961) and Anderson (1999).

unknown in others. Could this be what the great variability in national homicide rates is primarily about?

As you may recall from Chapter 1, Margo Wilson and I proposed in 1988 that cases in which killers and their victims are unrelated men constitute the most variable component of homicide rates. If we were correct, it follows that the task of explaining the variability in homicide rates is essentially the same task as that of explaining variability in the intensity of men's competition. It also follows that a major reason why economic inequality is such a good predictor of homicide rates is that greater inequality engenders more intense competition.

But *were* we correct in proposing that the variability in homicide rates resides primarily in these male–male cases? In 1988, we showed that both cross-national analyses and longitudinal evidence of changing homicide patterns in American cities supported our proposal, and the evidence that has accumulated since 1988 has added further support. Homicide victims are still overwhelmingly male where homicide rates are very high, and are about equally divided between the sexes where rates are at their lowest.[33]

Almost every country that has a very low homicide rate is a member of the OECD (the Organization for Economic Co-operation and Development), a club that consists of just thirty-four "developed" nations. Figure 3.4 portrays the *proportion* of each OECD country's 2012 homicide victims who were male, in relation to its total homicide rate. These two quantities could, in principle, have varied independently of one another, but they clearly don't. Instead, unusually low homicide rates are associated with a reduced tendency for victimization to be male-biased.

There were four OECD nations—Iceland, Japan, Korea, and New Zealand—in which female homicide victims slightly outnumbered the males in 2012, and a fifth—Switzerland—in which each sex made up exactly half the victims. These five countries all had very low overall homicide rates of fewer than ten victims per million citizens. On the figure's right-hand side stand the United States and Estonia, with homicide rates of 47 and 50 deaths per million citizens, respectively, and males constituting 78 percent and 77 percent of victims. The association

---

[33] Although longitudinal studies often find that as homicide rates increase, the proportion of male–male cases also increases (e.g., Block 1976; Rushforth et al. 1977; Verkko 1951), as expected, evidence from temporal trends is noisier than that from "cross-sectional" (e.g., cross-national) comparisons. Trying to understand how rates change from year to year raises complex issues, especially with respect to the "lagged" effects of certain predictors (i.e., effects that are delayed and/or persistent); we'll come back to this problem in Chapter 8.

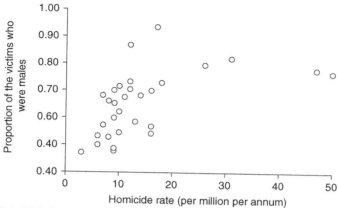

Figure 3.4. Male bias in homicide victimization in OECD countries in 2012, in relation to the overall homicide rate. Low levels of male bias are associated with low homicide rates, as expected if male-male contests are the most variable component of the homicide rate. (Data for Iceland, Luxembourg and Mexico are omitted; see text.)

obviously isn't perfect: Greece is a notable outlier at the top of the figure, with a modest overall homicide rate of 16, but with more than 90 percent of its victims male. However, the positive association between these two measures should be evident. Three OECD countries are omitted from the figure: Iceland, in which there was only one homicide in 2012; Luxembourg, in which there were only four; and Mexico, whose homicide rate of 215 per million was by far the highest in the OECD, and in which the degree of male-biased victimization (89 percent males) was surpassed only by Greece.

All in all, these 2012 data continue to support Margo's and my proposal: The higher the homicide rate, the more male-biased is the population of victims. Another way to say the same thing is this: Where homicide rates have fallen to the lowest levels, that's primarily because of an exceptionally low rate of male victimization, not of female victimization. The implication is surely that if we want to understand what drives the variability in homicide rates, we must seek the factors that cause variability in the intensity of competition among men. And that brings us back, once again, to inequality.

Or does it? Can we be sure that the problem isn't simply that men who find themselves in desperate material circumstances are apt to resort to violence, irrespective of inequality? That is an alternative that we will examine, and dispose of, in the next chapter.

4

Inequality, or Just Poverty?

As soon as we extend our gaze toward other people, richer than us, and let their incomes influence our own welfare, too, we move from concern with poverty alone to concern with inequality as well. . . . In reality, people are much more likely to think about and be concerned with those who have more than they than with those who have less. In other words, it is "envy" that is much more likely to enter our welfare function than "concern."
—Branko Milanovic, *Why We All Care about Inequality (But Some of Us Are Loathe to Admit It)*, 2007

Relative or Absolute?

If you happen to be well to do, you may be attracted to the proposition that social problems derive solely from the "absolute" deprivation of hunger, homelessness, and destitution, and not at all from the "relative" deprivation of inequality. It would be convenient for the rich if they could persuade themselves—and everyone else within earshot—that inequality is not a problem, indeed that it is a necessity in order for all of us to reap the benefits of a productive, growing economy. And when you consider the fact that the privileged dominate media ownership, governments, the academy, think tanks, and the blogosphere, it should be no great surprise that the drumbeat for this self-serving world-view is loud and incessant. Any redistribution of wealth from the rich to the poor would destroy the incentive structure that supports innovation and prosperity, or so we are told. The rising tide of extreme wealth supposedly raises all our boats.

In introductory economics courses, students are typically taught that there is an inevitable "trade-off" between incompatible societal goals of greater equality, on the one hand, and economic productivity, growth, and innovation, on the other. Facts and figures are seldom marshalled in support of this claim. Rather than trying to demonstrate that it can withstand scrutiny as an evidence-based generalization, professors and textbooks portray the trade-off as a logical deduction from first principles. Their argument goes like this. To eliminate inequality, you would have to compensate everyone identically, regardless of their efforts or the value of their labor. In such a world, there would be no incentives to innovate, nor indeed to work at all. Therefore, equality can only be achieved at the expense of productivity, and vice versa.

So far, so good, although some simplistic assumptions about what inspires people may already have aroused your skepticism. Were the game-changing innovations of the twentieth century motivated solely by anticipated monetary gains? Of course not. The people who discovered penicillin, invented the computer, split the atom, worked out how to transplant organs, created the internet, deciphered the genetic code, and so on and on, were salaried scientists who made their contributions with no hope or expectation of financial rewards.

But let's set that very large qualm aside for a moment, and grant that compensating everyone identically, regardless of their efforts, would have a disastrous effect on productivity. Nobody has ever succeeded in implementing the communist ideal of "from each according to his ability, to each according to his needs" and nobody ever will. The theory of human nature that underpins that particular ultra-egalitarian dream is no more realistic than the contrary theory that people care *only* about personal wealth.

So the reason why it is pointless to argue that rewarding everyone equally, regardless of their contributions, is a sure-fire recipe for disaster is not that the argument is false. The problem with that argument is that it's an irrelevant critique of a straw man, an attack on policies that no one is advocating. In the real world, debates concern the feasibility, efficiency, and justifiability of various possible inequality-*reducing* policies, not inequality-*abolishing* policies. And when the trade-off argument is stretched to discredit the economic utility of any and all efforts to reduce inequality, it goes completely off the rails.

The over-extended version of the trade-off argument goes like this. Because unequal rewards are needed to incentivize productivity, it follows that higher levels of inequality must be associated with greater incentives and with all the positive economic consequences that flow from those incentives. Any redistribution from the rich to the poor would therefore have to be justified on non-economic grounds, since its effect on the economy will necessarily be negative.

A moment's thought should suffice to show that this can't be right. As inequality increases, wealth is concentrated in the hands of a shrinking minority, which at the extreme becomes a despot with a huge harem. That's no foundation for innovation and entrepreneurship! So although too little inequality may indeed hamper productivity and growth, too *much* inequality must surely hamper them, too. And indeed, the evidence is now overwhelming that inequality begins to hurt economic performance long before we reach the extremes of despotism. What the evidence now indicates is that even if policy-makers had *no other aim* than to maximize economic growth and productivity—even if they had no interest whatsoever in goals like combatting poverty and injustice—the levels of inequality that prevail in rich countries are *already too high*. How economists have come to this conclusion, and *why* extreme inequality inhibits growth and innovation rather than fostering them, are topics that we will examine in some detail in Chapter 9. In this chapter, I want to retain a narrower focus on violence. Does the argument that absolute poverty is the real culprit and that inequality is a red herring have any merit when we are seeking explanations for the variability in homicide rates?

Before proceeding further, let me stress that there's no reason why "poverty or inequality?" must be an either-or issue. I am persuaded—and I'll try to persuade you—that inequality has genuine effects, but I would never suggest that "absolute deprivation" must therefore have none. There is no question that desperate material circumstances can inspire desperate measures. Just think about some grisly news story that you once read, in which starving castaways lost their compunctions about killing and cannibalizing their fellows. Yes, that really happens; I'll spare you case histories, but it's no mere urban myth.[1]

That said, it is equally implausible that one's absolute level of deprivation could turn out to be the whole story either, for reasons that we have already discussed. Throughout the course of any species' time on earth, its passions and preoccupations are constantly being shaped by natural selection to contribute to the single end of *relative* reproductive success. And in human societies, relative reproductive success has clearly been determined, in part, by relative rank. Evolutionists therefore expect social animals to be highly sensitive not only to their absolute material circumstances, but to indicators of where they stand in comparison to their fellows, as well. We humans most certainly fulfill that expectation.

---

[1] Regarding murder and cannibalism as a response to imminent starvation, see Mallin (1967) and Hutchinson (2011).

Unfortunately, few criminologists are evolutionists, and the force of this argument is lost on them. Most criminologists have nevertheless been persuaded by the evidence that inequality affects homicide rates, but there is a minority who remain skeptical, continuing to champion a counterclaim that it's really all about poverty in an absolute, not a relative, sense.

Blaming It All on Poverty

Let us begin our evaluation of that counterclaim with a point that both sides of this debate can agree on. Quantifying the extent to which income or wealth is unequally distributed will not, in and of itself, shed light on the material circumstances of the poor. Why not? Because if all that you know about a certain country's economy is its Gini index of income inequality, you will still be in the dark about how many of its people, if any, are homeless or starving. There could, in principle, be great inequality even though everyone has adequate food, housing, and other essential resources. And there could, in principle, be very little inequality where everyone is in desperate straits.

That said, if a *rich* country has a highly equitable distribution of both income and wealth, it is necessarily the case that few if any of its citizens are destitute. Moreover, it is a simple matter of fact, at least in the developed world, that a relatively high level of economic inequality usually tends to go hand in hand with a relatively large proportion of the population living in material circumstances that place them below some designated "poverty line." Thus, wherever there is severe inequality, there is usually going to be a lot of poverty, too.

And that, in a nutshell, is the basis for questioning whether inequality itself is truly relevant to the social problems, including violence, with which it is demonstrably associated. Could it be the case that poverty is the real culprit, and that the inequality with which poverty tends to be associated is a red herring?

We have already reviewed some evidence bearing on this question. In Chapter 2, we saw that the level of income inequality in the different US states was a strong predictor of their respective homicide rates, whereas the state-specific average income—whether a state is rich or poor—had no demonstrable relevance. Moreover, we saw that exactly the same was true in comparisons across the provinces of Canada, in spite of a striking difference between the two countries: In the United States, inequality was most extreme in the poorest states, whereas in Canada, inequality was most extreme in the richest provinces. These facts strengthen the argument that inequality makes a difference. But they cannot fully resolve the issue of the respective roles of inequality and poverty.

In recent years, the most forceful advocate of the hypothesis that poverty, not inequality, is the economic variable that affects homicide rates has been University of Indiana criminologist William Alex Pridemore. His argument can be summarized as a set of four claims.[2]

First, Pridemore notes, as I just did, that inequality and poverty are often correlated with one another: In many comparisons, the poorest jurisdictions are also the most unequal jurisdictions. When this is so, in the jargon of statistics, inequality and poverty are "confounded," and without adequate statistical controls, the effects of one of these two variables could be misattributed to the other.

Second, Pridemore maintains that although a large body of cross-national research has implicated inequality as a reliable correlate and probable cause of variations in homicide rates, all of this research suffers from the very problem just mentioned: Cross-national studies don't include measures of poverty among their predictor variables, and may therefore be misattributing poverty's effects to inequality. The authors of these studies typically maintain, or at least imply, that they have dealt with this potential problem by including measures of absolute well-being, such as median income or GDP (gross domestic product) per capita, in their analyses. But Pridemore insists that that is no remedy. Why not? Because, as I noted above, knowing a country's average income doesn't tell us whether many or few are poor.

The third prong of Pridemore's argument concerns research comparing across jurisdictions within the United States. Unlike the cross-national research, these studies typically *have* included measures of absolute deprivation as well as inequality, and he maintains that this kind of research has consistently implicated absolute poverty as the more relevant factor.

Finally, Pridemore claims to have incorporated a novel measure of poverty into his own original cross-national analyses, and to have shown that when he does so, he gets the same result as that which he attributes to the US studies: Poverty is a robust predictor of homicide rates whereas inequality is not.

---

[2] See Pridemore (2008, 2011). In both papers, he makes the four-point argument that I discuss here, using somewhat different data sets and analyses.

If this argument were correct, it would be devastating to my thesis. In reality, however, only the first of Pridemore's four points is valid. Thus, although a point-by-point rebuttal of his argument must be rather technical, I feel that I have no other choice than to provide just that. I also fear that my point-by-point rebuttal may strike some readers as an *ad hominem* attack. It is not. I focus on Pridemore because his is the most thorough argument that anyone has made for the primacy of poverty over inequality, and his work has been widely cited as authoritative, even by authors whose own analyses support contrary conclusions. If the proposition that inequality is a distraction and its apparent effects are really due to absolute poverty is ever to be laid to rest, dissecting Pridemore's arguments is obligatory. Readers who find the dissection tedious may wish to skip ahead to the next chapter.

So let us begin with the first of the four claims. Yes, inequality and absolute poverty are often "confounded": The most equitable developed countries have the lowest rates of poverty, and the same is true with regard to US states. In 2010, for example, there was a modest but statistically significant correlation between state-level income inequality and the percentage of a state's populace whose family income placed them below the federal poverty line. Please recall, however, that a positive association between inequality and poverty is neither inevitable nor universal. As we saw in Chapter 2, for example, the most equitable Canadian provinces have had the lowest homicide rates, despite being the poorest provinces, with *larger* proportions of the populace living in poverty than in the richer, more unequal provinces. But let's give a modicum of credit where it's due: Pridemore is right that mistaken inferences could, in principle, result from the confounding of inequality with absolute poverty.[3]

Pridemore's second claim is that the many cross-national analyses that have implicated inequality as a predictor of homicide suffer from this very confound: They lack controls for "absolute" poverty. There is a kernel of truth to this criticism, too, but only a kernel, and the implications are actually problematic for Pridemore's argument. The kernel of truth is that the researchers who conduct cross-national analyses don't

---

[3] In 2010, the correlation between income inequality (measured as the Gini coefficient of pre-tax household income) and poverty, across the fifty US states plus the District of Columbia, was 0.472. Data for both measures are from the *American Community Surveys* conducted by the US Census Bureau. This correlation is lower than that which prevailed for 1990 (see Chapter 2), mainly because some relatively rich states, especially New York, had moved up in the inequality rankings, but it is still highly significant.

Regarding the contrast between Canada and the United States, see Daly, Wilson and Vasdev (2001).

typically try to include a direct index of poverty such as the percent below the poverty line. The reason why they don't incorporate such an index is that none is available; the *United Nations* uses distinct measures of poverty for "developed" and "developing" countries. But why is that? The answer is that "poverty" is not adequately conceived of as absolute material deprivation. In much of the world, impoverished people lack shelter, clothing, and enough to eat, but in rich countries, the poor are seldom at risk of starvation and often live in material circumstances that most of our ancestors and billions of our contemporaries might envy. Conservative defenders of inequality are fond of noting these facts, but my point is very different from theirs. I mention this not to belittle the very real suffering and humiliation of those living in poverty in the midst of affluence, but to illustrate how dichotomizing "absolute" *versus* "relative" disadvantage misrepresents the lived experiences of the poor. Poverty is, in large part, a matter of being deprived relative to others.

That the experience of poverty entails more than "absolute deprivation" is widely, if not universally, appreciated. According to British sociologist Peter Townsend's influential definition, for example, people "can be said to be in poverty when they lack the resources to obtain the types of diet, participate in the activities and have the living conditions and amenities which are customary, or are at least widely encouraged or approved, in the societies to which they belong." Similarly, according to the European Commission's *Joint Report on Social Inclusion 2004*, "People are said to be living in poverty if their income and resources are so inadequate as to preclude them from having a standard of living considered acceptable in the society in which they live. Because of their poverty they may experience multiple disadvantages through unemployment, low income, poor housing, inadequate health care and barriers to lifelong learning, culture, sport, and recreation. They are often excluded and marginalised from participating in activities (economic, social, and cultural) that are the norm for other people and their access to fundamental rights may be restricted."[4]

For the sake of argument, however, we can set aside the issue of what role social context and social comparisons play in the experience of poverty, and we can go along with Pridemore by *defining* "poverty" (or "absolute poverty") as a matter of falling short of a specified income

---

[4] For the first quoted definition of poverty, see Townsend (1979, 31). The second is from page 8 of the European Commission's *Joint Report on Social Inclusion 2004* at http://ec.europa.eu/employment_social/soc-prot/soc-incl/final_joint_inclusion_report_2003_en.pdf.

threshold, the so-called "poverty line." We can then conduct analyses designed to distinguish the effects of inequality from those that are due simply to poverty thus defined. Pridemore's criticism of the cross-national research is that incorporating average income (or GDP per capita) into a multivariate analysis fails to address the confounding of inequality and absolute poverty. In this, he is simply mistaken.

Here's why. It is true that average income, *by itself*, is not necessarily informative as regards how many people live in poverty, and neither is inequality, *by itself*. It does not follow, however, that controls for average income are therefore meaningless additions to tests of the predictive power of inequality, because *together*, the two carry information about poverty levels that could not be derived from either variable alone. For a given level of average income, a reduction in the number of people living in poverty can only be achieved by a reduction in inequality. Thus, poverty and inequality are not statistically independent of one another. If either of the two were to increase while average income remained constant, the other would increase, too.

An example using real data should help make this clearer. On the basis of its most recent income survey in 2010, the US Census Bureau has reported both the median household income and the Gini index of household income inequality, for each of the fifty states plus the District of Columbia (the national capital district encompassing the city of Washington). The Census Bureau has also reported the percentage of each state's population whose absolute incomes placed them below the federal poverty line. But let's imagine, for a moment, that we didn't have access to that last poverty statistic. If we didn't know what proportion of the population had incomes that placed them below the poverty line, could we get away with using median income and income inequality as predictors of a social problem like homicide, and still claim to have controlled, at least to some degree, for absolute poverty? Yes, we could.

How so? Well, in the first place, median household income alone is actually a pretty good proxy for poverty in this case: All by itself, it predicts 63 percent of the variability among the states in the proportions of their respective populations that are living below the poverty line. But having information on inequality permits us to do even better than that. In 2010, there was no association whatsoever between the median household income of a state and the value of its Gini coefficient of income inequality, and yet *both* were significantly related to poverty. What this implies is that some of the variability across states in the incidence of poverty was predictable from average income, and some *additional* variability in the incidence of poverty was predictable from inequality. And that is indeed the case. Together, median household income and income inequality predicted 84 percent of the variability in the percentage of the population living below the poverty line, and that's a fairly impressive degree of statistical control of poverty's effects. Pridemore's assertion that adding average income to your statistical model provides no remedy for the confounding between poverty and inequality is therefore incorrect.[5]

Is Poverty a Better Predictor of Homicide than Inequality?

So much for Pridemore's second point: In the cross-national research that he disparages, possible effects of absolute poverty have actually been controlled much more effectively than he understands or will admit. So what about his third claim: that when both inequality and poverty have been used as simultaneous potential predictor variables in research comparing across jurisdictions within the United States, poverty has consistently outperformed inequality as a predictor of homicide rates.

This is a very curious conclusion to have drawn from a very messy literature. The first two published studies to address the relative importance of poverty and inequality both appeared in 1982. One, by State University of New York sociologists Judith and Peter Blau, was a sophisticated statistical analysis of possible determinants of homicide rates in the 125 most populous US cities. Interestingly, the Blaus concluded that economic inequality between individuals and economic inequality between "races" were distinct predictors, and that controlling these inequalities abolished apparent effects of (absolute) poverty, of region (south *versus* north), and of "race" itself. These conclusions, which are still widely cited and accepted, are diametrically opposed to Pridemore's generalization.[6]

Coincidentally, while the Blaus were conducting this pioneering research, Columbia University criminologist Steven Messner was independently doing something quite similar. He too focused on the variability in homicide rates across US cities, but he used data from a larger sample of cities than the Blaus had done, and he used some

---

[5] Data are again from the US Census Bureau's 2010 *American Community Survey*. Across the fifty states plus D.C., the bivariate correlations among median household income ("income"), the household Gini index of income inequality ("Gini"), and percent below the poverty line ("poverty") are as follows: income and Gini, $r = -0.016$; income and poverty, $r = -0.791$; Gini and poverty, $r = 0.472$.

[6] See Blau and Blau (1982).

different predictors, including both population size and population density. Messner's results weren't as straightforward and readily interpretable as those of Judith and Peter Blau, but they too were inconsistent with Pridemore's assertions about what the US homicide literature supposedly shows. Like the Blaus, Messner reported that both income inequality and poverty were significant correlates of homicide, and that income inequality was the stronger of the two predictors. But when Messner threw these and a bunch of other candidate predictors into a multivariate analysis, income inequality ceased to be a significant predictor of homicide and poverty became a significant *negative* predictor. In other words, with all other correlates statistically "controlled," it seemed that the more poverty a city had, the *lower* its homicide rate! Messner had no interpretation to offer for this surprising result, which was almost certainly an artifact of the particular combination of (mutually correlated) predictor variables that he used.[7]

Subsequent research hasn't upheld Messner's odd result, and I wouldn't even have mentioned it, were it not for the fact that it illustrates what I mean by a messy literature. Pridemore can indeed find studies in which poverty apparently outperforms inequality, but that is by no means a clear and consistent finding. Other analyses show precisely the opposite. There isn't *any* clear and consistent finding from all the various studies of homicide across the United States, arguably because many of them have entailed tossing a hodgepodge of predictor variables, which are highly correlated with one another and thus partly redundant, into analyses that have weak theoretical rationales. What shakes out as the most important predictor in that kind of everything-but-the-kitchen-sink analysis has a large element of chance.[8]

---

[7] See Messner (1982).

[8] This problem is known technically as "multicollinearity." The Wikipedia entry on the subject (http://en.wikipedia.org/wiki/Multicollinearity) explains it well, noting that when "two or more predictor variables in a multiple regression model are highly correlated . . . the coefficient estimates may change erratically in response to small changes in the model or the data." Thus, "a multiple regression model with correlated predictors can indicate how well the entire bundle of predictors predicts the outcome variable, but it may not give valid results about any individual predictor, or about which predictors are redundant with respect to others." See Belsley et al. (2010) for a full explication.

One study that seems to me much sounder than most in this regard was a study of "crime" in US cities, not just homicide; econometrician Morgan Kelly (2000) ran various regression models with well-thought-through combinations of control variables, and concluded that measures of absolute poverty predict property crimes, but not violent crimes, whereas measures of inequality predict violent crimes, but not property crimes. A concern here, however, is that most crime is less reliably recorded than homicide, and it is plausible that the magnitudes of bias in detection and recording of crime are themselves correlated with predictors in Kelly's models.

So let's simplify. Considering only poverty and inequality, is poverty really the better predictor of homicide? No, it is not, and data for the fifty states plus D.C. in 2010 can again be used to make the point. It turns out that both poverty and Gini are significant correlates of homicide, but Gini is much the stronger of the two, predicting fully half of the variability in homicide all by itself, whereas poverty alone predicts less than a fifth. Because Gini and poverty are also significantly correlated with one another, however, the crucial question is which of the two predicts homicide better when the other is statistically controlled. The answer is unequivocal. Gini remains a strong, significant predictor of the homicide rate when poverty is "held constant" by statistical methods. Poverty, by contrast, loses its predictive power when Gini is "held constant." In sum, the literature is messy, but we can say with confidence that Pridemore got it wrong: In research that incorporates measures of both "absolute" poverty and inequality to predict the variability in homicide rates across jurisdictions within the United States, poverty *does not* consistently outperform inequality.[9]

So far, we have seen that Pridemore's dismissal of previous cross-national findings is unfounded, and that his summary characterization of the results of research comparing jurisdictions within the United States is simply wrong. What, then, of his fourth and most provocative claim, namely that he has at last incorporated a measure of poverty into cross-national comparisons, and has shown that it trumps inequality? To avoid any risk of misrepresenting him, I quote from the opening summary (the "abstract") of his 2011 article in the *British Journal of Criminology* entitled "Poverty matters."

> Dozens of cross-national studies of homicide have been published. Virtually all have reported an association between inequality and homicide, leading scholars to draw strong conclusions about this relationship. Unfortunately, each of these studies failed to control for poverty. In the present study, I replicated two prior studies in which a significant inequality–homicide association was found. After the original results were replicated, models that included a measure of

---

[9] I computed homicide rates for 2010 from counts in the FBI's *Uniform Crime Reports*—and in the case of Florida, which is missing from the FBI data, from that state's own *Uniform Crime Reports*—in conjunction with populations as reported by the US Census Bureau. The economic data are again from the 2010 *American Community Survey*. The bivariate correlation between Gini and homicide is 0.710, and between poverty and homicide 0.419. The partial correlation between Gini and homicide controlling for poverty is 0.640 ($p < 0.0000001$); the partial correlation between poverty and homicide controlling for Gini is 0.136 ($p = 0.341$).

poverty were estimated to see whether its inclusion had an impact on the inequality–homicide association. When effects for poverty and inequality were estimated in the same model, there was a positive and significant poverty–homicide association, while the inequality–homicide association disappeared in two of three models.

This sounds like a powerful case, but wait. How is it, you may be wondering, that Pridemore was able to find "a measure of poverty" to include among his predictor variables, when no previous analyst had been able to come up with one? The answer is that when he sought a cross-nationally valid measure of poverty, he had no more luck than his predecessors and therefore resorted to something completely different: a variable that seemed to him, on purely intuitive grounds, to be a likely indicator of absolute deprivation. A casual reader of his work could easily overlook this crucial point, because it is only after another eighteen dense pages of text and tables that we finally discover what his claims about the "effects of poverty" actually refer to: "The infant mortality rate was used as a proxy for poverty."[10]

At this point, your alarm bells should be going off. Sure, it's highly plausible that poverty will raise the infant mortality rate. But so will other factors. Infants die at relatively high rates where infectious diseases abound, for example, and differential exposure to disease vectors depends at least as much on latitude as it does on poverty. Pridemore's argument becomes even stranger when we consider the fact that infant mortality and homicide are two components of the overall death rate. His main result therefore boils down to this: Where mortality from one of these causes is high, so is mortality from the other. The obvious implication is that these two components of the death rate must have some causal factors in common, and the obvious question is what those common causal factors might be.[11]

Finally, even if it were reasonable to use infant mortality as a "proxy" variable, it would actually make a more defensible proxy for inequality

---

[10] The lengthy quotation is from Pridemore (2011, 739); the term "models" in this case refers to regression analyses that incorporate different sets of potential predictors of the various countries' homicide rates. The revelation that the word "poverty" in his abstract actually refers to the infant mortality rate appears on page 757.

[11] In other words, Pridemore's analysis treats infant mortality as if it were a potential cause of homicide, when both should be treated as outcome variables. Granted, it's just a regression analysis and every student of statistics has learned the mantra that "correlation does not imply causation." But the whole point of the exercise was to assess the merits of alternative hypotheses about the *causes* of homicide.

than for poverty! More than twenty years ago, economist Robert Waldmann conducted an extensive cross-national analysis of possible predictors of infant mortality, and was surprised by his results:

> Comparing two countries in which the poor have equal real incomes, the one in which the rich are wealthier is likely to have a *higher* infant mortality rate. This anomalous result does not appear to spring from measurement error in estimating the income of the poor, and the association between high infant mortality and income inequality is still present after controlling for other factors such as education, medical personnel, and fertility.[12]

Waldmann's result was not quite as original or "anomalous" as he imagined. Another economist, Anthony Flegg, had reported similar findings a decade earlier. And subsequent research reinforces Waldmann's and Flegg's conclusions. In response to Pridemore's claims that "absolute poverty" can be indexed by infant mortality, and that it is a better predictor of homicide than "relative poverty" (inequality), criminologist Steven Messner and colleagues analyzed the relationships among these and other variables in data more recent than Waldmann's, and got essentially the same result:

> This article assesses the extent to which the infant mortality rate might be treated as a 'proxy' for poverty in research on cross-national variation in homicide rates . . . The results reveal that the infant mortality rate is correlated more strongly with 'relative poverty' than with 'absolute poverty,' although much unexplained variance remains. In the regression models shown here, the measure of infant mortality and the relative poverty measure yield significant positive effects on homicide rates, whereas the absolute poverty measure does not exhibit any significant effects.[13]

Pridemore's argument is left in tatters. We have seen that a regression analysis with both inequality and average income among its predictors controls for poverty remarkably well, notwithstanding his claims to the contrary. He was wrong again in his blanket claim that poverty outperforms inequality in US studies. And now we see that his alleged

---

[12] The quotation is from Waldmann (1992, 1283; emphasis in original).

[13] Flegg (1982) anticipated Waldmann's finding. The passage quoted here is from Messner et al. (2010, 509). It was explicitly directed at Pridemore (2008), and yet in reiterating his argument, Pridemore (2011) cited Messner et al. (2010) without responding to, or even acknowledging, its devastating criticism of his "proxy" measure.

demonstration that poverty outperforms inequality in cross-national analyses used a putative proxy measure of poverty that is not in fact an indicator of absolute poverty at all!

A Legacy of Obfuscation

I'm sorry if my critique has become tedious, but I am not simply bullying an easy target. Pridemore's claims about the relative impacts of poverty and inequality on homicide continue to be cited respectfully, even by analysts whose results lead them to contrary conclusions, and his misinterpretation of infant mortality continues to muddy the waters.

Consider the following three examples. Brazilian epidemiologists Paulo Nadanovsky and Joana Cunha-Cruz conducted an innovative analysis indicating that income inequality and "impunity" (the probability that serious crime will go unpunished) jointly predict national homicide rates both in Latin America and in rich developed countries. Because of Pridemore's claims, they too employed infant mortality as a proxy for poverty, even though it added nothing to the prediction of homicide in their analyses. Similarly, political scientists Sean Fox and Kristian Hoelscher conducted analyses of homicide rates incorporating novel measures of the "political order" as predictors, and they too followed Pridemore by using infant mortality as a proxy for poverty alongside an index of income inequality. Finally, criminologists Amy Nivette and Manuel Eisner added an index of "political legitimacy" to yet another such cross-national study, with similar results: The new measure had an evident effect, as did income inequality, but infant mortality, which they too accepted as an unproblematic reflection of "poverty," did not. In all three of these studies, the accuracy of the researchers' quantitative estimates and the soundness of their interpretations would probably have been strengthened if they had left infant mortality out of the analyses.[14]

More recently, a June 2014 *World Bank* report concludes that income inequality is a powerful determinant of the variability in homicide rates across Mexican municipalities, but its authors still cite Pridemore as having demonstrated that statistical controls for poverty abolish the

---

[14] The cited studies are those by Nadanovsky and Cunha-Cruz (2009), Fox and Hoelscher (2012), and Nivette and Eisner (2013). I suggest that these authors' results and interpretations would probably have been improved by omitting infant mortality from their predictors because, as a better proxy for inequality than for poverty, its inclusion exacerbates the problems of collinearity without providing offsetting benefits.

apparent effects of inequality in cross-national studies. The fact of the matter is that he has demonstrated no such thing, and has only obscured the legitimate issues of whether, where, and in what ways poverty and inequality might both be relevant.[15]

The defenders of privilege will probably never give up trying to demonstrate that the social costs of economic inequality are statistical artifacts. But the evidence is running strongly against them. Op-ed assertions that inequality is a non-issue should be recognized for what they are: propaganda, and nothing more.

---

[15] For the World Bank study of homicide in Mexico, see Enamorado et al. (2014).

5

Jockeying for Position

It is not enough to succeed. Others must fail.
—Gore Vidal, speech at a memorial service,
December 8, 1976

Sensitivity to Relative Standing

Embedded within the orthodox theoretical framework of economics is a curiously counterfactual assumption: What you want is unaffected by what the people around you already possess. The theorists who make this strange assumption haven't tried to justify it. They don't even seem to notice that they're making it.

In the standard theorems concerning supply and demand, the "clearing" of markets, and many other things that every beginning student of economics is required to learn, the archetypal human consumer, whom I will refer to as *Homo economicus*, comes equipped with certain preferences that somehow combine to generate a "utility function," and rationally pursues the business of maximizing total utility. Utility is invariably assumed to increase with increasing wealth, but whether "goods" other than money, such as health or the number of one's children, generate utility is up to the theorist. Social influences on preferences and desires seldom enter into the calculations. Utility theories don't explicitly deny that you might be motivated to keep up with the Joneses, to dress fashionably, or to acquire the latest cool gadget before your brother-in-law, mister know-it-all, gets it first. They just tend to leave all that out.

Can this omission be justified in terms of a pragmatic division of labor among the social sciences? Not really. By ignoring social influences, economists have taken on board, albeit implicitly, a premise that whatever the determinants of preferences may be, they do *not* include social comparisons. Of course, a good scientific theory is, by its very nature, a simplification, but the messy details that a good theory strips away must be inessential details, and that's simply not the case when economic models ignore social influences. Consider, for example, the relationship between supply and demand. According to the orthodox neoclassical economics that is still being taught to students, the reason why scarcity makes prices rise is because scarcity reduces the supply while leaving the demand unchanged. Period. The obvious possibility that some commodities are coveted precisely *because* of their scarcity is not part of the standard theory, and failures of the theory to account for real-world behavior flow directly from this omission.

A few maverick economists have recognized that this presumption of an absence of social influence is essential to many cherished theorems in their field, and that it happens to be nonsense. Robert Frank of Cornell University has been particularly relentless and scathing on this subject, both in the *Economic View* column that he writes for the *New York Times* and in a series of books. Frank points out that people are deeply interested in what he calls "positional goods" for reasons that are every bit as self-interested and "rational" as the profit-seeking motives of the fantastic *Homo economicus*. People care about positional goods primarily because of social status and competition, and this rationale is often transparent. One of Frank's favorite illustrations concerns a competitive job interview. If only one of those who are being interviewed for a job can get it, and if wearing a more expensive suit than rival candidates raises one's chances of being the winner, then how much a job candidate is willing to spend on a suit will be affected by how much the *other* applicants are willing and able to spend.[1]

Once our basic needs have been met, many of the "goods" that we desire are positional goods of this sort. The result is often a social trap of the sort that Frank refers to as an "expenditure cascade," which he analogizes to the phenomenon that biologists call an "evolutionary arms race":

> A mutation for larger antlers served the reproductive interests of an individual male elk, because it helped him prevail in battles with other males for access to mates. But as this mutation spread, it started an arms race that made life more hazardous for male elk over all. The antlers of male elk can now span five feet or more. And despite their utility in battle, they often become a fatal handicap when predators pursue males . . .

---

[1] For evidence and arguments on the crucial importance of positional goods, see Frank (1985), Frank and Cook (1995), and Frank (1999).

Individual and group interests are almost always in conflict when rewards to individuals depend on relative performance, as in the antlers arms race. In the marketplace, such reward structures are the rule, not the exception. The income of investment managers, for example, depends mainly on the amount of money they manage, which in turn depends largely on their funds' relative performance . . .

In cases like these, relative incentive structures undermine [Adam Smith's] invisible hand. To make their funds more attractive to investors, money managers create complex securities that impose serious, if often well-camouflaged, risks on society. But when all managers take such steps, they are mutually offsetting. No one benefits, yet the risk of financial crises rises sharply . . .

It's the same with athletes who take anabolic steroids. Individual athletes who take them may perform better in absolute terms. But these drugs also entail serious long-term health risks, and when everyone takes them, no one gains an edge.

If male elk could vote to scale back their antlers by half, they would have compelling reasons for doing so, because only relative antler size matters. Of course, they have no means to enact such regulations.[2]

For these reasons, Frank has suggested, only half in jest, that the day will come when economists will celebrate Charles Darwin, not Adam Smith, as the intellectual founder of their science.

Frank has been an exceptionally eloquent critic of the hidden assumption that preferences have no social context, but he hasn't been the only one. A handful of economists who believe that theory in their field ought to aim for realism as well as elegance have decried this absurdity for more than a century. In 1899, in his first and best-known book, *The Theory of the Leisure Class*, Thorstein Veblen (1857–1929) mocked what was then, and still is, standard economics:

The end of acquisition and accumulation is conventionally held to be the consumption of the goods accumulated - whether it is consumption directly by the owner of the goods or by the household attached to him and for this purpose identified with him in theory. This is at least felt to be the economically legitimate end of acquisition, which alone it is incumbent on the theory to take account of. Such consumption may of course be conceived to serve the consumer's physical wants—his physical comfort—or his so-called

---

[2] The quotation is from Frank's *New York Times* column of July 12, 2009, as downloaded on July 8, 2013 from *www.nytimes.com/2009/07/12/business/economy/12view.html*.

higher wants—spiritual, aesthetic, intellectual, or what not; the latter class of goods served indirectly by an expenditure of goods, after the fashion familiar to all economic readers.

But it is only when taken in a sense far removed from its naïve meaning that consumption of goods can be said to afford the incentive from which accumulation invariably proceeds. The motive that lies at the root of ownership is emulation . . . The possession of wealth confers honour; it is an invidious distinction. Nothing equally cogent can be said for the consumption of goods, nor for any other conceivable incentive to acquisition, and especially not for any incentive to the accumulation of wealth.

As regards the word "invidious," Veblen was careful to explain that he was not deploying it pejoratively, but in a "technical sense as describing the comparison of persons with a view to rating and grading them in respect of relative worth or value—in an aesthetic or moral sense."[3]

In a nutshell, Veblen was saying that after basic subsistence needs are met, the motivation for economic activity is all about relative position. *The Theory of the Leisure Class* had many fans, especially among sociologists, and it is still being read today. But perhaps because he eschewed mathematical formalisms and scholarly citation of his sources, Veblen was always a bit of a black sheep in economics, where his influence faded more from neglect than as a result of contrary evidence or cogent counterarguments.

The fates of other dissenting voices have been similar. Harvard economist James Duesenberry, for example, noted in his 1949 doctoral dissertation that "There is little observational warrant for the independence of different individuals' preferences yet it is implicit in most economic theory" (13), and he suggested as an alternative that "impulses to consume . . . arise when an individual makes an unfavorable comparison of his living standard with that of someone else" (32). On the basis of this insight, Duesenberry built a substantial alternative theory of consumption and saving, in which each consumer's "utility index" was based in part on his or her observations of what salient others possessed and consumed.[4]

---

[3] The longer quotation is from Veblen (1899, 25–26); the explication of "invidious" is quoted from page 34. Ironically, *The Theory of the Leisure Class* was written while Veblen was an instructor in economics at the University of Chicago, soon to become the prestigious twentieth-century stronghold of the "neo-classical" economic theory that Veblen disparaged; Veblen was dismissed from the university in 1906.

[4] The thesis was published as a monograph: Duesenberry (1949).

Duesenberry went on to demonstrate that his theory could do a better job than the standard theory when the task was to explain real world data, such as how the amounts that people save change as their incomes change. But as Frank has lamented, Duesenberry's theory was scorned and is largely forgotten, while the theories that it out-performed continue to be taught in introductory economics courses. It is hard to avoid the suspicion that when it comes to the issue of "positional preferences," the usual scientific criteria of predictive validity and evidence have been subordinated to neo-liberal ideology. For an economic theory to find its way into the standard curriculum, it appears that it must sit well with the dogma that free markets produce socially desirable outcomes and should never be messed with.

Relative Deprivation

With certain laudatory exceptions, economists have resisted incorporating "positional" striving and "invidious" social comparisons into their explanatory framework. But other social scientists have not been so squeamish. Social psychologists and sociologists have long been aware that people care not only about their personal material circumstances—about food and shelter and other necessities—but also about how their circumstances compare with those of their fellow citizens. If you don't have enough food to maintain your body weight or to sustain a pregnancy, you are suffering from deprivation in an "absolute" sense. But well fed or not, if you have less than your neighbors, you may feel the pain of "relative deprivation."[5]

Criminologists sometimes use the term "relative deprivation" interchangeably with inequality. But although relative deprivation has an obvious affinity with the sort of economic inequality that can be quantified with a Gini index, that's not exactly what the term originally meant, nor what it means today in the substantial psychological literature on the subject. "Relative deprivation" refers not to the inequality itself, but to a subjective *response* to that inequality.

This two-word phrase entered the social sciences in 1949, in a report on the adjustment of soldiers to life in the US armed forces. The report's senior author, Samuel Stouffer, was a sociologist by training, but his interpretations of his data were unabashedly psychological. He coined

---

[5] In addition to Veblen, Duesenberry, and Frank, economists who have recognized the value that people attach to relative position and have analyzed its effects include Clark and Oswald (1996) and Luttmer (2005).

the phrase "relative deprivation" as a label for a particular state of mind: the feelings of dissatisfaction and resentment that people experience when they think they're getting the short end of the stick.[6]

Stouffer and his colleagues were led to focus on this issue by some puzzling contrasts in the questionnaire responses of various groups of soldiers whom the researchers had interviewed about their military experiences. One of these puzzling contrasts was that African-American soldiers stationed in the southern states were more satisfied with their treatment in the army than those stationed in the north, even though there was apparently no objective basis for their greater satisfaction. Another puzzling finding was that men in the military police expressed greater satisfaction with their prospects for promotion than men in the air force, despite the fact that the military policemen were far less likely than the airmen to actually get a promotion. To explain these and other anomalies, Stouffer suggested that people evaluate their circumstances by drawing comparisons with salient others around them. If the black soldiers compared their situations to those of the local African-American citizenry, then army life may have looked pretty good in comparison to civilian life in the relatively racist south, but not in the north. And if the airmen had acquaintances who had been promoted from their ranks, while the military policemen did not, perhaps social comparisons fed the former's disgruntlement.

Through decades of subsequent research and elaborations, Stouffer's psychological construal of what it means to be relatively deprived has predominated. In an influential review published in 1976, Boston University psychologist Faye Crosby declared that relative deprivation is an "emotion," and more specifically "a sense of grievance or of resentment" that constitutes "one type of *anger*." Many subsequent writers on the subject have cited Crosby's definition approvingly. It is therefore unfortunate that some criminologists continue to use the same term to refer to the simple fact that some people have less wealth than others, regardless of whether those who are thus "deprived" resent their relative disadvantage, indeed regardless of whether they are even aware of it.[7]

Redefining relative deprivation purely in terms of inequitable resource distribution may seem more "scientific" than Crosby's

---

[6] See Stouffer et al. (1949).

[7] Regarding relative deprivation as a psychological response to inequality, see Crosby (1976), Olson et al. (1986), and Smith et al. (2012).

definition because it's more "objective." That appears to be why the *Wikipedia* entry on the topic (or at least today's version) begins as follows:

> **Relative deprivation** is the lack of resources to sustain the diet, lifestyle, activities, and amenities that an individual or group are accustomed to or that are widely encouraged or approved in the society to which they belong. Measuring relative deprivation allows an objective comparison between the situation of the individual or group compared to the rest of society. Relative deprivation may also emphasise the individual experience of discontent when being deprived of something to which one believes oneself to be entitled, however emphasizing the perspective of the individual makes objective measurement problematic.[8]

But the subjective element, however problematic it may be methodologically, cannot simply be ignored. If a relative "lack of resources" really does affect violence—or anything else—that effect must be mediated by the ways in which deprived persons apprehend their relative disadvantage and by the ways in which they react to it. And *that* appears to be why the same *Wikipedia* entry immediately switches gears. With no acknowledgment that the preceding sentence is now being contradicted, the next paragraph explains that relative deprivation "is a term used in social sciences to describe feelings. . ." and that its "preconditions" include that "Person A does not have X," that "Person A knows of other persons that have X," and that "Person A wants to have X."

Of course, an internal contradiction in a *Wikipedia* entry should be no great surprise, given the multi-authored process of serial correction by which these little essays are assembled. The important question is this: How does any particular, "objective" degree of inequality have its effects on people's thoughts and actions? And when you put it that way, the question sounds like one that might reside within the purview of social psychologists.

Social Comparison Processes

In 1954, Leon Festinger, then at Stanford University, published a paper entitled "A theory of social comparison processes." He proposed that we humans are "driven" to assess our opinions and abilities, and that in order to do so, we seek information about the opinions and abilities of other "similar" people. This paper and his

---

[8] The quoted passage was downloaded from *http://en.wikipedia.org/wiki/Relative_deprivation* on September 6, 2014.

ensuing theory of "cognitive dissonance" made Festinger (1919–89) the most influential social psychologist of his generation. Following his lead, hundreds of experimental and survey studies have addressed questions about the phenomena that he dubbed social comparison processes. How does the "drive" to make these comparisons vary across situations and across content domains? Are there systematic changes in this drive over the course of the lifespan? What makes someone else similar enough to be treated as a salient reference person to whom one might compare one's self? In what contexts do we attend preferentially to those who are of greater or lesser status or ability than ourselves?[9]

This massive research effort should be of great relevance to the question of how inequality affects our behavior, including violent behavior, but it has been less informative than one might hope. That's partly because Festinger's initial focus was on how we assess our *opinions* and *abilities*, not our material circumstances. But it's also because of three more general weaknesses of social psychology as a field.

The first of these weaknesses is a propensity to draw grand generalizations from the results of idiosyncratic experiments in highly artificial laboratory settings. For example, there have been scores of papers reporting the results of experiments that take the following form. Psychology students are brought to the laboratory and handed a paper-and-pencil personality inventory to fill out; are then given false feedback about how they scored and about their scores' implications; are then told that they can ask to see one other person's score; and, finally, are instructed to choose which single other score they would like to see (the highest, lowest, next highest above their own, etc.). Although devoid of actual social interaction or realistic social information, these studies are nevertheless treated as critical tests of hypotheses about social cognition and action, such as whether "threat" induces us to compare ourselves preferentially to our inferiors. And then, when small differences in methods produce seemingly contradictory results—as they regularly do—further research is undertaken to make the conflicting results compatible by invoking the contingent effects of an additional variable such as engagement or privacy or mood. The permutations are sufficiently numerous to keep a platoon

---

[9] Festinger (1954) launched the "social comparison processes" research area. For reviews of that research, see, for example, Suls and Miller (1977), Olson et al. (1986), and Suls and Wheeler (2000, 2012).

of researchers occupied from dissertation to retirement, without once facing up to the possibility that their experiments speak weakly, if at all, to real-world social processes.[10]

A second compromising weakness of social psychology is its implicit premise that the students who enroll in introductory psychology courses can be considered representative of all human beings. Anthropologists and cross-cultural psychologists have criticized this surprising ethnocentrism harshly, and I cannot do better than to quote from the abstract of a particularly forceful and thorough recent critique by Joseph Henrich, Steven Heine, and Ara Norenzayan of the University of British Columbia:

> Behavioral scientists routinely publish broad claims about human psychology and behavior in the world's top journals based on samples drawn entirely from Western, Educated, Industrialized, Rich, and Democratic (WEIRD) societies. Researchers—often implicitly—assume that either there is little variation across human populations, or that these "standard subjects" are as representative of the species as any other population. Are these assumptions justified? Here, our review of the comparative database from across the behavioral sciences suggests both that there is substantial variability in experimental results across populations and that WEIRD subjects are particularly unusual compared with the rest of the species—frequent outliers. The domains reviewed include visual perception, fairness, cooperation, spatial reasoning, categorization and inferential induction, moral reasoning, reasoning styles, self-concepts and related motivations, and the heritability of IQ. The findings suggest that members of WEIRD societies, including young children, are among the least representative populations one could find for generalizing about humans.

If you find these strong claims provocative, you might enjoy reading the full twenty-three-page harangue, which was published along with twenty-eight commentaries and a "last word" by the original authors.

---

[10] Gartrell (2002) notes that the standard social comparison experiment "uproots people from the moorings of ongoing social relationships" and yields results of scant relevance to real-world social comparison processes, which occur largely within social networks of close acquaintances (p. 165).

Excessive optimism about the meaningfulness of artificial experiments is a central aspect of Festinger's legacy. In a hagiographic obituary, Zajonc (1990) quoted the great man delighting in social psychology's supposed ability to bring major issues (e.g., "autocratic vs. democratic atmospheres") into the lab, and concluded that without Festinger's influence, it is "doubtful if experimental social psychology would have emerged as a discipline at all."

Research on "downward comparison" as a (sometime) response to "threat" began with Hakmiller (1966).

Although the critique is surely overstated in some particulars, and although the cute acronym WEIRD highlights an incomplete and somewhat arbitrary list of reasons why your typical research subject is *not* your typical human being, there can be little doubt that the basic indictment is fair: Many social scientists—and social psychologists in particular—have been blithely ethnocentric in drawing inferences about the human animal's "mental nature."[11]

As Henrich and his collaborators appropriately caution, their diatribe should not be misread as a denial that a complex psychological "human nature" exists. There are many cross-culturally "universal" aspects of thought and behavior, society and culture, ranging from bipedal locomotion, through various aspects of our language faculty, to such surprising specifics as eating socially at scheduled mealtimes. But experimenters can be too eager to conclude that their results have revealed one of these "universals," and Festinger's followers in the study of social comparison processes have fallen repeatedly into that trap. I have already mentioned the premature generalization that "threat" leads people to compare themselves preferentially to their inferiors. More generally, researchers persist in defending an even broader claim that "people" attend to their inferiors rather than their superiors in order to boost their "self-esteem," in spite of extensive evidence that such tendencies are localized at best.[12]

This notion that social comparisons are sought for the purpose of enhancing or defending "self-esteem" illustrates the third major weakness that compromises the usefulness of social psychological research in this area: a shallow, pre-Darwinian concept of adaptive function that is strictly intrapsychic. All psychological scientists recognize that our brains / minds have a functional organization that serves to accomplish specific things. In perception research, basic processes are *named* for those functions: sound localization, motion detection, object recognition, and so forth. Cognitive psychologists have a respectable grasp of adaptive function, too, agreeing that our brains contain specialized machinery for solving such specific problems as similarity assessment, selective attention, and short term

---

[11] The quoted passage is from Henrich et al. (2010, 61). Even earlier, Arnett (2008) raised the alarm about psychological science's undue reliance on a narrow subject pool.

[12] For an outstanding discussion of cross-cultural universals, see Brown (1991). For a summary of the debate about "self-enhancing" social comparison in the pursuit of "self-esteem" and for citation of the relevant experimental literature, see the commentary by Gaertner et al. in Henrich et al. (2010) and the authors' reply.

and long term memory storage and retrieval. In social psychology, by contrast, it is less obvious exactly what the useful things that our brains / minds are organized to accomplish might be, and theories are often unconstrained by pragmatic considerations of what constitutes effective functioning in the world.

Because the structure of the brain/mind has been "designed" by natural selection, its basic organization must be such as to promote the individual's reproductive fitness, or at least to have done so in ancestral environments. But you don't always need to think evolutionarily to generate sound hypotheses about more immediate ends. Figuring out how we detect an edge in our visual field or store a memory requires no explicit recourse to Darwinism, because the task demands are relatively transparent and you are unlikely to postulate fantastic objectives. Unfortunately, that seems not to be the case in social psychology, whose history is a succession of theoretical ideas about what social information processing is designed to achieve that have no clear connection to anything that the human animal must accomplish to survive and reproduce. There have been any number of theories, for example, claiming that we expend costly effort and even deceive ourselves about reality in the pursuit of nothing more than consistency or "balance" in our attitudes and beliefs. Indeed, there is a sort of premium placed on "counter-intuitive" theories—the professor who taught me social psychology decades ago insisted that a worthy theory must be one your grandmother would have scoffed at—making implausibility, even zaniness, a virtue. The result is a succession of fads such as the currently popular "terror management theory" which posits that we engage in the costly mental gymnastics of social comparison and self-enhancement for the sole purpose of distracting ourselves from an awareness, which would otherwise paralyze us, of our eventual mortality. (I am not making this up.) Unanchored by any consideration of external, real-world demands, such theories wax and wane in popularity while making little contribution to a cumulative understanding of social behavior and the mind.[13]

---

[13] Influential "balance" theories in social psychology include those of Festinger (1957), Heider (1958), and Higgins (1987). Festinger (1954, 138) even suggested that competitive behavior is a mere byproduct of "the drive for self-evaluation," and some of his followers (e.g., Garcia et al. 2006) still accept this baseless proposal.

For terror management theory, see, for example, Solomon et al. (1991); regarding its many failings, see, for example, Buss (1997), Leary and Schreindorfer (1997), and Kirkpatrick and Navarette (2006).

We can be confident that the function of self-esteem is not to "manage terror." But what is it? If enhancing or maintaining self-esteem costs time and effort, and requires that we deceive ourselves about our social standing to boot, why bother? Why, in other words, would natural selection not have eliminated this wasteful obsession? To make the defense or maintenance of self-esteem a plausible function of any aspect of the evolved human mind, you have to specify how it helps us interact effectively with the world outside our heads. One response to this challenge has been provided by Duke University psychologist Mark Leary who proposes that self-esteem functions as a "sociometer": a sort of gauge of one's apparent social value to significant others, whose "read-outs" motivate efforts to repair damaged or fragile relationships and to be a more valuable partner when such efforts are needed. To this I would add that such a gauge will also tell us how we measure up against others and against our ideals for ourselves, providing crucial information for the modulation of social initiative-taking. Experiences that lower self-esteem are indicators that certain overtures are likely to fail and certain contests likely to be lost, helping us know when to back off. Experiences that boost self-esteem convey the opposite message. It would be a bizarre, dysfunctional psyche that ignored the signal in self-esteem's ups and downs, and merely responded by artificial, intra-psychic "regulatory" strategies that elevate our self-esteem without addressing our actual shortcomings.[14]

These ideas don't just make better evolutionary sense than the alternative view that self-esteem is an end in itself. They also fit the facts better. Do people outside the psychology lab really engage in useless mental contortions to defend self-esteem? Various sorts of perfectly reasonable behavior are often interpreted in those terms, but such interpretations are not persuasive. In one recent study in an organizational setting, for example, decision-makers responded positively to excellence when making hiring recommendations except when the job candidate was apparently superior in the particular domain within which the decision-maker himself excelled; bizarrely, the researchers interpreted this transparently self-interested bias as a mere attempt to maintain self-esteem. More generally, studies often find that failures and setbacks inspire people to turn to new "comparison groups," especially groups of lower status or accomplishment. Again, this phenomenon

---

[14] For the sociometer hypothesis of self-esteem, see Leary et al. (1995) and Leary and Baumeister (2000).

is routinely interpreted as an effort to defend self-esteem and nothing more, although there is an obvious, more plausible interpretation: If you can't be one of the big frogs in your present pond, maybe you should look for a new pond where your past humiliations are unknown and you might be able to rank higher.[15]

Festinger's "theory of social comparison processes" has garnered well over twelve thousand *Google Scholar* citations, but the immense volume of psychological research on this topic has shed little light on relative deprivation in people's everyday lives or on its links to violence. Artificial experiments and an obsessive focus on intrapsychic "regulatory strategies" are partly to blame, but the crucial weakness of social psychology in this context has surely been its reliance on a subject pool of reasonably affluent, nonviolent American college students with above-average social standing and relatively rosy future prospects. Can criminologists, whose remit specifically includes the study of lethal violence and its perpetrators, serve us better?

Turf Defense in the Social Sciences

A majority of criminologists have been convinced by the evidence that economic inequality affects homicide rates. Unfortunately, with the partial exception of those who maintain that criminal offending is often a "rational choice," they have said little of value about *why* inequality should have this particular effect. Perhaps it is their abhorrence of violence that leads many criminologists to interpret it, implicitly or explicitly, as a pointless, pathological "lashing out" in response to frustration, rather than as a sadly predictable consequence of escalating tactics of social competition. In this regard, they are on the same (wrong) page as the social psychologists who, following Faye Crosby, routinely dichotomize responses to "relative deprivation" into those that are "productive" *versus* those that are "destructive," and consider the latter category, which of course includes violence, to be maladaptive by definition.

The isolation and parochialism of social scientists within their separate fields doesn't help. Most criminologists were trained as sociologists, and have taken on board that field's concern that sociology remain uncontaminated by attention to the individual actors who make up

---

[15] The study of bias in hiring recommendations is Garcia, Song, and Tesser (2010). For other research in which defending self-esteem has been seen as an end in itself, and for criticism thereof, see Leary and Baumeister (2000).

society. Émile Durkheim (1858–1917) is commonly credited, along with Max Weber (1864–1920), as a founding father of modern sociology. In the first paragraph of his 1895 manifesto, *The Rules of Sociological Method*, Durkheim declared that sociology must have a "subject matter exclusively its own" so that its domain could not be "confused with that of biology and psychology." Later in the same work, he laid down a famous dictum: The "determining cause of a social fact should be sought among the social facts preceding it" (110). If you seek an understanding of social phenomena in the intentions, beliefs, motives, or emotions of the actors involved, not only are you not doing sociology, but your efforts are furthermore doomed to failure. "Every time a social phenomenon is directly explained by a psychological phenomenon, we may rest assured that the explanation is false" (104).[16]

In his flawed efforts to elevate the effects of "absolute poverty" over inequality, William Alex Pridemore provides an unabashed example of the sort of intellectual circling of the wagons that Durkheim advocated: "Unfortunately, what are claimed to be structural-level theories too often resort to reductionist explanations about individual behavior." The phenomenon that Pridemore was complaining about is real: "Sociological" theories of crime, such as those that invoke "strain," often consist largely of psychological claims, even if they avoid psychological terminology. But why call this "unfortunate"? Sooner or later, a workable sociological theory *must* "resort to reductionist explanations about individual behavior." Poverty, inequality, or any other "structural-level" variable can exert its hypothesized influence only through its effects on individuals. To declare those individual effects off limits is to leave your theory devoid of a mechanism.[17]

"Strain" theories have long ranked high among criminologists' favorite explanations of how it is that economic variables influence crime, and depending on the particular theorist, the word "strain" is more or less synonymous either with stress or with thwarted goal-seeking. In the leading contemporary version, Robert Agnew's "general strain

---

[16] The quotations and page numbers are from a 1958 English translation of Durkheim's (1895) *Les règles de la méthode sociologique*. In his most famous work, *Suicide*, Durkheim (1897) continued to beat the same drum: "Sociological method as we practice it rests wholly on the basic principle that social facts must be studied as things, that is, as realities external to the individual." For an exceptionally cogent, evolution-minded evaluation of the strengths and weaknesses of Durkheim's vision for sociology, see Cohen and Machalek (1994).

[17] The quoted sentence is from Pridemore (2008, 147); I promise that this is the last time I'll pick on him.

theory," strain's consequences are explicitly attributed to the elicitation of "negative emotions," namely anger and frustration. So what makes this a "sociological" theory, and not a "psychological" one? As far as I can see, the answer is the particular choice of jargon and nothing more. "Strain" is a term coined by sociologists; psychologists use other words. Regrettably, however, by marginalizing the contributions of psychologists, physiologists, and other outsiders who have actually *studied* anger, stress, and frustration, strain theorists risk reinventing the wheel, and often an obsolete wheel like the tired old "frustration–aggression hypothesis" at that.[18]

When Margo Wilson and I began attending criminology meetings in the 1980s, we would sometimes join a group of fellow homicide researchers for a drink after the day's sessions. Like us, many of these researchers had assembled data sets from the investigative case files in some city police department's homicide division, and as human beings are everywhere wont to do, we would sometimes chat in a gossipy way about our respective experiences. One of our new colleagues might then become animated while discussing the tragic dramas recorded in police files and the human passions that they reflect: sexual jealousy, perhaps, or the humiliation of barroom mockery. And then, on two or three such occasions, something astonishing ensued: With a half-smile, a member of our little party would introject "You realize, I hope, that you're engaging in psychological reductionism?", and the shamed story-teller would fall silent. We didn't know whether to laugh or cry.

The reason why these cocktail hour exchanges struck Margo and me as both funny and sad is of course that "psychological reductionism" is exactly what is *required* if the responses of actual human beings to their social and economic circumstances are ever to be fully understood. The probability that Johnny Badass will go so far as to kill the

---

[18] Robert K. Merton's (1938) *Social structure and anomie* is usually credited as the first "strain theory." The "anomie" in Merton's title refers to a mismatch between legitimate social goals and legitimate means to attain them, but it is also an implicitly psychological sort of angst; Merton considered it the main source of deviance, including crime. Psychological reductionism is even more overt in Robert Agnew's "general strain theory," which emphasizes the emotions that allegedly link strain to action; see, for example, Agnew (1992). Unfortunately, Agnew, a past-president of the *American Society of Criminologists*, invokes emotions in a commonsensical or "folk psychological" way, largely ignoring actual research on emotions and their elicitors and other properties.

In *Frustration and aggression*, psychologists Leonard Doob et al. (1939) proposed that "the occurrence of aggression always presupposes the existence of frustration, and, contrariwise, frustration always leads to some form of aggression" (p. 338). These authors soon backed away from these excessive claims.

rival who dissed him at Swillers Bar doesn't rise or fall because he's just been informed of the latest changes in the Gini coefficient of income inequality. If such an abstraction as economic inequality indeed affects Mr. Badass's behavior, it can only do so via the conduit of his personal experiences, whether in the recent past, as an adult, or in childhood. Any explanation of violent crime rates that confines its explanatory apparatus to aggregated societal variables is therefore incomplete at best, and mystical at worst. Facing up to the reductionist question of *how* the structural-level variables that you believe to be relevant are able to exert their hypothesized influence on individual behavior is an essential part of assessing the plausibility and validity of any such explanation.

Don't get me wrong. I am not suggesting that sociologists are uniquely hobbled by parochialism. Many psychologists fear and loathe the bogeyman of "biological reductionism" with an intensity rivaling that of the staunchest sociologist's distaste for "psychological reductionism." And if economists appear to be more open to outside influences, that is largely because their field's ground rules entitle them to take credit for any recycled idea that no other economist has previously poached. We need to move beyond these sectarian habits of thought. Knowledge about the psychology, endocrinology, and neurobiology of competition and violence is growing rapidly, and this knowledge will play an essential role in our eventual understanding of how inequality influences homicide rates. But we're not there yet. Too many social scientists seem to view progress in sister disciplines as a threat rather than an opportunity, and defend their turf by ignoring or even denigrating the insights that such progress might provide.

There is nothing shameful about synthesizing the contributions of complementary disciplines. To the contrary, such synthesis is sorely needed.

The Genes of the Conquerors

People clearly care about relative position. But why? If you've read this far, you already know the answer. Darwinian fitness is itself relative, by definition: The traits that natural selection favors are traits that help individuals reproduce more reliably and prolifically than their same-sex, same-species rivals. A strong interest in maintaining and improving one's social and economic standing is undoubtedly such a trait. Throughout history, one's relative position in society has had a huge effect on personal reproductive prospects, especially for men, and on the survival, well-being, and eventual reproduction of one's children.

Our ancestors surely acquired their intense interest in relative social standing long before they were human. In research on nonhuman primates and many other animals, social rank is inferred primarily from pairwise interactions in which the "dominant" individual can displace the "subordinate," and therefore has priority of access to mutually desired goods. A dominance-subordinance relationship may be established only after fighting, and it may be reversible at some future time or in some specific contexts, but by and large, acceding to subordinate status is how a predictable loser avoids the costs of a dangerous confrontation. Both parties recognize which of the two is dominant, and other members of their social group clearly know, too.[19]

So how does this jockeying for hierarchical position relate to reproductive success? The short answer is that there is almost always a strong correlation between dominance rank and procreation. High-ranking male mammals typically have relatively large numbers of offspring, and high-ranking females tend to have relatively high rates of offspring survival. Subordinate individuals of both sexes are often shut out of breeding altogether. That is certainly the story with the red deer on the Isle of Rum that you met in Chapter 3, and it is similarly true of species more closely related to ourselves. In group-living monkeys, early studies typically showed, unsurprisingly, that males of relatively high dominance rank also had relatively high mating frequencies. Subsequent studies using DNA evidence to confirm paternity tend to reveal an even greater advantage for the dominant males than the observational data had suggested, apparently because the monkeys can tell which females are fertile better than human observers can, and dominant males preferentially guard those fertile females while allowing the subordinate males sexual access to females who are unlikely to conceive.[20]

The correlation between rank and reproduction isn't perfect, and recent research has brought new considerations to the fore, such as the importance of female rank in group-living monkeys and the fact that a female may sometimes try to escape the attentions of a dominant male and mate with someone who is a better bet to be a solicitous father. But these complications don't negate the basic facts that male mammals

[19] For reviews of the substantial theoretical and research literature on contests and the establishment of dominance among nonhuman animals, see Hardy and Briffa (2013) and Riechert (2013).
[20] Regarding the association between rank and reproduction in nonhuman animals, see, for example, Ellis (1995), Alberts et al. (2006), and Wroblewski et al. (2009).

compete intensely for social rank and that success in that competition pays off reproductively.

Anthropological, historical, and genetic studies confirm that *Homo sapiens* is no exception to this generalization. Across the gamut of human societies, the men with the most power and resources have consistently tended to leave the most descendants. Military conquerors provide some extreme illustrations of this more general point.

The Mongolian warlord Genghis Khan (1162–1227) was the greatest conqueror in human history. He rose to prominence as the commanding officer of an army that defeated the Tatars in 1202, whereupon he ordered that all the men should be killed, and that after he had had his pick of the women, those remaining should be distributed among his supporters. Shortly thereafter, he became the adopted heir of a more powerful warlord, and within a few years he united the Mongol tribes under his own rule and was elected the great Khan, or emperor. In 1211, he conquered Zongdu (modern Beijing), and in 1219 Samarkand and Bukhara in what is now Uzbekistan. Azerbaijan, Armenia, and Georgia fell like dominos before his troops, and by 1223, he had conquered most of present-day Russia and Ukraine.

Where they met resistance, the Mongols sometimes destroyed whole cities and massacred their inhabitants, which had the useful effect that terror preceded them. But their rapid sweep across Asia was more than just a spree of murder, rape and pillage. Genghis Khan co-opted the expertise of non-nomadic administrators to establish colonial governments, and after his death in 1227, the sons and grandsons among whom he had divided his empire continued to expand it. In 1258, one grandson sacked Baghdad and destroyed the remaining power of the Abbasid caliphate in the west, while another finally subdued Korea in the east. The last great conqueror in the lineage was yet another grandson, Kublai Khan, who, after a long campaign, subdued all of present-day China by 1279. The expansion of the Mongol empire finally ground to a halt when Kublai twice failed to annex Japan. By then, Genghis's descendants ruled over a loosely federated empire extending from the Black Sea to the Pacific, and from Siberia to the mouth of the Indus river.[21]

Two ways to increase your share of future gene pools are to reproduce at a relatively high rate, and to interfere directly with the reproductive

---

[21] For a fuller chronicle of the many thirteenth-century Mongol wars of conquest, see Benson (2006).

prospects of unrelated rivals. Genghis Khan and his immediate descendants excelled at both. They routinely killed all the men in any city that tried to resist them, thereby annihilating genetic competitors. (One recent analysis concludes that massacres during the Mongol conquest had a greater ecological impact than the Black Death or any other major depopulation event in human history.)[22]

As regards personal reproduction, Genghis sired children by women he married, by courtesans, by slaves, and by rape victims. In the *Tobchi'an*—a history of the early Mongol conquests that was written in the thirteenth or fourteenth century and is considered authoritative even though its authorship remains unknown—it is taken for granted that fertile women were booty. To save themselves, the men of conquered tribes would offer their daughters to the great Khan. When an officer named Naya'a was suspected of sampling the wares before delivering a girl to Genghis, he protested his innocence by declaring "Foreign people's girls and women with beautiful complexions. Geldings with fine rumps. When I encounter these, I always say 'These are the Khan's!'" Genghis examined the girl, confirmed her virginity, and rewarded the loyal Naya'a with a promotion. Another translation from the *Tobchi'an* illustrates what the author refers to as the great Khan's "magnanimity and generosity" with a story in which he told a supporter to "Seek out the most beautiful maidens and women from the subjugated tribes and select thirty for yourself." Genghis's sons and grandsons followed his polygynous example. Kublai Khan had only four official wives, but according to Marco Polo, an Italian visitor to Kublai's court who greatly admired him, he maintained a harem of thousands of concubines.[23]

In 2003, a team of geneticists headed by Tatiana Zerjal of Oxford University announced a remarkable discovery. The Y-chromosomes of an estimated sixteen million men, constituting about 8 percent of all the men now living within the geographical area of the Mongol empire at the time of Genghis Khan's death, are so similar that they must have descended from a common ancestor who lived only about a thousand years ago. The geneticists dubbed this family of closely related Y-chromosomes the "star cluster." No other family of Y-chromosomes

---

[22] For massacres perpetrated during the Mongol conquests, see Man (2005). Regarding those massacres' ecological impact, see Pongratz et al. (2011).

[23] The story of Naya'a's exoneration is from Onon (1990, 102); that of the thirty-woman reward is from Ratchevsky (1991, 147). Both are translated from passages in the *Tobchi'an*, sometimes called *The secret history of the Mongols*. Regarding Kublai Khan's harem, see Polo (2005).

has both migrated and proliferated at a remotely similar rate. The geographical distributions of the star cluster and of other Y-chromosomes that are more or less distantly related to it furthermore indicate that it originated in Mongolia. Moreover, on the opposite side of the continent, men whose oral traditions tell of an unbroken male-line genealogical descent from the great Khan have turned out to be especially likely to possess a star cluster Y. Thus, although Genghis Khan's tomb has never been found and his remains may never be genotyped, there can be little doubt that the star cluster Y was his.[24]

The news of Genghis Khan's abundant descendants fascinated people throughout the world. In the popular press and even in the scientific literature, much has been made of the astonishing fact that they now number in the millions. A typical example is this: "Studies conducted in the early 2000s showed that Genghis may be a distant ancestor of as many as sixteen million men living in modern Asia and Europe - or approximately one of every two hundred men in the world." But the real implications, which Zerjal and her collaborators explained very clearly, are far more astonishing than just that. The oft-repeated estimate of sixteen million represents only the strictly patrilineal descendants of Genghis (or at least of one of his close male ancestors): the sons of the sons of the sons, etc. The story gets more interesting when we realize that for every such pure male line, extending back approximately thirty generations to Genghis himself, there are necessarily many *thousands* of lineages passing through some combination of his male *and female* descendants. The contemporary human horde that can count the great Khan among their ancestors surely numbers in the *hundreds* of millions, perhaps even in the billions.[25]

Although Genghis Khan probably cornered a larger share of future human gene pools than any other despot in history, his proclivities were not exceptional. According to the evolutionary anthropologist

---

[24] The original report by Zerjal et al. (2003) of the probable discovery of Genghis Khan's Y-chromosome is a richly detailed exemplary piece of scientific reasoning, and well worth reading.
[25] The quote that I refer to as "typical" is from Behnke (2008, 127).

You have two parents, four grandparents, eight great-grandparents, etc. If you could trace back thirty generations, you would find yourself with more than a billion "28 x great"-grandparents, only one of whom passed his Y-chromosome down an all-male line to your father. But note, too, that a thousand years ago, there were fewer than a billion human beings; many of the ancestors in that family tree must therefore be duplicates. It follows that countless numbers of Genghis Khan's descendants could, if full genealogical information were available to them, count him as an ancestor repeatedly through numerous distinct lineages.

and historian Laura Betzig, whenever men in the ancient world attained positions of limitless power, whether in Asia, Europe, Africa, or the Americas, they were repeatedly struck by the same brainwave about what they should do with that power: collect and sequester fertile women. The resultant harems were invariably guarded, often by eunuchs, and breaches of security were always treated severely. The numbers of nubile women maintained for the exclusive use of the despot not infrequently exceeded a thousand.[26]

In a lively review of mating practices in highly stratified human societies, the American anthropologist Mildred Dickemann has written:

> It may be wondered whether such large numbers of harem inmates could have any reproductive significance. I think it well not to underestimate their masters' capacities. Van Gulik's description of Chinese Imperial Harem procedures, involving copulation of concubines on a rotating basis at appropriate times in their menstrual cycles, all carefully regulated by female supervisors to prevent deception and error, shows what could be achieved with a well-organized bureaucracy. Given nine-month pregnancies and two- or three-year lactations, it is not inconceivable that a hardworking Emperor might manage to service a thousand women ... An early 20th-century observor reports that the Nizam of Hyderabad became the father of four children in the space of eight days, with nine more expected the following week, though how long this rate of achievement persisted is not stated.[27]

Rank and Reproduction

Before going further, I need to make a few things clear. The reasons why I've been telling you about imperial conquest and harem polygamy have nothing to do with the effects that these phenomena may (or may not) have had on human evolution. Whether the proliferation of Genghis Khan's particular genes has left a mark on the statistics of human temperament—or on anything else—is an interesting question, but it's not what I'm concerned with here. What I find intriguing about the behavior of conquerors, and about their recurrent, independent inventions of the harem, is what these things imply about the human male's tastes and ambitions. Let a man gain access to unchecked power, and what does he typically do with it? History tells us the answer, and

---

[26] Regarding harems and the variance in male reproductive success in historical societies, see Betzig (1986, 2012, 2014).
[27] The quote is from Dickemann (1979, 175–76).

it's not pretty: He converts that power into a hugely disproportionate share of the sexual and reproductive pie.

Despotic power and extreme polygyny arose relatively recently in human history, after our ancestors invented agriculture and began to form large, sedentary communities with elaborate divisions of labor. Before all that, until just a few thousand years ago, all people were hunter-gatherers who lived in societies that tended to be relatively unstratified, and in which marital and reproductive opportunities were distributed much more equitably than was the case after the rise of civilizations. It was in those hunter-gatherer societies that the basic, cross-culturally universal aspects of human nature, such as our unique language capacity, evolved, and it was in those societies that selection refined the characteristic motives of the human male, including his inclinations to care about relative position, to get one up on the other guys, and to acquire another wife whenever his abilities and his social environment made that a possibility.[28]

Brute force isn't always what it takes to achieve these goals, and that's another *caveat* that probably warrants emphasis. Hunter-gatherers are renowned for their "leveling" practices: Those who persist in trying to put themselves above others may be collectively ridiculed, ostracized, or even killed. In such a social milieu, gentle persuasion and tactful mediation may be the most useful social skills. It is a mistake, however, to interpret this social leveling as evidence that human nature is fundamentally peaceful and cooperative, rather than violent and warlike, as some scholars have done. Practices aimed at preventing social ascendancy exist precisely *because* men will dominate one another aggressively if they are undeterred, and leveling can even take the form of the consensual execution of men whose aggressivity could not otherwise be controlled. We'll come back to this in Chapter 10.[29]

Violent domination of others is one major route to higher rank, but it is neither a sure route nor the only route. Anthropologist Napoleon Chagnon famously showed that among the Yanomamö Indians of

---

[28] Hunter-gatherer societies are often stereotyped as devoid of social stratification, but as several authors have recently noted, the studies that have led to this view were conducted in low-productivity settings, such as the Kalahari Desert, into which hunter-gatherers were pushed by agriculturalists. Earlier hunter-gatherers may have occupied more bountiful habitats that permitted more stratified societies like those of the native North American populations exploiting the salmon rivers of the Pacific northwest coast. Nonetheless, extreme stratification and harem polygyny are unlikely to have antedated agriculture-based civilization.

[29] Regarding leveling practices in hunter-gatherers, see Kelly (1995) and Boehm (2000).

Venezuela, those men who had killed someone had more wives and children, on average, than those who had not, and it is likely that the same has been true of other tribal horticulturalists in Amazonia and New Guinea. And yet even among the "fierce" Yanomamö, Chagnon has described alternative routes to headman status, which can be attained not solely by intimidation, but by persuading others that you're *not* a hothead and can be counted on for coolness, bravery, and wisdom.[30]

These *caveats* are important reminders that the bloody, ignoble savage and the gentle egalitarian are both simplistic caricatures of the evolved nature of the human male. But it is also important to note that a capacity for self-interested violence has helped countless men attain and hold on to high rank, all over the world, and that those high-ranking men are disproportionately our ancestors. Personal violence is not simply the lashing out of society's losers. The classic duel in defense of one's "honor" was a contest between high-status men defending their eminence. And if you think that it's only in exotic tribal societies that killing your rivals could possibly carry you to the top, think again. For centuries, ascent to the thrones of Europe routinely left a trail of blood. In any society without strong judicial institutions and an independent, dispassionate constabulary, claims on property and status need to be backed up by credible threats of violence. Until very recently, that meant pretty much everywhere.[31]

In the developed nations of the modern world, this ancestral social situation has been transformed to such a degree that we have become accustomed to thinking of violence as something resorted to mainly by men at the bottom of the social order. In fact, violence is an under-class specialty only where the state has laid claim to the legitimate use of violence and provides other mechanisms to defend the interests of the propertied, for it is only then that high-status men are willing to relinquish the onerous requirement that they deter and punish tres-passes at their own expense. Violence has become the recourse of the poor largely because they don't have access to the law's protections and remedies in the same way as the rich. We should never lose sight of just what a novel state of human affairs this is.

---

[30] See Chagnon (1988) for the increased marital and reproductive success of Yanomamö killers, and Chagnon (1992) for the contrast between popular headmen and those whose position was based on instilling fear.

[31] Regarding violence as a route to monarchy, see Eisner (2011). Williams (1980) is a good source on dueling.

6

The Arena of Competition

Envy is, of course, closely connected with competition . . .
Beggars do not envy millionaires . . . [They] envy other
beggars who are more successful.
—Bertrand Russell, *The Conquest*
of Happiness, 1930

Competition Is Local

Every experienced homicide detective is familiar with a handful of fatal scenarios that crop up again and again. When Margo Wilson and I were reading case files in the Detroit police department, many years ago, one of the recurrent varieties that we encountered was what we called an "escalated showing-off dispute." Here's an example:

> B.B. (male, age 19) and A.S. (male, age 23), were drinking with mutual acquaintances in a private home. B.B. was a boxer and was talking about his fights. A.S. placed his night stick between B.B.'s legs and hoisted him in the air. B.B. was embarrassed and had to ask to be let down, then accused A.S. of tearing his pants and demanded that A.S. pay for them. By then, A.S. and others were laughing at B.B., who punched A.S. Both were then asked to leave. B.B. left the house first, and when A.S. followed, B.B. allegedly struck him again, whereupon A.S. shot B.B. dead.

Among the solved homicides in Detroit in 1972, there were twenty-six such cases in which two men had traded boasts and insults in the company of witnesses before one killed the other. Circumstantial evidence suggested that the 178 homicides that had never been solved probably included many more.

Slightly different are those cases in which the antagonists parted company after their initial confrontation, and one then went looking for the other with violent intent. We put those into a second category called "retaliation for previous verbal or physical abuse." Here is one example:

> P.T. (male, age 23) publicly accused acquaintance G.K. (male, age 17) of a break-and-enter robbery of P.T.'s home, and administered a beating for the alleged offense. G.K. left the scene, borrowed a gun from a friend, and returned and shot P.T. dead before several witnesses.

In addition to being provoked by prior assaults or accusations of theft, these retaliatory homicides might be acts of revenge for prior public mockery or insults, or for an accusation of cheating at cards or dice. Interestingly, these payback killings after a potential cooling off period were even more numerous than the uninterrupted escalated disputes: We counted seventy-five male–male cases of this sort among that one calendar year's solved homicides.[1]

When a killer and his victim are low-status acquaintances, and especially when they are members of the same minority ethnic group, the case is likely to be lamented by commentators, on both the left and the right sides of the political spectrum, as an example of "fratricidal violence" that has been tragically misdirected against the killer's "own people." The authors of a recent academic discussion of how "black rage" is expressed in rap music, for example, apparently consider the following a truism: "Very often the oppressed direct their rage against their own people and other subaltern groups, thus furthering their own oppression and subordination." But if we accept the idea that the violence perpetrated by men at the bottom of society against their equally disadvantaged peers is a mistake—a mere manifestation of "redirected" aggression against inappropriate targets—we are failing to respect the protagonists' circumstances, options, and motives.[2]

---

[1] One reason for distinguishing these types of cases is that the delayed retaliatory killings meet the criteria for a murder charge better than nonstop escalated incidents, which are arguably acts of unpremeditated manslaughter. In actuality, however, overworked Detroit prosecutors only prosecuted about half of all solved cases, abjuring any mutual combat case with a plausible self-defense plea, and they accepted plea bargains that reduced the charge to manslaughter in over 90 percent of the cases that they pursued. For a fuller description of Detroit's homicides in 1972, including conflict typologies and summary characteristics of the protagonists, see Wilson and Daly (1985).

[2] The quotation is from Best and Kellner (1999). Wilson (2005) provides an insightful critique of the racialized rhetoric deploring "black-on-black violence" in the United States, a trope that is embraced by conservatives and liberals alike and that deflects attention from remediable economic and class issues.

One problem with this way of thinking is that it entails an error that we have discussed before: misattributing pathology to phenomena we find distasteful. Even medical practitioners are guilty of this confusion. In a 1992 treatise on the "deadly epidemic" of violence, psychiatrist James Gilligan, then Director of the Harvard Institute of Law and Psychiatry, insisted that in order to understand and prevent violence, we must "think of violence as a symptom of life-threatening pathology, which, like all forms of illness, has an etiology or cause, a pathogen." The trouble with Gilligan's prescription is that although violence surely does have an "etiology," it is *not* a "form of illness." Interpersonal violence is an evolved capability of normally functioning, healthy organisms, defending their interests in a world that is not always benign.[3]

The Merriam-Webster online dictionary defines "social pathology" as the "study of social problems (such as crime or alcoholism) that views them as diseased conditions of the social organism." This approach has fallen out of fashion in sociology, and deservedly so, for it was never anything more than a value judgment masquerading as a causal theory. An *organism* is a genetic *individual*, whose constituent parts have an indissoluble integrity of purpose because they have all been sculpted by the evolutionary process to promote the same end, namely that individual organism's fitness. The individuals who constitute a so-called "social organism," by contrast, have no such integrity of purpose because they have been shaped by natural selection to promote their *separate* fitnesses, often in competition with one another. If your liver and your kidneys are behaving at cross purposes, you have grounds for suspecting that something is malfunctioning. If two men are behaving at cross purposes, you have none.[4]

The second crucial misconception that is embedded in the standard litany deploring "fratricidal violence" is its implicit presumption that a disadvantaged man who attacks his "own people" is the dupe of a false consciousness, and has failed to grasp that the elites who are his real oppressors should be his targets. But how preposterous—how insulting—to imagine that if men at the bottom of the social hierarchy only understood their situation better, they would direct their violence

---

[3] The quote is from Gilligan (1992, 92).
[4] Influential proponents of the faulty metaphor of "social pathology" include sociologists such as Lemert (1951) and philosophers such as Honneth (2009). The misconstrual of social problems as the malfunctioning of a social "organism" goes back at least to Aristotle, and infected Durkheim's sociology from its beginnings.

against those at the top! A low-status man cannot reasonably hope to assume the mantle of a high-status man by attacking him. What he *can* reasonably expect to reap from such an act is a punishment more certain and more severe than that for assaulting a low-status rival.

In a troop of monkeys, or a flock of chickens, or any other animal group with a dominance hierarchy, you don't see low-ranking individuals launching attacks on the alpha. If you see overt aggression at all, it is almost invariably directed against someone close in rank to the aggressor. The situation facing human beings is similar: The social arena within which one has the most realistic chance of making gains—and in which one must be most vigilant against being taken down a peg—is the arena of competition among near equals.[5]

The Age–Crime Curve

In the illustrative scenarios with which this chapter began, the killers and their victims were in their teens and early twenties. That's not unusual. Not only are the protagonists in fatal confrontational conflicts disproportionately men, they are disproportionately *young* men. Figure 6.1 shows the most recent available worldwide homicide victimization rates by age group and by sex. No such compilation is possible for the killers, but all available evidence indicates that the picture would be similar, except that the proportion male would be even higher and the peak in young adulthood would be even more pronounced. Moreover, the competitive confrontations that I have been focusing on—and that are major drivers of the variability in homicide rates—are even more concentrated among young men than is homicide in general.[6]

This familiar pattern has been called the "age–crime curve," and in 1983, two prominent American criminologists, Travis Hirschi and Michael Gottfredson, provoked a minor furor by insisting that criminology had no explanation for it. More specifically, Hirschi and Gottfredson declared that (1) "the age distribution of crime is invariant across social and cultural conditions," and (2) "the age distribution of crime cannot be accounted for by any variable or combination of variables currently available to criminology." Their indignant colleagues responded to the first of these assertions with

---

[5] Regarding dominance hierarchies and rank-related aggression, see, for example, Mazur (2005).
[6] Homicide victimization is biased toward young men wherever homicide rates are highest, whereas in low-rate countries, the age pattern is flatter and risk is often maximal after age thirty (United Nations Office on Drugs and Crime 2013). Regarding the demography of the killers and of homicides in which victim and killer are unrelated male rivals, see Daly and Wilson (1990b).

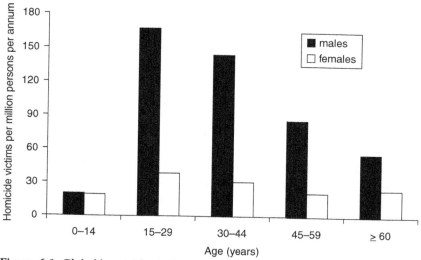

Figure 6.1. Global homicide victimization rates by age and sex in 2012 (or, for some countries, in the most recent available prior year). Source: United Nations Office on Drugs and Crime (2013).

evidence that the age at which offending is maximal differs to some degree across criminal offenses and populations, and to the second by insisting that one or another sociological stand-by—"strain theory" or "labeling theory" or "social control theory"—could account for the age–crime curve perfectly well, thank you very much. Ironically, these lame refutations only served to underscore the substantial element of truth in Hirschi and Gottfredson's polemic. Quibbles about their first claim have highlighted the robustness of an age–crime curve and its relatively youthful peak in the specific realm of crimes of violence. Attempts to dismiss Hirschi and Gottfredson's second claim have demonstrated only that *no* predictions about demography can be derived from the leading criminological theories, which can be and are invoked as empty *post hoc* "explanations" for whatever age pattern happens to turn up.[7]

The age–crime curve *is* attributable in part—but only in part—to social factors associated with age. At any given age, men who are unemployed are relatively likely to commit crimes, including homicide.

---

[7] The quotes are from Hirschi and Gottfredson (1983, 554). Regarding the furor that their claims provoked, see Daly and Wilson (1990b).

The same goes for men who are unmarried, and for men who are child-less. It follows that if twenty-year-olds are relatively often unemployed, unmarried, and childless, compared to, say, thirty-five-year-olds—and of course, they are—then twenty-year-old men would be expected to have a higher homicide rate than thirty-five-year-olds for these reasons alone. That said, however, the familiar age–crime curve shows up, only slightly attenuated, within the married and the unmarried, the employed and the unemployed. It appears, then, that these age-asso-ciated risk factors affect the precise shape of the age–crime curve, but cannot explain it away. And it would be surprising if they could, for there is a great deal of complementary evidence that the human male is adapted for maximal competitive formidability in young adulthood. That is the life stage at which strength and aerobic capacity and sen-sation-seeking and the "taste for risk" are all both at their peaks and maximally different between the sexes. That is the life stage at which men are most physically formidable and most dangerous.[8]

Why dangerous confrontational competition should be predomi-nantly a young man's game is actually something of a puzzle from an evolutionary perspective. If this reality were not so familiar, one might have predicted a very different demographic pattern, reasoning as fol-lows. Aggressive confrontation is a *risky* social strategy, whereby one accepts big potential costs of injury or death in the pursuit of potential gains. This being so, a competitor whose decision-making has been shaped by natural selection should be more willing to pursue the risky option when the costs are lower, all else equal, and all else equal, the costs of risky behavior decrease with age. Why? Because your expected future fitness is shrinking anyway, so what you will have lost if you get killed is shrinking, too.

An example may help make this logic more intuitive. Imagine that you're an aging male baboon, facing a challenge from a strapping up-and-comer. Your molars are already worn down to nubs, and you'll surely be out of the game within months. So why not see if a show of recklessness will hold that punk off and enable you to get one last mating? The younger male would probably win a fight to

---

[8] Wilson and Daly (1985) showed that unemployment is a risk factor for homicide, but that there is a clear age–crime curve among employed and unemployed alike; Daly and Wilson (2001) showed the same with respect to marital status and that this is not simply due to a "selection into marriage" confound. Regarding the life-span trajectory of human physical performance, see, for example, Thomas and French (1985), and for that of risk-taking and related phenomena, see, for example, Gove (1985), Wilson and Daly (1985), and Wang et al. (2006).

the death, but he's got a potentially long future, so maybe he'll back off: "I'm not messing with that crazy old bastard! He doesn't care if he lives or dies!" Well, nonhuman animals sometimes do appear to behave like that—that is, to be less deterred by danger the older they get—and so, perhaps, do human mothers in defense of their babies. But there is abundant evidence that confrontational violence and other sorts of risk-taking increase rapidly during human adolescence, especially in males, reach a peak in young adulthood, and then gradually decline over decades. And I'm not convinced that anyone fully understands why.

Is this aspect of the human life-course truly exceptional? We can't even answer that with certainty. It is possible that a tendency to become more risk-tolerant with age, and a postprime escalation of willingness to fight dangerously, are typical of most other mammals, but research bearing on the question remains sparse. If the human pattern that is reflected in the age–crime curve *is* indeed unusual, it seems likely that the explanation resides in other unusual aspects of human social life. In most mammals, fathers do nothing for their young, and male reproductive efforts consist solely of the competitive pursuit of matings. But the parental contributions of human fathers are substantial, impactful, and exceptionally prolonged, and we are probably unique in the extent to which we can influence the life prospects even of our grand-offspring. An aging red deer stag who makes a last-ditch effort to defeat a rival or to force himself on an unwilling female imposes no fitness costs on his relatives. An aging man who behaved similarly might do his genetic posterity serious harm.

Personal reputations are uniquely important in human affairs, and probably provide the key to understanding many odd aspects of human development and psychology. Utah anthropologist Alan Rogers has shown that a life-span trajectory of risk-proneness and impatience that looks very much like the age–crime curve could, in principle, be favored by natural selection, if the effects of personal reputation and of inheritance on the life prospects of family members are incorporated appropriately into the optimality analysis. And perhaps even more important are the "sticky" effects that the reputations which we acquire in young adulthood continue to exert on our own life prospects. This is the life stage in which men in traditional face-to-face societies come to be known as brave or cowardly, staunch or unreliable. This is the life stage at which they must impress potential fathers-in-law. And this appears to have been the life stage at which men have been selected to be maximally competitive.[9]

Men and Women

Competition is certainly not confined to men. But the competition among women tends to be less confrontational, and much less violent. In our Detroit homicide study, in addition to the twenty-six "escalated showing-off disputes" in which both parties were men, there was a single such case in which the killer and the victim were both women. In addition to the seventy-five delayed acts of "retaliation for previous verbal or physical abuse" in which men killed other men, there were five analogous cases in which women were slain by female rivals.

As we have noted repeatedly, a very large majority of the world's killers are men, and so are a substantial majority of their victims. And when we narrow our focus to those killings that arise from competitive confrontations, the predominance of males gets even larger. The relative numbers given above for Detroit in 1972—six fatal contests between women *versus* 101 between men—are unremarkable, except perhaps for the fact that there *were* several cases of lethal female competition. Often, there are none.

Still, you might wonder, are there *no* reversals? After all, women can and sometimes do kill one another, as witness those few Detroit cases. Perhaps you have a vague recollection of having read about an exotic land, far away, in which the warriors are women, and the behavioral and temperamental differences between the sexes that we thoughtlessly take for granted are startlingly reversed. Where was that, anyway? Somewhere up the Amazon? Sorry, but it was a fiction. No such society has ever been found. The perpetration of violence is overwhelmingly the business of men, everywhere, and all available evidence indicates that it always has been.[10]

If you have taken a psychology course, you may also have encountered textbook assertions that women and men do not in fact differ in their levels of "aggression," but only in how they manifest that aggression. The basis for this recurrent claim is fatuous, and not simply

---

[9] Regarding the human lifespan trajectory of risk-taking and (im)patience, see Daly and Wilson (1990b, 2005). Rogers (1994) presents a theory of the conditions for that developmental trajectory to be favored by natural selection.

[10] See Chapter 7 of Daly and Wilson (1988b) regarding the fantasy of "sex-role-reversed" societies and what the ethnographic record actually says. Regarding human sex differences more generally, especially behavioral and psychological sex differences, see Geary (2010).

because it lumps assaults and snide remarks together as manifestations of the "same" thing. The actual evidence for claiming that the sexes don't differ consists of subjective ratings of feelings on a scale that might range, for example, from "1 = not at all aggressive" to "7 = extremely aggressive." It is neither surprising nor informative when such measures produce similar female and male means, because people anchor their ratings to their notions of what is normal for their comparison groups, including their own sex. Concluding that the sexes don't differ in aggression (or jealousy, or whatever) on the basis of such measures is the logical equivalent of (1) asking people to describe themselves on a 7-point scale ranging from 1 "very short" to 7 "very tall"; (2) finding identical means for men and women, and (3) concluding that the sexes don't *really* differ in height after all, but only in how they manifest it. So forget about whether "aggression" differs between the sexes. The perpetration of potentially lethal assaults most assuredly does.

The well-known sex difference in the intensity of reproductive competition provides a satisfying explanation for this cross-culturally reliable aspect of human affairs. Ultimately, the reason why men are readier to resort to dangerous confrontational aggression than women is the same as the reason why stags compete more dangerously than hinds: because male fitness has been more variable than female fitness for countless ancestral generations, resulting in the evolution of a broad array of complementary differences between female and male bodies and minds.

Our anatomical differences are of course the most conspicuous of these. Adult human skeletons can be reliably classified as female or male, and men grow to be taller and more muscular than women, on average, even when they are equally well nourished and equally active. The physiological sex differences that influence differential combat-readiness are more subtle, but they, too, are uncontroversial. Just one of many examples is that men have a higher resting metabolic rate than women, even among people of equivalent aerobic fitness.[11]

Psychological and behavioral sex differences are the most difficult ones to characterize with precision, and it is often reasonable to question whether a particular sex difference has any direct basis in an evolutionary history of differential selection on females *versus* males

---

[11] Regarding sex differences in basal metabolic rate, see, for example, Arciero et al. (1993). For further evidence on metabolic sex differences and their endocrine and enzymatic correlates and causes, see, for example, Cortright and Koves (2000) and Tarnopolsky (2008).

at all. Could some particular difference in which we are interested be explicable as the result of relatively arbitrary and culturally variable differences in how girls and boys are treated? Intuition may not be a good guide to the correct answer. Surely little girls play with dolls and little boys play with trucks because those are the toys that their parents give them, right? Well, don't be too hasty. Many an anti-sexist parent has begun to suspect that the reality is more complicated when her toddler insisted on pretending that his doll was a truck or a gun. As naïve infants, even male *monkeys* differ from their female counterparts by preferring toy trucks to dolls.[12]

My point is *not* that sex differences are unaffected by "nurture." Consider something as apparently straightforward as a "reaction time": how long it takes to react to something that suddenly pops up out of nowhere. In a wide variety of experiments, men and boys have been found to have faster reaction times, on average, than women and girls, and it is easy to imagine that the human male's relatively quick responses might be an evolved aspect of masculine physical prowess. However, it is also easy to imagine that people's reaction times might respond to training, and indeed there is evidence that playing video games, driving, and participating in sports can all make you that little bit quicker. It should therefore be no great surprise that in a systematic analysis of the many reaction time studies that have been carried out over several decades, psychologist Irwin Silverman discovered that sex differences have been getting smaller over time in the United States, and also that there are significant differences among nationalities.[13]

None of this proves that reaction times have *not* been differentially affected by Darwinian selection in men *versus* women, and I know of no case in which the sex difference in simple reaction times has been abolished, much less reversed. But you would certainly be justified if you were to demand additional evidence and arguments before accepting a claim that quick reaction times represent a male adaptation. Any proposal about the universality of an alleged sex difference warrants

---

[12] Regarding the toy preferences of infant monkeys, see Alexander and Hines (2002) and Hassett et al. (2008).

[13] In one study, Dykiert et al. (2012) reported that males have quicker "simple" (i.e., stimulus detection) reaction times than females throughout the life span—the youngest children tested were four years old—but that there was no sex difference when the task was to make the right four-choice response to one of four possible stimuli. Orosy-Fildes and Allan (1989) report that playing video games improves reaction times. For the evidence that sex differences in reaction time vary between countries and have been shrinking in the United States, see Silverman (2006).

careful scrutiny, as does any hypothesis about why it evolved and what functional significance, if any, it might have.

That said, we know with certainty that the brains and minds of men differ in systematic ways from those of women, and that many of those differences cannot be explained away as the reversible consequences of differential treatment and sex role socialization. We can be sure that these things are so both because male and female brains exhibit various anatomical and biochemical differences even before birth, and because identical postnatal experiences affect the development of girls and boys in different ways.[14]

Rivalrous Males

I am not actually obsessed with sex differences. The reason why I have brought them up yet again is simply this: If we wish to pinpoint the ways in which men are specialized for competing with one another, examining how men's thoughts and actions differ from those of women is illuminating. Consider, for example, the issue of willingness to compete. If I were to suggest that men possess an "appetite for competition," which plays some role in the dramas that can leave them dead on city streets, you might want a standard against which to evaluate my suggestion. In what sense are men more attracted to competition than they might be? An obvious standard of comparison is the behavior of women in comparable situations.

Economists have become interested in how women and men differ in their competitive inclinations and behavior because of the implications for labor markets and career trajectories. Gender inequality in the workplace and the predominance of men in top management positions have been hot-button issues for at least twenty years. Sexist discrimination certainly bears much of the blame, but the stubborn persistence of inequality, even in the face of aggressive strategies to combat discrimination, has persuaded researchers that sex differences in preferences play some role, too. One well-established difference is that men are generally more inclined than women to take risks.[15]

---

[14] On sex differences in the human brain, see, for example, Hines (2010), Pfaff and Christen (2013), and Lentini et al. (2013). Lytton and Romney (1991) reviewed the data on parental treatment of boys *versus* girls and concluded that the differences and their impacts are smaller than is generally believed. Regarding differential impacts of identical experiences on male *versus* female development, see, for example, Bee et al. (1984) and Topçuoğlu et al. (2014).

[15] On sex differences in risk-taking and "risk attitudes," see Wilson and Daly (1985), Byrnes et al. (1999), Daly and Wilson (2001), Croson and Gneezy (2009), and Charness and Gneezy (2012).

In addition to this difference in "taste for risk," men and women apparently differ in other, more subtle, aspects of how they respond to the social context. In an experiment that Margo Wilson and I conducted, not only did male students choose riskier options than their female counterparts in a gamble for real money, but they also responded to witnesses differently: Men who made their choices in front of an audience of their peers made riskier bets than those who chose in privacy, regardless of whether the audience consisted of men, women, or both, whereas women's choices were unaffected by witnesses. Others have replicated and extended these findings by showing that the ways in which men's decisions are affected by witnesses depend on the witnesses' perceived status relative to that of the decision-maker himself.[16]

More recently, economists Muriel Niederle and Lise Vesterlund have provided evidence that, in addition to their greater "taste for risk," men have a greater "taste for competition" than women in the context of a risky bet: When the high-risk option took the form of entering into a winner-take-all competition, the sex difference in preference for that high-risk option got bigger. Niederle and Vesterlund used a speed-arithmetic task in which the sexes performed equally well, and let women and men choose between "piecework" compensation for each correct answer, or a competitive top-performer-takes-all payoff scheme instead. The winner-take-all option was preferred by 73 percent of the men in their study and only 35 percent of the women. Partly, this was due to women's relative risk-aversion, but additional data and analyses showed that the men's greater taste for risk wasn't the whole story. The men's greater degree of overconfidence—another trait for which there is broad evidence for a sex difference—also played a role, and so did the pure and simple appeal of participating in a competition.[17]

The sex difference in "taste for risk" was well known to economists, but Niederle and Vesterlund's 2007 report of a further sex difference in "taste for competition" excited fresh interest. Subsequent research has typically replicated the finding that men and boys are keener on turning a task into a competition than are women and girls, regardless

---

[16] Daly and Wilson (2001) reported sex-differential effects of an audience on risky bets. Ermer et al. (2008) found similar effects, and also that men are less affected by higher- or lower-status audiences than by status peers.

[17] The piecework-versus-competition experiment was reported by Niederle and Vesterlund (2007). Regarding male overconfidence, see, for example, Beyer and Bowden (1997), Kamas and Preston (2012), and Jakobsson et al. (2013); for an explanation of why overconfidence persists despite its costs, see Johnson and Fowler (2011).

of whether it's a task in which males excel. In one study, this sex difference was apparently fully formed by three years of age, but there is also evidence that it can be abolished in certain settings. According to one report, English children attending coed (mixed-sex) schools exhibit the usual sex difference, but girls from single-sex schools are no less inclined to compete than boys. And in the matrilineal Khasi of northern India, a society in which men have unusually little economic power, women have been found to opt for a competitive payoff regime slightly (although not significantly) more often than men.[18]

These mixed findings speak to the lability of the taste for competition. In this, as in most domains, experience clearly matters. However, it would be a mistake to conclude that the typical sex difference is therefore arbitrary and indicates nothing about human nature. In one study using Niederle and Vesterlund's experimental protocol, University of Amsterdam economist Thomas Buser found that whether women chose the competitive payoff regime was affected by their stage in the menstrual cycle and by birth control pills; the findings indicated that high levels of circulating progesterone engender an aversion to competition that is not mediated by changes in performance, confidence, or risk-aversion.[19]

Relatively few people live, or ever did live, in societies with sex roles like those of the matrilineal Khasi, and few children are, or ever were, sequestered from the opposite sex in single-sex schools. In typical human environments, boys and girls interact with one another, and in the process, robust, sex-typical characteristics that owe little or nothing to active sex role socialization by adults emerge from those peer interactions. One major consideration is that boys engage in rough-and-tumble play with one another from a very early age to a much greater extent than do girls, and in their tussles, they sort themselves

---

[18] Niederle and Vesterlund (2011) review experiments on sex differences in competition; see also Croson and Gneezy (2009), and Gupta et al. (2013). Niederle and Vesterlund (2011) cite an unpublished study as showing that the sex difference in preference to compete is age-invariant and already evident at age 3. For the contrasting behavior of girls from coed *versus* single-sex schools, see Booth and Nolen (2012); testing was done at 14 years of age, so sex differences in pubertal maturation may have played a role. Gneezy et al. (2009) report the study of the matrilineal Khasi of India, contrasting them with the "patriarchal" Maasai of Kenya, who exhibited a more typical (and significant) contrast of men choosing to compete more than women. See also Cárdenas et al. (2012) who found the expected sex difference in taste for competition among school children in Sweden, but not in Colombia, whereas the usual sex difference in taste for risk was seen in children from both countries.

[19] For the study implicating progesterone levels, see Buser (2013).

into a dominance hierarchy that children of both sexes recognize. (Although boys' aggressiveness is often attributed to parental encouragement, observational studies indicate that boys are in fact punished for aggression more often than are girls, mainly because they aggress more than girls regardless of the consequences.) In mixed-sex groups, children from preschool onward usually agree about which boy is the "tougher" of any two. The girls cannot be ranked as reliably, nor is there any analogous consensus about which child of two is "smarter" or "nicer" or "has the most friends." In other words, being "tough" seems to have a special salience, and the girls are as cognizant of the male toughness rankings as the boys. These phenomena have been most thoroughly documented among children in the modern west and may, of course, be cross-culturally variable, but observational studies of Kalahari hunter-gatherers, whose sons and daughters are apparently not differentially socialized by their parents in these domains, suggest an essentially similar developmental process.[20]

Boys and men are apparently attracted to competitions that sort out who can dominate whom, in a wide variety of situations. Girls and women, not so much.

Take It or Leave It

Imagine the following situation. You're a student in Arts & Sciences at the University of California at Berkeley, and you receive an e-mail inviting you to earn a little money by taking part in an experiment in the Economics Department. When you show up, you are instructed to sit at a desk in a room with other students, and are given some pages, stapled together, each of which presents you with a choice. The first explains that you have been randomly paired with someone else in the room, but you can't know whom—let's call your partner "X"—and that you have furthermore been randomly assigned to be the sole decision-maker; X has no say. Now here's the choice you're asked to make: Should you and X each get $4, or should you get $3.75 and X get $7.50? In other words, would you forgo twenty-five cents to bestow an extra $3.50—fourteen times as much—on your anonymous partner? Well, would you? After all, your partner is someone similar to you, and your role as the "dictator" was randomly assigned, so you may feel that you have no greater entitlement than X to the experimenter's money.

---

[20] Classic studies of small children's dominance hierarchies, including those of American preschoolers and Kalahari San children, are reviewed in various chapters in Omark et al. (1980).

In fact, exactly half the Berkeley students who were confronted with this problem in a study by economists Gary Charness and Matthew Rabin chose to be generous and half chose to be selfish. Spanish students at the University of Barcelona did almost exactly the same.[21]

Now, let's consider a slightly different decision. Suppose, instead, that the choice had been between $4 each, or $4 for you and $7.50 for X. In this case, it will cost you nothing to make the generous choice. "There but for fortune," as they say: Your role and X's might just as readily have been reversed. Nevertheless, 31 percent of the Berkeley students who were presented with this choice opted for $4 each. (This version of the experiment wasn't run in Barcelona.) In other words, generosity was more common when it was free than when it cost a quarter, but not all that much more common. A substantial minority stiffed their partners anyway. Unfortunately, Charness and Rabin didn't proceed to ask whether some students might even be willing to pay a cost to *prevent* their playing partners from receiving a higher payoff than their own, nor did they mention whether the decisions made by women differed from those made by men. But other research has shed light on these questions.

Of all the laboratory tasks devised by experimental economists, the most popular has been the "ultimatum game." In its typical form, introduced over thirty years ago by Werner Güth and his collaborators at the University of Köln, there are two players who make successive decisions. Player A first proposes how a sum provided by the experimenter should be split between the two, and Player B either accepts the proposal, in which case the sum is divided accordingly, or rejects it, in which case both players get nothing. Before making any decisions, everyone is informed of these contingencies in full, and in the basic experiment, the players are furthermore sequestered and anonymous, in order to make reputational or retaliatory consequences impossible. A's offer is an "ultimatum" because B cannot negotiate; all B can do is take it or leave it.[22]

So let's say Player A has been given ten 1-euro coins and has to decide how he will offer to split them with B. If everyone could be relied on to make the "rational" decisions that maximize their personal income, A should keep nine euros and offer B one, thus providing the smallest possible incentive required to induce B to accept the offer, since one

---

[21] These "dictator game" results are from Table 1 of Charness and Rabin (2002). Whereas the Berkeley students' decisions split exactly 50:50, the Barcelona students exhibited a very slight preponderance of selfish choices.

[22] The "ultimatum game" was introduced by Güth et al. (1982).

euro is better than nothing. But of course, that isn't what real people do. The most common offer is a 50:50 split, and anyone who offers less runs a risk of having his offer rejected; if he proposes that "rational" 9:1 split, he will almost certainly leave the experiment with nothing. This should surprise no-one (other than economists attached to the most simplistic model of self-interest), but it raises some important questions. Does the prevalence of 50:50 offers by players in the A position reflect a preference for fairness, or a rational disinclination to risk a rejection, or something else? And why exactly is it that some—but not all—players in the B position are willing to pay the price of rejecting an offer that, albeit inequitable, is nevertheless better than nothing?

Changing the rules so that one player becomes a "dictator" goes some way toward explaining why ultimatum game players in the A position so often make equitable offers; indeed, that is why dictator games like those conducted by Charness and Rabin were invented. Will A still be as generous if B has no choice but to accept the split that A dictates? The answer is that 50:50 splits are often bestowed even in dictator games, but not as often as they are proposed in the ultimatum game. The usual interpretation is that equitable divisions reflect a preference for fair play in some cases, and a prudent response to anticipated rebuffs in others. But again, why is a rebuff by ultimatum game player B a genuine risk? Here, insight is provided by considering *who* is relatively likely to reject an inequitable offer, as well as who is relatively likely to make one. And this brings us back to sex differences.

In what was apparently the first ultimatum game study to look for possible sex differences, Keith Murnighan and Michael Scott Saxon reported that girls made more generous offers than boys over a range of ages, indeed even in kindergarten when playing for candies. The youngest children made their offers and responses face-to-face, but the sex differences persisted in trials in which older children knew neither the identity nor the sex of their playing partner. Later studies have created all possible gender pairings with players knowing the partner's sex; in general, if either sex is more generous in their offers, it will be the women, but it's often neither.[23]

---

[23] Murnighan and Saxon (1998) reported on ultimatum game (UG) play of schoolboys and girls from kindergarten up; besides making lower offers, boys exploited an "information asymmetry" condition in which their partners didn't know how much they had to divide, more than did girls, at all ages. Eckel and Grossman (2001) found that women made higher UG offers than men; Solnick (2001) found both that higher offers are made *to* men, and that both sexes will accept lower offers *from* men than from women. See also Garcia-Gallego et al. (2012).

The significance of the fact that women usually tend to make somewhat higher offers than men remains ambiguous. Maybe women value equity or fairness more than men, but maybe they're just more risk-averse. Of greater interest is the question of who rejects inequitable offers. Sex differences have been somewhat inconsistent, but studies of what predicts men's decisions have been enlightening. In 2007, economist Terry Burnham proposed that "If low ultimatum game offers are interpreted as challenges, then high-testosterone men may be more likely to reject such offers," and tested that hypothesis by assaying hormone levels in his experimental subjects' saliva. As expected, men who rejected unequal divisions had higher testosterone (T) levels than those who acquiesced to being low-balled, although there was no significant link between hormone levels and the offers that one made as Player A. Interdisciplinary research of this sort has since boomed, and a couple of years later, economist Paul Zak and collaborators tried artificial administration of the hormone. Men's decisions when their T levels were artificially boosted by means of a skin patch were compared to the same men's behavior when the patch was an inert placebo. The men themselves couldn't tell the difference, and yet an active T patch made them more punitive in the role of Player B, as expected from Burnham's results, and also made them less generous as Player A. Zak's work also replicated and extended Burnham's by showing that higher levels of naturally circulating male hormones (both T and dihydrotestosterone) were associated with less generous offers and more punitive responses, quite apart from the additional impact of artificial hormone supplementation.[24]

Winning and Losing

Effects of castration on masculine behavior have been known for centuries. Testosterone was first isolated and synthesized in 1935, and direct study of its many effects on body, brain and behavior immediately blossomed. Every literate lay person is now aware that sex-typical hormones influence sex-typical behavior. If you blame an act of stupid risk-taking or bone-headed perseverance on "testosterone poisoning," everyone gets the joke.

Well, maybe not everyone, because some people won't understand that "testosterone poisoning" *is* a joke. The things "everyone knows"

---

[24] See Burnham (2007) and Zak et al. (2009) for the experiments described here.

about hormone effects are over-simplified, and it is therefore worth pointing out that a T assay is *not* in fact a very good predictor of risk-taking, nor of violent aggressiveness, nor of anything at all. That's partly because a single T assay isn't even a very good predictor of a second measure from the same man. Blood hormone levels rise and fall over the course of the day, and change rapidly in reaction to a wide range of experiences and circumstances. On the one hand, this variability is a nuisance, because you have to conduct a lot of repeated sampling before you can safely say that someone is a chronically high-T or low-T individual. On the other hand, the vicissitudes within individuals are interesting in their own right. What provokes a quick surge or decline in circulating T? And how do these short-term fluctuations influence social response? This, it turns out, is where the action is.[25]

Of particular interest are testosterone responses to success and failure. A substantial body of research indicates that men commonly experience some elevation of T in anticipation of a competition, and once the contest has been resolved, the winner's T levels are typically found to be elevated and the loser's to be depressed. These effects are largest and most consistent when the outcome was clearly determined by the competitors' relative performance, and may be absent if success or failure was obviously determined by pure luck, such as by a lottery. T responses also tend to be stronger when the opponents are well matched, and weak or absent if the outcome was never in doubt because the skill levels of the opponents differed greatly. These effects are seen in boxing and judo matches, but the contest doesn't have to take the form of a fight. T responses to winning and losing were first demonstrated in tennis players, and they have been found to occur even in competitions as cerebral as a chess match.[26]

What is the function of these testosterone responses to competition and its results? Why, in other words, did they evolve? The answer apparently resides in the fact that success or failure in a competitive context carries predictive information about what is likely to transpire in the near future. A recent victory or defeat tells you something about your chances of success in social initiatives ranging from aggression to

---

[25] Regarding the poor predictive power of a T assay, and the overwhelming evidence that T nevertheless plays a causal role in aggressive behavior, see, for example, Dabbs and Dabbs (2000), Archer (2006), and Nelson (2011).

[26] Regarding T responses to victory and defeat, see, for example, Gladue et al. (1989) and Booth et al. (1989, 2006).

courtship. Your physiological responses to contest outcomes, including those T responses, then play a role in determining whether you will launch those initiatives or will instead elect to withdraw and keep out of trouble for a while.[27]

Competing as Teams

It is noteworthy that T responds to success or failure not only in mano-a-mano competitions, but in team sports as well, and not only in the contestants themselves, but also in their supporters. Psychologist Paul Bernhardt and collaborators were the first to report T effects in fans. In one study, they collected pre-game and post-game saliva samples for T assay from men attending a 1991 college basketball game between arch-rivals Georgia and Georgia Tech. In a second study, they collected pre-game and post-game saliva samples from fans watching the 1994 World Cup football final between Brazil and Italy on television sets in public venues in the United States. Both games turned out to be nail-biters that were settled only at the very end, and in both studies, the supporters of the winning side exhibited an elevation of T over their pre-game levels within minutes of the contest's end, while the supporters of the losing side exhibited a drop in T of roughly the same magnitude.[28]

These "hurray for our side" physiological responses presumably reflect adaptations for competition between coalitions. Such group-level competition is relatively rare in the animal kingdom. It can be seen to some degree in chimpanzees, and it is highly evolved in ants and some other social insects, but the human capacity to make war stands out, at least among vertebrates. In this light, shared T responses to "our" side's victories and defeats are intriguing, perhaps alarming. As the authors of that first study of basketball and football fans aptly mused at the end of their report:

> Could small changes in testosterone in individuals lead to large cognitive and behavioral changes in a group? The mood of a community changes when its team wins or loses a game, and the mood of a nation

---

[27] An early, influential argument that the social responsiveness of T serves to modulate social initiative-taking was advanced by Wingfield et al. (1990), with reference mainly to bird behavior. Regarding behavioral consequences of T response to victory and defeat in human beings, see Archer (2006), Mehta and Josephs (2006), Zilioli and Watson (2014), Carré et al. (2013), and Carré and Olmstead (2015).
[28] Regarding T response among participants in team competition, see Booth et al. (2006), Archer (2006), Gonzalez-Bono et al. (1999), and Flinn et al. (2012). For the initial studies of fan effects, see Bernhardt et al. (1998).

changes when its army wins or loses a battle. Physiological factors in individuals, including changes in hormone levels, may affect these group phenomena.[29]

Because this book is about inequality and homicide, you have read a great deal about competition and rather little about cooperation. But we should never forget that the human animal is unsurpassed in its capacity to organize large-scale cooperative ventures, nor should we take that capacity for granted. Cooperation requires explanation, and that turns out to be a more interesting and subtle problem than explaining competition, mainly because the stability of cooperation is always threatened by individual incentives to loaf, to cheat, and to dominate others.

Overcoming those incentives sufficiently to permit large-scale cooperation has been a major feat of human evolution. How did we do it? Perhaps surprisingly, the testosterone research discussed above, including the vicarious effects on fans, may help point the way to an answer. Rather than being the antithesis of competition, cooperation is its handmaiden: We evolved our capacity to cooperate in order to compete more effectively at the level of coalitions. We'll come back to this idea in our concluding chapter.

---

[29] The quotation is from Bernhardt et al. (1998, 62).

7

Culture of Violence?

Critics often accuse economists of failing to appreciate the extent to which human behavior is shaped by cultural forces. But many people also fail to appreciate the extent to which cultural norms and practices are themselves shaped by economic forces.
—Robert Frank, *The Economic Naturalist's Field Guide*, 2009

A Love Affair with Violence?

I recently began typing a phrase into Google. I had only got as far as *"americans lo"* when the clever search engine suggested that what I might be looking for was *"Americans love their guns."* Well, yes, as a matter of fact, that was exactly what I had intended to type, and when I clicked on it, Google coughed up more than fifteen million results. I looked at the first dozen. Some were comical or ironic. Others were threats, directed at snake-in-the-grass "liberals" bent on confiscating freedom-loving Americans' primary defense against tyrannical governments and marauding hippies.

H. Rap Brown, a prominent black power activist of the 1960s, famously declared that "Violence is as American as cherry pie!" Some cultures legitimize violence, glorify violence, "valorize" violence. Others do not. And this has seemed to many analysts to provide an important "explanation" for variability in homicide rates.[1]

Why are murder rates higher in the United States than in other rich countries? A popular answer is the so-called "cowboy culture" of the United States, grounded in its expansionist history. As Americans of European descent spread out from their Atlantic beachheads, the Native Americans whom they displaced sometimes tried to stand their

---

[1] The former H. Rap Brown, who changed his name to Jamil Abdullah Al-Amin, is now serving a life sentence for the murder of a policeman who tried to arrest him in 2000 for a speeding violation.

ground. When Andrew Jackson, the seventh president of the United States, signed the "Indian Removal Act" of 1830, he created a legislative basis for banishing woodland-dwelling eastern tribes to semi-arid, sparsely populated Oklahoma, as well as a precedent for denying native land claims more generally. The Euro-Americans then moved west *en masse*, often before any sort of government or police force had been put in place, and in the absence of an effective justice system to help them resolve their disputes with one another, successful settlers had to be willing and able to dispense their own "self-help justice."[2]

No doubt, the need to deter cattle rustlers was one reason why men in the wild west were armed, but the frontier culture that made a virtue of being willing and able to use violence wasn't restricted to cowboys. Jackson himself had been raised on an earlier frontier in Tennessee, where he was indoctrinated with essentially the same value system. His dying mother's last words to the 14-year-old Jackson allegedly included this advice:

> Never bring a suit in law for assault and battery or for defamation. The law affords no remedy for such outrages that can satisfy the feelings of a true man . . . If you ever have to vindicate your feelings or defend your honor, do it calmly. If angry at first, wait until your wrath cools before you proceed.

In defending his honor, Jackson fought several duels and killed at least one political opponent.[3]

So is the problem of violence in the United States essentially a cultural problem? Policy makers often seem to think so. In 1998, the *American Bar Association* held its annual meeting in Toronto, Canada, and the keynote speaker, US Attorney General Janet Reno, took the occasion to highlight a contrast between the two neighboring countries: "In the five years from 1992 through 1996, the city in which we're meeting now, Toronto, experienced exactly 100 gun homicides. Chicago, an American city of comparable size, had 3,063." Reno then went on to discuss what the lawyers in her audience could do, putting her emphasis on changing values and attitudes: "We need to teach these young people that television and gratuitous violence is not real, that guns really do kill. They are not

---

[2] Black (1983) introduced the useful concept of "self-help justice" into criminology. Regarding the *Indian Removal Act* of 1830, see Prucha (1984).
[3] Courtwright (1996) is an outstanding source on the multiple origins of America's violent frontier culture. For Andrew Jackson's mother's advice to her son, as well as his duels, see Brands (2006).

status symbols. They are not glamorous . . ." Policy remedies got a mention, as well, but Reno made policy sound more like a tool for bringing about cultural change than a means by which democratic governments might alter incentives or rectify injustices. "And if we really work hard at it," she concluded, apparently forgetting momentarily that she was speaking in Canada, "we can end the culture of violence in this nation."[4]

Media commentators are similarly inclined to portray the problem of violence in the United States as a cultural problem. In the aftermath of a 2012 massacre of small children in a Connecticut school, for example, the *New Yorker* posted an article entitled "America's Culture of Violence." Its author, Nicholas Thompson, argued that although gun control legislation was obviously needed, restricting access to guns wouldn't be nearly enough. "American violence doesn't just come from the assault weapons we buy and the gun shows we frequent. It's much deeper than that." The United States, Thompson noted, supplies most of the world's arms, and most of its violent entertainment. "Firearms have long been identified with masculinity in popular culture. Ever more they are identified with femininity, too."[5]

Pointing an accusing finger at popular culture appeals to those on the political right even more than to those on the left. In the same week in which Thompson's *New Yorker* blog lamented America's love affair with guns, another headline blared "NRA blames Hollywood for culture of violence." The acronym NRA refers to the National Rifle Association, a powerful US lobbying organization that focuses its activism and spending on opposing gun control.[6]

Opinions clearly differ regarding who's to blame, but there seems to be a broad consensus that the United States suffers from a culture of violence.

Cultural Diversity

At this point, we need to take a little detour to consider in detail what it means to blame violence—or anything else—on the prevailing culture. What is this thing called "culture," anyway? The first definition that the Merriam-Webster on-line dictionary offers is this: "the beliefs, customs,

---

[4] Reno's American Bar Association address was downloaded on September 27, 2014, from *http:// www.americanbar.org/content/dam/aba/migrated/gunviol/docs/renoadd.authcheckdam.pdf*
[5] Nicholas Thompson's *New Yorker* blog was downloaded on September 27, 2014, from *http:// www.newyorker.com/online/blogs/newsdesk/2012/12/americas-culture-of-violence.html*
[6] The "NRA *versus* Hollywood" item was downloaded on September 27, 2014, from *http://tv.msnbc. com/2012/12/21/nra-blames-hollywood-for-culture-of-violence-and-hollywood-responds/*

arts, etc., of a particular society, group, place, or time." That's not bad, but it leaves something crucial unstated: the *social acquisition* of those beliefs, customs, etc.

"Culture" is etymologically akin to "cultivate." It originally referred primarily to the care and nurture of plants: to the arts of *agri*culture. Its meaning was eventually extended to the refinement of human tastes and manners, a meaning that has not entirely vanished. (You might still hear boorish behavior disparaged as "uncultured.") But when anthropologists took custody of the culture concept, they turned it into something that encompasses everything about how we think and act that we derive from experiences with our fellow human beings.

Here's a definition that captures more of what people have in mind when they decry the "culture of violence" in the United States: Culture is "that complex whole which includes knowledge, belief, art, morals, law, custom, and any other capabilities and habits acquired by man as a member of society." This was the definition concocted by the English anthropologist Edward Tylor in his 1871 tome *Primitive Culture*, and apart from Tylor's politically incorrect use of "man" to encompass women, it still sounds quite modern.[7]

Like all of us, Tylor was shaped by his natal culture, namely that of Victorian England, and like other Victorians, including Darwin, he did not doubt that each society fell somewhere along an "evolutionary" trajectory from savagery to civilization. But while he referred explicitly to the evolution of society, there was nothing truly Darwinian in Tylor's claims. He did not suggest that natural selection had created cultural diversity or culture itself, nor did he propose that the differences between "savages" and civilized Englishmen reflected distinct biological natures. What he *did* mean by societal evolution was that as any society accumulates knowledge and technology, social practices change in ways that are to some degree predictable and repetitive, and that some societies have progressed farther along this shared trajectory than others.

Ethnocentrism is the presumption that the attitudes and values that prevail in one's own society are superior to everyone else's, and by the twentieth century, views like Tylor's stood accused of that sin. Under the influence of Franz Boas and others, decades of strenuous efforts to eliminate every sort of overt or latent value judgment from

---

[7] Cross-cultural management guru Geert Hofstede defines culture as "the collective programming of the mind which distinguishes the members of one group or category of people from another"; http://geert-hofstede.com/national-culture.html

cross-cultural analysis followed, and it became the mainstream view of anthropologists and other social scientists that cultures cannot usefully be called more or less advanced, higher or lower. This "cultural relativism" has subsequently come under fire in its turn, for in its more extreme versions, it often seems to entail an odious *moral* relativism as a sort of corollary: If no society can be considered more "advanced" than any other, and if civilizing trends are therefore ethnocentric illusions, what basis have we for deploring child labor or clitoridectomy or slavery or genocide, where these are deemed righteous?[8]

Debates about these issues will continue, but for our purposes here, some things are clear. Cultures differ in more than just their languages, technologies, and supernatural beliefs. Most importantly, they differ in *values*, and the differences can astound those who take their own values for granted. Killing your own daughter for engaging in premarital sex may be a despicable crime where you come from, but elsewhere it's a moral duty.

Cultural diversity presents a challenge to those who wish to apply insights from evolutionary biology to the study of human affairs. If you seek to understand why some languages rely on word order to encode what other languages accomplish with suffixes, or why a nutritious foodstuff is relished by one population and excluded from the realm of the edible in the next, it is not obvious how Darwinism can help you. This is not to say that there is nothing adaptive about human psychology and behavior. But so much of what people think and do is local, and is apparently arbitrary, irrational, and wasteful to boot. How are we to explain this? A popular answer is that the only sound "explanation" for any cultural phenomenon is a detailed reconstruction of the unique history leading up to it. This view, which is sometimes called "historical particularism," was championed by the American anthropologist Robert H. Lowie almost a hundred years ago, when he famously declared "Culture is a thing *sui generis* which can only be explained in terms of itself . . . *Omnis cultura ex cultura*."[9]

---

[8] For conflicting perspectives on cultural relativism, see, for example, Benedict (1935), Steward (1948), Herskovits (1958), Jarvie (1975), and Rachels (2003). (An 1887 letter by Franz Boas to the journal *Science* is commonly cited as the first statement of "cultural relativism," but it is unclear why. Boas's letter was a straightforward plea that ethnographic museum displays should be organized by ethnic groups rather than by the aggregation of functionally analogous artifacts from different societies.)

[9] The historical particularist manifesto appeared in Lowie (1917); the quotation is from pages 25–26. In his ambitious review of the history of anthropological theories, Marvin Harris (1968) characterized Lowie as the "most sophisticated advocate . . . and most effective defender" of this stance.

If we followed Lowie's dictum too strictly, social science would be reduced to a collection of disconnected narratives, and it is therefore tempting to interpret his words as a hissy fit of turf defense against the dual threats of psychological reductionism and Marxist materialism: Hands off, culture is *our* bailiwick! But we cannot dismiss Lowie quite so easily, because historical particularism contains an undeniable grain of truth. Idiosyncratic historical trajectories surely *do* create cross-cultural differences that are "arbitrary" in the following sense: Nothing extrinsic to the cultural phenomenon itself presently favors maintaining it in one form rather than another. Lexicon provides obvious examples: There is no "first principle" from which we can deduce that *Canis familiaris* should be a *dog* in English, a *hund* in German, a *chien* in French, and a *perro* in Spanish. The only "explanation" for this Babel of names must be pure historical narrative: Then this change took place, and then this, and then this.

What such examples can *not* demonstrate, however, is that *all* variability is arbitrary and that a science of cross-cultural comparison is therefore a pipe dream. And yet that is what many anthropologists and sociologists appear to believe, imagining that they have delivered a devastating critique when they call some line of thought "reductionist." Reductionism—the quest to explain phenomena in terms of more basic phenomena at lower levels—is an essential part of the scientific method, but Lowie and his followers wanted no part of it, and rejected out of hand the possibility that there could be any such thing as principled cross-cultural analysis. They were mistaken. Such analysis is not only possible but highly enlightening. Local ecologies and economies constrain and shape cultural forms, leading to convergent cultural "syndromes" of similar institutions, ideologies, and values among peoples with distinct histories.

Consider, for example, what anthropologists call the "pastoral" way of life, and its "culture of honor." In various parts of the world where rainfall is inadequate for farming, people keep domestic livestock and move with their herds in search of forage. The animals that pastoralists depend on differ from place to place—cattle in sub-Saharan Africa, camels farther north, sheep in the eastern Mediterranean—but one common denominator is that these beasts are the primary source of sustenance and the foundation of wealth. Rangelands aren't usually very productive, and pastoralist populations therefore tend to be widely scattered and low in density. Thus, although one can sometimes travel with kin and allies, it's often better to split up and take smaller herds in different directions. Twenty-first century shepherds carry cell phones, but it is less than a generation since a herdsman could never know the precise whereabouts of anyone who wasn't right there with him, nor, for that matter, whether those friends and relatives whom he hadn't seen for a while were even alive.

The combination of mobility and low density makes it difficult for pastoralists to establish an effective constabulary or any other form of central authority, and their herds invite thievery. In the absence of police and judiciary, rustling must be deterred by sincere, credible threats of a violent response by those who are victimized or by their kinsmen. How better to advertise such a threat than by bristling at any minor affront and exhibiting a reckless willingness to face up to any antagonist?

The ecological commonalities of pastoralist life surely help explain why geographically scattered herding societies who have had no contact with one another since the domestication of the animals on which they depend have nevertheless converged on a shared cultural "syndrome" with a number of common attributes. Pastoralists typically stress patrilineal kinship ties while ignoring or even denying kinship through maternal links, and they practice strictly patrilineal inheritance down male lines. A bridegroom's family typically pays a substantial "bridewealth" to the new wife's natal family, usually in the currency of livestock, and by so doing acquires rights to her labor and her reproduction, which the groom's kinsmen retain even in the event of his death. Having more than one wife is a perquisite of clan leaders with large herds. Men's "honor" is tightly bound to their patrilineage's ability to deliver properly socialized, chaste brides to their allies. Patrilineages are construed as corporate entities to such a degree that killing a close kinsman of a rapist, a murderer, or a cattle rustler is seen as an honorable alternative to retaliating against the offender himself. And there is a code of manly behavior that justifies violent response to relatively minor personal affronts. This complex suite of attitudes, values, and practices constitutes the pastoralist *culture of honor*, and it has apparently been invented independently several times.[10]

Subcultures of Violence?

Has it ever struck you that there is something odd about the clichéd description of the prevailing culture of the United States of America as a "culture of violence"? If that is indeed the case, then the general

---

[10] Regarding the pastoralist culture of honor, see Peristiany (1965) and Nisbett and Cohen (1996).

public doesn't seem to have been very effectively enculturated! Millions of Americans may love their guns, but opinion polls consistently indicate that a majority would prefer stricter limitations on gun availability. Brutal mixed martial arts matches draw big pay-per-view television audiences, but those who find this spectacle repugnant continue to outnumber its fans.

The important general point here is that attitudes and values differ among the individual persons who compose a cultural group. Ethnographers often gloss over this reality of diversity and dissent, but theories that treat culture as a major determinant of our behavior will not take us far if they simply ignore it. One approach to this complication has been to try to identify "subcultures" within the larger culture: groups whose members share a worldview that is socially reinforced within the subculture, while departing in some, but not all, of its constituent attitudes and values from the predominant normative culture surrounding it.

The concept of a subculture is in a sense uncontroversial, even trite. Does anyone doubt that the larger society contains subgroups—some organized, some informal—whose members influence one another? And does anyone doubt that these subgroups often demarcate themselves not only by their shared enthusiasms, but by a socially reinforced contempt for aspects of the mainstream culture as well? There are peaceniks and punks, wiccans and white supremacists, not one of whom constructed her suite of beliefs and values in isolation. The fact that these and other subcultures exist is easily confirmed. More controversial, however, is the question of the extent to which the concept of a subculture actually explains anything, as opposed to being merely descriptive.

In 1967, Marvin Wolfgang (1924–98), the criminologist whose earlier study of Philadelphia police department files had set the standard for American homicide research, collaborated with an Italian psychiatrist, Franco Ferracuti (1927–92), to produce an influential book entitled *The Subculture of Violence*. Wolfgang and Ferracuti's analysis focused rather little on violence *per se*, but it dealt at length with the concept of a subculture, the essential feature of which was said to be the distinctiveness of its values:

> There are shared values that are learned, adopted, and even exhibited by participants in the subculture, and that differ in quantity and quality from those in the dominant culture. (99)

Then, facing up to the problem of defining exactly what they meant by *values*, Wolfgang and Ferracuti listed seven definitional criteria, the first of which was this:

> They arise outside the individual, are the products of group living, and make us captives of conformity. (115)

Violent capability and the willingness to use it are valued, they argued, in "certain male groups" that "retain notions of machismo [and] continue to equate maleness with overt physical aggression" (259), and in which a young man "seeks reinforcement from others . . . for his commitment to these values of violence" (260). Wolfgang and Ferracuti called their vision of the "subculture of violence" both a "theory" and their "thesis," and they immodestly subtitled their book *"Towards an integrated theory in criminology."* Both enthusiasts and critics have taken their hubris seriously.[11]

There was much to admire about *The Subculture of Violence*. It was unusually scholarly and synthetic in its respectful citations of the writings of sociologists, psychologists, and anthropologists, and it rose above the blithe Americocentrism that mars many criminological works. Also impressive was the serious attention that the authors paid to methodological issues, such as the subtle problem of how to measure values without falling prey to either the uncritical acceptance of socially desirable cheap talk or the circular logic of ascribing values on the basis of the behavior that those values are being invoked to explain.

That said, there was also much to criticize. Striving to be dispassionate analysts, Wolfgang and Ferracuti explicitly rejected blame—violent men, like all of us, are after all just "captives of conformity"—and yet their pejorative view of the subculture they sought to describe repeatedly leaked through the cracks. (Did you notice, for example, the words "retain" and "continue" in a phrase that I quoted two paragraphs back, and the gratuitous implication that valuing violence is atavistic?) Nor did Wolfgang and Ferracuti try to hide the fact that what they were describing was the specifically *black* subculture in cities like Philadelphia, to which they ascribed a wholesale, positive valuation of violence:

> It is not far-fetched to suggest that a whole culture may accept a value set dependent upon violence, demand or encourage adherence to violence, and penalize deviation. (155)

---

[11] All quotations are from Wolfgang and Ferrcutti (1967).

Wolfgang and Ferracuti made explicit (if not entirely successful) efforts to preempt accusations of racism, and yet they seemed oblivious to their own *classist* biases. Ignoring phenomena ranging from elite duelling to murderous potentates, they portrayed the valorization of violence as strictly a lower class phenomenon, and even as a value system subscribed to by men who cannot "reason" as well as their betters. "The middle- or upper-class actor," they wrote, might plan a "rational, premeditated murder," but his culturally ingrained revulsion at the thought of using violence and his "ponderous assessment of the probabilities of apprehension" would combine to reduce the likelihood that he would ever follow through. The lower-class man, by contrast, "acts with quick, yet socially ingrained aggressivity" and "Neither reasoning nor time for it are at his disposal."[12]

The Subculture of Violence has attracted fire not only for its biases, but for empirical failings as well. Researchers who have tried to test the theory have concluded that people who *perpetrate* violence don't necessarily, or even typically, *approve* of it any more than the rest of us. But as important as that may be, it does not discredit the reality of subcultures in which willingness and ability to perpetrate violence are admired and even glorified. The ethnographic literature on urban ghetto life provides abundant testimony to the fact that such value systems exist. Yale University sociologist Elijah Anderson has described what he calls the "code of the streets" in African-American ghettoes as follows:

> The code revolves around the presentation of self. Its basic requirement is the display of a predisposition to violence. Accordingly, one's bearing must send the unmistakeable if sometimes subtle message to 'the next person' in public that one is capable of violence and mayhem when the situation requires it, that one can take care of oneself. The nature of this communication is largely determined by the demands of the circumstances but can include facial expression, gait, and verbal expressions—all of which are geared mainly to deterring aggression . . .

> Even so, there are no guarantees against challenges, because there are always people around looking for a fight to increase their share of respect—or 'juice,' as it is sometimes called on the street. Moreover, if a person is assaulted, it is important, not only in the eyes of his opponent but also in the eyes of his 'running buddies,' for him

---

[12] For phrases quoted in this paragraph, see Wolfgang and Ferracuti (1967, 259, 262, 263).

to avenge himself. Otherwise he risks being 'tried' (challenged) or 'moved on' by any number of others. To maintain his honor he must show he is not someone to be 'messed with' or 'dissed.'[13]

Other social groups in other lands subscribe to similar codes, as illustrated by this description of attitudes among the traditional Mafia of Calabria:

> Among the *mafiosi* of the Plain of Gioia Tauro the act of homicide, if carried out in a competition for supremacy of any sort whatever, indicated courage and the capacity to impose oneself as a man. It brought an automatic opening of a line of credit for the killer. The more awesome and potent the victim, the more worthy and meritorious the killer.[14]

I could pile on additional examples from many cultures and subcultures whose common denominator is *self-help justice*. But I doubt that I need do so in order to convince you that value systems in which violent men are admired and emulated *exist*. My primary qualm about the "subculture of violence thesis" concerns the imputation of *causality*: the implicit or explicit suggestion that by establishing the reality of these values, we have explained why acts of violence occur.

A demonstration that attitudes and values *predict* behavior tells us nothing about what is cause and what is effect. A few years ago, Alfred McAlister of the University of Texas School of Public Health reported a significant association between a country's homicide rate and the extent to which its citizens expressed agreement with the following three propositions:

(1) A person has the right to kill to defend their (sic) property.
(2) I would approve if a parent kills someone who has raped his/her child.
(3) I approve of the death penalty for certain crimes.

What can we infer from the association between homicide rates and the endorsement of these statements? It is certainly possible that adherence to the values implied by these attitudes drives up homicide rates, but it is no less plausible that living in a relatively violent milieu drives up

---

[13] Prominent studies that purport to have tested Wolfgang and Ferracuti's theory and failed to support the hypothesis that violent behavior reflects pro-violence values include Ball-Rokeach (1973), Erlanger (1974), and Cao et al. (1997). The "code of the streets" passage is quoted from Anderson (1994, 87–88).
[14] This description of mafia values is from Arlacchi (1983, 111–13).

people's willingness to endorse the use of retaliatory and deterrent violence. If violence is locally prevalent, that fact provides a strong rationale for wanting to be ready and able to perpetrate violence. Indeed, people explicitly strive to inculcate violent capabilities and attitudes in their children where they perceive that the children will need them.[15]

Blaming violent behavior on a violent culture or subculture sheds no light on the reasons for the concomitant variability in behavior and culture across locales and over time. Either that variety is capricious, or it hangs on something else. My concern here is the same one that Margo Wilson and I expressed a quarter century ago, and that I quoted in Chapter 1:

> If we think we can explain why poor young men behave violently in terms of the 'transmission' of 'values' within a 'subculture', then we are unlikely to seek more utilitarian explanations. In fact, poor young men have *good reason* to escalate their tactics of social competition and become violent.[16]

And that is more or less the reservation that I still have concerning the "southern culture of violence" thesis, which is widely accepted as an explanation for regional differences in homicide within the United States.

Homicide and the Culture of Honor in the Southern United States

American criminologists have long been aware that homicide rates are substantially higher in the southern states than in the northern states, and they have long debated why. Is this regional difference best understood as deriving from "structural" differences between south and north, such as differences in adult sex ratios or institutionalized racism or the economic importance of agriculture? Or should we be seeking explanations for regional differences in violence in regional differences in such "cultural" factors as beliefs, attitudes, and values?[17]

---

[15] McAlister (2006) reported the cross-national correlation between these attitude items (which were also significantly correlated with one another) and the homicide rate. Many writers have described parental encouragement of violence in dangerous milieus such as urban ghettoes; a good example is Anderson (1999).

[16] The quote is from Daly and Wilson (1988b). In Chapter 6 of that work, we reviewed further evidence that violence enhances male prestige and achievement in many societies.

[17] Regarding debates about the relative importance of "structure" and "culture" as explanations for "southern violence" in the United States, see Lee et al. (2007).

In the 1990s, a fresh perspective that goes some way toward synthesizing structural and cultural accounts emerged from the multimethod research program of social psychologists Richard Nisbett and Dov Cohen. By focusing on the behavior and attitudes of "white" men, these researchers circumvented some of the complications engendered by US race relations, and assembled a strong case that white southerners, unlike white northerners, adhere to a "culture of honor."[18]

The prototypical culture of honor entails a suite of interrelated attitudes, values, and norms, such that a man's familial and personal honor resides largely in the "virtue"—the chastity and subservience—of his female relatives, and in his being respected as one who will brook no trespass. This suite of attitudes, values, and norms tends to be characteristic of societies with strong patrilineal family loyalties, institutionalized eye-for-eye family feuds, and, most importantly, self-help justice. As we saw earlier in this chapter, it is particularly prevalent among pastoralists, and the economic / ecological reasons why pastoralists should adhere to such a value system seem clear.

The traditional duel—a gentlemanly and potentially lethal fight conducted with great decorum—is a classic manifestation of the culture of honor in the US south. Duelling is now rare, at least among the propertied classes, but its underlying values live on. In one survey study, Cohen and Nisbett showed that southerners don't endorse violence in general to a greater degree than do northerners, but in certain specific contexts, they do: Southerners condone violent responses to trespassing, insults, and sexual advances against one's female partner or relatives. In an ingenious experiment, Cohen then showed that "southernness" is more than skin deep. University of Michigan undergraduate men were exposed to a staged insult—each was bumped in a narrow hallway by a large man who then muttered "asshole" under his breath—and men from the south responded very differently from those raised in the north. Questionnaire responses and actual behavior showed that the southerners were more upset by the insult, and more motivated to react aggressively, but the most remarkable difference was physiological: The insult induced a rapid spike in the levels of testosterone circulating in the southern men's blood, and in their levels of the "stress hormone" cortisol, while the northerners exhibited no hormonal response at all. Finally, as regards contemporary homicides, analyses by Nisbett and

---

[18] Nisbett and Cohen's (1996) book, *Culture of Honor: the Psychology of Violence in the South*, provides a highly readable account of their research methods and results.

others indicate that it is specifically in the context of "arguments" rather than "felonies" that white men from the southern states are more likely than their northern counterparts to kill.[19]

What could be the historical origin of these regional differences? Surprisingly, Nisbett and Cohen propose that the answer resides in the same ecological basis of honor cultures elsewhere: in pastoralism. Citing historical evidence, they maintain that the northern states received their predominant economic and cultural influences from Puritans, Quakers, and Dutch farmers and townsmen, who brought with them a strong ethic of neighborly cooperation. The Europeans who settled the southern states, by contrast, were mostly "Scotch-Irish" folk from the fringes of Britain, who had made their living there as shepherds, and to some extent, continued to do so in the new world. The pastoralist ethic of self-help justice accompanied them to the new world, with all its baggage about "real men" being ready and able to act violently when they must.[20]

According to Nisbett and Cohen, herding retained its economic importance in the southeastern United States into the nineteenth century, and in the southwest even longer, but it is now a minor source of employment and economic activity throughout the country except very locally. In short, their proposal is that southerners and northerners brought distinct cultural baggage from Europe centuries ago and have transmitted their distinct cultures with sufficient fidelity that they persist to this day, even though their material foundations have largely evaporated.

Cultural Inertia?

In my opinion, Nisbett and Cohen have assembled an airtight case that white men from the southern United States differ from their northern counterparts in their attitudes and behavior, and even in their physiological responses to being disrespected. These regional differences are nicely summarized by saying that southerners adhere to a "culture of honor."

---

[19] For surveys showing south–north differences in attitudes toward the use of violence, see Cohen and Nisbett (1994). The primary report of the experimental study of hormonal responses to an insult is Cohen et al. (1996). For evidence that it is specifically "social conflict homicides," and not "felony homicides," that are elevated in the southern United States, see Nisbett (1993) and Lee et al. (2007).

[20] Nisbett (1993) and Nisbett and Cohen (1996) make the case for a pastoralist origin of "southern violence." For a counter-argument, see Chu et al. (2000).

The proposal that this culture owes its existence to Scotch-Irish pastoralism is more speculative, but Nisbett and Cohen never pretended that it's not, and little of importance hangs on whether this particular historical hypothesis is correct anyway. Of much greater importance is their equally speculative suggestion of *massive cultural inertia*: The culture of honor has allegedly continued to reproduce itself in generation after generation of southerners via the social transmission of its essential values, long after any material basis for it has disappeared. This is an important hypothesis because it has implications about what, if anything, can be done about southern violence.[21]

In their book's concluding section, Nisbett and Cohen argue against the usual suspects on which southern violence is often blamed: hot climate, poverty, and racism. Without reprising their arguments, let me just say that their skepticism about the explanatory power of these factors is justified. Then, having rejected what they see as the leading "material"—or, as a criminologist would say, "structural"—hypotheses, they attribute the honor culture's persistence to pure cultural transmission more or less by default. Moreover, while they concede that the southern culture of honor may yet wither and die for want of an enduring material foundation and rationale, that's not where they would place their own bets:

> Because culture is taken in without reflection, because we acquire it more by *absorbing* it than by studying it, the ultimate reason for why we do things (or why a behavior is functional) is often hidden from us. We do not reexamine cultural rules every generation or analyze how functionally adaptive they are before we internalize them. So, as long as they do not get us in too much trouble in some way that is manifest and as long as there is no far more attractive alternative, they will continue. Indeed, as long as there is social enforcement of the norms, it may be profitable to continue to behave in accord with such norms and costly to defy them even when one consciously, personally rejects them.

> An important implication of that analysis is that one should speculate not merely on whether the culture of honor will wither when material circumstances cease to make it rational but also whether the culture of honor could maintain itself, or even grow, for nonmaterial reasons . . .[22]

---

[21] The arguments and evidence to follow are revised from Daly and Wilson (2010).
[22] The quoted passage is from Nisbett and Cohen (1996, 93–94).

This proposal has caught the fancy of many readers, and even though Nisbett and Cohen stressed that they were "speculating," it seems to have become every social scientist's go-to example of culture's supposed inertia in the absence of material supports. Evolutionists are especially fond of citing it, perhaps to disarm inane accusations of "biological determinism" by demonstrating that they, too, take culture seriously.[23]

Biologist Peter Richerson of the University of California at Davis and anthropologist Rob Boyd, now at Arizona State University, argue that culture should be thought of as a second "inheritance system," of no lesser importance than so-called "biological inheritance" for explaining human behavior. In a 2005 book entitled *Not by Genes Alone: How Culture Transformed Human Evolution*, Richerson and Boyd used the honor culture of the US south as their opening "hook." They began by summarizing Nisbett and Cohen's results and arguments, then elaborated on how this example illustrates their own thesis as follows:

> *Culture is crucial for understanding human behavior* . . . Murder is more common in the South than in the North. If Nisbett and Cohen are right, this difference can't be explained in terms of contemporary economics, climate, or any other external factor. Their explanation is that people in the South have acquired a complex set of beliefs and attitudes about personal honor that make them more polite, but also more quick to take offense than people in the North. This complex persists because the beliefs of one generation are learned by the next.[24]

And what, you may ask, is wrong with that? Southerners clearly do have behavior, beliefs, and attitudes that differ, on average, from those of their northern counterparts, and people undoubtedly learn these things from their families and neighbors. There's no controversy about all that. The only thing that I want to call into question is the suggestion

---

[23] Evolutionists who have cited Nisbett and Cohen's book as having *demonstrated*—not just suggested—that the culture of honor has persisted in the US south "for nonmaterial reasons" include Runciman (1998, 183), Cosmides and Tooby (1999, 461), Alvard (2003, 138), Gangestad et al. (2006, 91), and Norenzayan (2006). The latter then generalizes the lesson as follows, "The best explanation for the persistence of honor cultures is social transmission . . . Perhaps a common scenario across cultures is that ecological differences evoke an initial cultural response that adaptively varies but then is picked up by processes of transmitted culture, amplified, and perpetuated even when the initial conditions are no longer present." (Norenzayan 2006, 126).
[24] The quote is from Richerson and Boyd (2005, 3).

that "contemporary economics" has been disposed of as a candidate explanation. Yes, average income and how many live in poverty are poor predictors of local homicide rates, but if you've read this far, that shouldn't surprise you. What, you should be wondering, about income *inequality*?[25]

Figure 7.1 presents the same 1990 homicide data that you saw in Chapter 2 (figure 2.1 on page 24), with one addition: The "southern" states are now represented by filled (black) circles. The regional difference in homicide rates should be obvious: Most of the states with very high rates in 1990, and *none* of those with very low rates, were in the south. The average southern state had 108 homicides per million

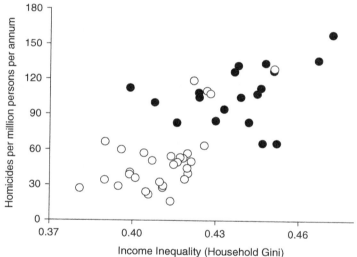

Figure 7.1. Homicide rates in the fifty US states in 1990, as a function of the state-specific Gini coefficient of income inequality, with "south" and "non-south" distinguished.

---

[25] Although Nisbett and Cohen (1996) omit income inequality from their list of "alternative explanations for southern violence," they have not totally ignored this variable. Nisbett et al. (1995) reported that Gini was a significant bivariate correlate of city-level homicide rates, but that it dropped out in multivariate models. This result cannot justify their subsequent ignoring of inequality, however, especially since the homicide data were for "white" men only, whereas the Gini estimates were based on the cities' full multiracial income distributions. Subsequent authors who have cited Nisbett and Cohen's work as having ruled out economic explanations for southern violence, including Richerson and Boyd, have then failed to consider income inequality at all.

persons per annum, and the average non-southern state had 57. That's a huge difference.[26]

But the regional difference in homicide rates isn't the only thing that becomes apparent when we highlight the southern states. In addition to the fact that most of the black circles are located in the upper half of figure 7.1, where homicide rates are high, you may have noticed that most of the black circles are also located on the right-hand side of the figure, where income is relatively unequally distributed. In other words, inequality tended to be more extreme in the south than in the north in 1990, and it looks as if that fact could be largely responsible for the regional difference in homicide rates. Could it be that "contemporary economics" has some relevance to southern violence after all?[27]

In 2004, Margo Wilson and I presented these data at a small conference on the topic of *Mind, Culture and Evolution* at the University of British Columbia in Vancouver, concluding that the "pure cultural transmission" explanation for the persistence of southern violence may have been overstated, and that an economic basis for north-south differences cannot yet be ruled out. Richard Nisbett was one of the conference participants, and he immediately raised an objection.

One of the strengths of the research that Cohen and Nisbett have conducted is that by singling out the behavior and attitudes of "white" men, they have been able to zero in on regional differences that cannot be dismissed as artifacts of regional variability in the relative proportions of the so-called "racial" groups. Now Nisbett proposed that we needed to do the same before we could conclude that variations in income inequality can account for the lion's share of regional differences in homicide, and he did not hide his skepticism that state-level

[26] Averages here, as well as the appearance of Figures 7-1 and 7-2, differ slightly from their counterparts in Daly and Wilson (2010) because of a few changes in categorization, which I made to bring my definition of the US "south" into line with Nisbett and Cohen's. Nisbett and Cohen (1996, 15) divide the contiguous forty-eight states into seven regions. My "south" now encompasses their "southern" (AL, DE, FL, GA, KY, MD, MS, NC, SC, TN, VA, WV) and "southwestern" (AR, LA, OK, TX) regions. (These state name abbreviations can be found in any online list of the United States of America.) The categorization remains somewhat arbitrary—one could argue for removing Oklahoma from the south and for adding Missouri—but this makes no practical difference.
[27] If we "partial out" the apparent effect of income inequality by computing the residual differences between the observed homicide rate for each state and what would be predicted on the basis of its Gini coefficient, the "southern effect" shrinks from a highly significant excess of 51 homicides per million persons per annum ($p = 0.000001$ by t-test) to an excess of 18 (still statistically significant, at $p = 0.024$).

variability in the severity of income inequality among "white" men would remain a significant predictor of the variability in *their* homicide rates.

I suppose Margo and I might have protested that insofar as the competition among men takes place within a multiracial pool, confining attention to the statistically advantaged Euro-American population would wipe out a crucial component of the inequality that affects men's behavior. But there was no denying that Nisbett had a point, and it happened to be a point that we could address with further analyses. For reasons of his own, Princeton University economist Angus Deaton had already computed state-level Gini coefficients for the incomes of "non-Hispanic white" men, and he kindly shared these estimates with us. The same category of "non-Hispanic white" men could then be picked out from the case-by-case victimization data in the FBI's *Supplementary Homicide Reports*, and it was therefore possible to repeat our analyses with both the Gini coefficients and the homicide rates computed with respect to this particular subpopulation.[28]

Figure 7.2 presents the results of this new analysis, and as you can see, they look a lot like the results portrayed in figure 7.1. The southern states again tend to be located mainly in the upper (high homicide) half of the figure, and they again tend to be located mainly on the right-hand (high inequality) side. The average southern state had 97 "white" male homicide victims per million such men per annum, and the average non-southern state had 61. Especially remarkable is the fact that the correlation between inequality and homicide was virtually undiminished when we narrowed our focus from the entire population (figure 7.1) to "white men" (figure 7.2), even though both the average level of inequality and its range of values were substantially reduced in the latter comparison. The homicide-Gini correlation was again in excess of 0.7, again indicating that income inequality alone could predict (or "account for") half the variability across the fifty states. Moreover, contrary to Nisbett's intuition, there was even less evidence in the "white" male data than in our original analysis that region makes any difference at all, once income inequality is duly considered.[29]

---

[28] Deaton's rationale for computing income inequality within "races" and his method of doing so are described in Deaton and Lubotsky (2003).

[29] If we again "partial out" Gini, the "southern effect" shrinks from a statistically significant excess of 36 homicides per million "white" men per annum (p = 0.004 by t-test) to an excess of just 5, which is no longer statistically significant (p = 0.558).

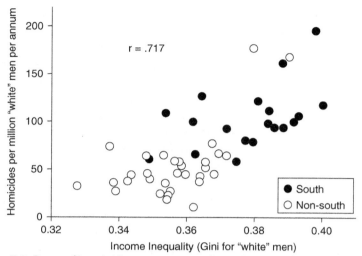

Figure 7.2. Rates of homicide victimization of non-Hispanic "white" men in the fifty US states. in 1990, as a function of the state-specific Gini coefficient of that demographic group's income inequality, with "south" and "non-south" distinguished.

In sum, then, Nisbett and Cohen have *not* demonstrated that long-standing regional differences in US homicide rates constitute a proof of the inertial power of culture in the absence of material supports. To suggest, even tentatively, that a cultural difference cannot be explained by *any* material factor is of necessity an argument by exclusion. Such arguments are always inconclusive, because eliminating one potential explanatory variable (such as average income) cannot rule out the possibility that another (such as income inequality) will do a better job. And in fairness, I should stress again that Nisbett and Cohen never *claimed* to have proven this point, which they explicitly called a speculation. Nevertheless, the hypothesis of pure cultural transmission without material supports is clearly an interpretation that they found attractive, and secondary sources have been less cautious about the implications of their research than have Nisbett and Cohen themselves.

For my part, I do not doubt that bits and pieces of arbitrary cross-cultural variation may persist for generations for no material reason other than that beliefs, attitudes, and values are taught to accepting youngsters who later pass them on, and that nonconformists are often scorned. But in this case, I'm skeptical. How likely is blind adherence to tradition when what we are talking about are life-or-death situations in which people exert some control over their level of participation?

Elite duelling is a thing of the past. Once elites had acquired safer means to defend their interests—safer means that were backed up by law—the "cultural transmissions" of Andrew Jackson's mother and her ilk were no longer sufficient to keep that particular tradition alive. Defy local norms by filing a lawsuit for defamation of character, and gentlemen may initially mock and ostracize you for your cowardice. But once they see you taking the proceeds of your successful lawsuit to the bank, you just might become a new cultural role model yourself!

Incentives Matter

Please don't misunderstand me. It is not my claim that because culture is immaterial, it is therefore a fantastical substance, the phlogiston of the social sciences. Culturally transmitted attitudes, values, and beliefs have undeniable behavioral consequences. Men who were raised in the southern states have different hormonal responses to insults than their counterparts raised in the north. Real people rally around flags, burn heretics, die for their beliefs.

My disagreement with Nisbett and Cohen, and with Richerson and Boyd, is more subtle and, in a sense, rather minor. In their discussion of the culture of honor in the southern United States, Nisbett and Cohen maintain, as do I, that a panhuman evolved psychology underlies our capacity to develop cultural construals and practices; Richerson and Boyd stress the same point while arguing that human evolution has proceeded "not by genes alone." And we are all on the same page again with respect to the point that cultures of honor tend to emerge for utilitarian reasons in particular social and ecological settings that oblige self-help justice. In pointing out the possible confounding effects of north-south differences in income inequality, I should not be misread as proposing that invoking culture in the explanation of regional differences is wrong or superfluous, not even in this specific case. Instead, it seems quite likely that the north-south difference in economic inequality itself reflects cultural differences in the value placed on self-reliance and in other ideological foundations of the culture of honor.

As I see it, the one important question on which we are *not* entirely in agreement is this: How robust, how self-sustaining is a local culture or subculture? Those who are most enthusiastic about the idea of cultural inertia in the absence of continuing material supports apparently doubt that well-chosen policies can counteract the problem of southern violence, on the grounds that its cultural supports are strong. Even Nisbett and Cohen, who express much more caution on this point than many of those who cite them, conclude their book on the psychology of violence in the US south by suggesting that "the culture of honor of the South might retain some force indefinitely" and might "even grow," and explain why they consider this a possibility as follows: "The ideals of the culture of honor are built into one's social identity and may become divorced from ideas about economic survival. Once those ideals are separated from their initial reasons for their existence and incorporated into gender roles, they may become much more impervious to change."[30]

Is this pessimism about the potential for change really warranted? Think about bicultural people whom you know: people who move back and forth between two different cultures without evident distress, functioning appropriately in both. There are a great many such people in the modern world, and their very existence proves that human beings are not the unthinking puppets of cultural indoctrination that a strong cultural inertia hypothesis supposes us all to be.

Nisbett and Cohen maintain that "culture is taken in without reflection" and that "we do not reexamine cultural rules every generation." That is surely true of many aspects of social learning, such as language acquisition, but it is not true of all domains. Rather than simply internalizing the attitudes and values of their elders, young people manifest a rather annoying *skepticism* about the wisdom of their elders, a stance that arguably serves them well as a defence against being easily manipulated into serving other people's agendas. One effect of this healthy skepticism is that people can and do jump ship, abandoning belief systems that they perceive to be obsolete and ineffectual. Elite duelling seemed to have great cultural inertia thanks to the shame associated with opting out, and then, quite quickly, it disappeared. Incentives had changed. Or consider, as another example, the phenomena of messianic movements and cargo cults, which can be interpreted as attempts to negotiate new deals with supernatural forces who are being insufficiently responsive to the old ways. Nothing undermines the sanctity of tradition more powerfully than the example of outsiders who don't buy into your group's beliefs and practices, and who are apparently more successful as a result.[31]

---

[30] Quotes are from Nisbett and Cohen (1996, 92–94).

[31] The quoted phrases are again from Nisbett and Cohen (1996, 94). Regarding cargo cults, see, for example, Trompf (1990).

As for homicide rates, they are far from immutable: They can and do change remarkably rapidly, in either direction, a phenomenon that we will examine in Chapter 8. In the United States as a whole, the homicide rate fell by more than 30 percent between 1991 and 1997; in New York City, it fell by more than 60 percent, and in Boston by more than 70 percent. Meanwhile, the Russian homicide rate doubled in the five years prior to the collapse of the Soviet Union, and doubled again in the ensuing five years. Such rapid changes tend to consist primarily of increases and reductions in precisely the sorts of killings that are our focus here, namely those that arise from social conflicts between unrelated men in a context of competition over status, respect, and the maintenance of personal manly honor. So if the subculture that Elijah Anderson called the "code of the streets" makes men kill in response to disrespect, its cultural impact evidently waxes and wanes on a time-scale much shorter than a generation. How inertial—how "impervious to change"—is that?[32]

There are at least two important "material" foundations for these lethal honor contests: inequitable access to resources, which inspires escalated and sometimes dangerous competition, and a lack of access to law enforcement, which obliges self-help justice. In their book's concluding section, Nisbett and Cohen seem pessimistic about the prospects for an amelioration of the southern culture of honor, but they propose on their very last page that this culture has "allure" specifically for "those who have little to gain by playing by society's rules and little to lose by standing outside of them."

In other words, the fervor with which people who are exposed to the culture of honor embrace its value system is affected by incentives and opportunities. And adjusting incentives and opportunities is something that social and economic policies most certainly can do.

---

[32] Regarding the decline in the US homicide rate between 1991 and 1997, see Blumstein and Rosenfeld (1998). Regarding the Russian homicide rate before and after the collapse of the Soviet Union, see Pridemore (2006).

8

Lags and Lifetimes

Early stress becomes deeply embedded in the child's neurobiology, with an astonishing range of long-term effects on cognition, emotion and behavior...Are those effects entirely maladaptive, or do they reflect a more complex balance of costs and benefits? ... [T]he field is undergoing a conceptual revolution, as traditional approaches founded on notions of "toxic stress" are revised in light of the potential of early stress to shift the developing organism along alternative adaptive trajectories.
—Marco del Giudice, "Early Stress and Human Behavioral Development," 2014

Ups and Downs

Up to this point, our efforts to understand the variability in homicide rates have focused on the differences across political boundaries, such as those between states, provinces, or entire nations. You may recall, for example, that according to the *United Nations Demographic Yearbook*, the homicide rate in Japan was 6 victims per million population per annum in 1990, while in the United States it was 98, and in Colombia 744. And as we have seen, the best single predictor of this diversity among nations is their respective levels of income inequality.

There is, however, another kind of variability in homicide rates which we have scarcely yet considered, namely the year-to-year changes that occur within one and the same jurisdiction. These temporal trends will be the focus of this chapter. In the relatively short term—one human lifespan, let us say—this "longitudinal" variability is rarely as extreme as the "cross-sectional" variability across nations at a given time, but it is remarkable nonetheless, and it is remarkably poorly understood.

Consider the recent ups and downs of murder in the United States. Estimates of the US homicide rate before about 1930 are suspect for various reasons, but in the early 1930s, it can safely be estimated that there were almost 100 homicides per million persons per year. Then, with the Great Depression in full roar, killings unexpectedly plummeted, cutting that 1930 level in half by the Second World War, and after a brief post-war reversal, the homicide rate continued down to a low of about 40 in the 1950s. Sadly, that relatively peaceful state of affairs didn't last, and after a steep rise in the 1960s and 1970s, the rate briefly surpassed 100 around 1980. It stayed high into the mid-1990s, when another big decline began. In 1993, there were an estimated 94 homicides per million US citizens. By 2000, that rate had plunged to 55, and in 2013, it reached a new fifty-year low of 45.[1]

A common intuition is that changing rates of crime, including violent crime, must surely track economic trends, especially changes in the unemployment rate. The fact that unemployed men are far more likely to kill, and to be killed, than their employed counterparts supports that intuition, but the history summarized above does not. For reasons that continue to be debated, the US homicide rate began its fall in the 1930s while unemployment was still close to its twentieth century maximum level of about 20 percent. The big increase in homicides during the 1960s and 1970s took place while unemployment was fairly steady at about 5 percent, the conventional criterion of "full employment." Homicide fell again during the roaring 90s, and it continued downward during the economic travails of 2008–2010. The unemployment rate *does* seem to have an impact on rates of property crime in the United States, but on violent crime, apparently not.[2]

What the volatility that we are examining means in terms of human lives may become more vivid if it is expressed in raw numbers rather than rates. In 1993, the total population of the United States reached 257 million, almost twenty-five thousand of whom were slain by their fellow citizens. Twenty years later, the nation's population had increased by a further 22 percent to 316 million. If the per capita rate of homicide

---

[1] Eckberg (1995) has shown that pre-1930 estimates of the US homicide rate cannot be trusted for multiple reasons, including incomplete and shifting coverage of the country, biased extrapolations from low-homicide regions, high proportions of deaths with no attributed cause, and changing definitions of homicide itself.

[2] Wilson and Daly (1985) showed that unemployment is a major risk factor both for killing and for being killed. Nevertheless, the simple correlation between each year's unemployment and homicide rates in the United States over the last half century is 0.180 (p = 0.211). For time-series analyses indicating that US unemployment levels affect property crime but have no demonstrable effect on violent crime, see Raphael and Winter-Ebmer (2001).

mortality had remained constant throughout those twenty years, the number of victims in the year 2013 would have surpassed thirty thousand for the first time. But in fact, the death toll wasn't even half that many. And no one knows why.

There is, of course, no shortage of theories, and several of those theories surely have at least a little validity with respect to trends in particular parts of the country during particular stretches of a few years. The issue is complicated and the relevant variables are many. Nevertheless, the inability of experts to predict even short-term trends suggests that a lot of their barking has been directed up the wrong trees. In 1996, *Scientific American* magazine profiled Northeastern University's Jamie Fox, "the country's most quoted criminologist," who predicted a coming wave of lethal violence that "will get so bad that it will make 1995 look like the good old days." The changing age structure of the US population was the sole basis for Fox's gloomy forecast, and age structure almost certainly *is* important, as we shall see. Nevertheless, he could hardly have been more wrong: Even as Fox was speaking, the US homicide rate had already begun a steep decline, and as I write, in May 2015, it has not yet undergone a substantial upturn.[3]

Figure 8.1 shows the rates of criminal homicide in three developed, predominantly English-speaking countries over the past half century. At least three things deserve our attention. First, the volatility that we have been discussing is not peculiar to the United States, whose highest rate in the period portrayed (101.4 homicides per million in 1980) was 2.26 times its lowest (44.9 in 2013). In Canada, that highest:lowest ratio is 2.42, and in England and Wales, it is 3.16.

A second noteworthy point is that the three patterns are not all in synch. America-centric commentators often say that homicide was in steep decline in "the West" during the 1990s. Not so in England, nor for that matter, elsewhere in western Europe. This simple fact—that the homicide rates of developed countries may be moving in different directions, even in this "globalized" era—is informative when we seek to evaluate proposed explanations for the trends, both by speaking against overly general proposals that attribute changes to economic or other processes that truly *are* global, and by providing leverage for testing other hypotheses.

A third noteworthy point about the trajectories portrayed in figure 8.1 is that we shouldn't overstate the second point. Yes, Britain has evidently been marching to a different drummer, but the trends and turnabouts

---

[3] See Yam (1996) for Fox's erroneous forecast of an imminent violent crime wave.

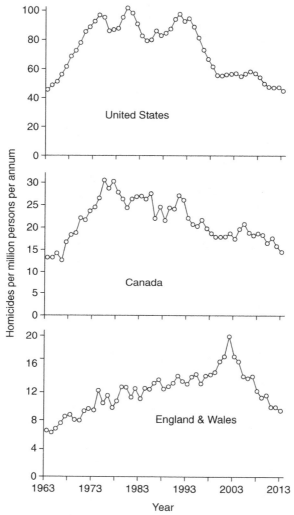

Figure 8.1. Criminal homicide rates in three developed nations, 1963–2013.[4]

in Canada and the United States *have* been in step with one another to a degree that is unlikely to be due to chance. This, too, is potentially informative. Some of the phenomena touted as explanations for recent

---

[4] Data in Figure 8-1 are from the FBI (United States), Statistics Canada, and the Home Office (Britain). Counts include only "criminal" homicides and not those deemed "justifiable," so the rates should, in principle, be lower than those based on World Health Organization cause of death data. The general trends, however, are robust.

trends in the United States—changes in policing practices, the waxing and waning of a crack cocaine epidemic, skyrocketing prison populations—are of lesser relevance to the Canadian situation, or have at least differed in their timing. This should inspire skepticism about any proposal that such a factor has played a determining role in generating a pattern of ups and downs that is essentially identical in the two countries.[5]

Unrelated Trends?

This book's central argument is simple, and at least to my way of thinking, it is compelling. When the goods that men desire are distributed relatively unevenly, the appeal of risky competitive tactics in pursuit of those goods tends to be relatively high, and for that reason, economic inequality is one important source of the variability in homicide rates. The temporal trends that we are now considering present a challenge to my argument. Although income inequality has repeatedly been shown to be an excellent predictor of cross-sectional variability in homicide rates at scales ranging from neighborhoods to nation states, it seems to have little or no predictive utility in longitudinal analysis.

In 1947, the United States Census Bureau began generating yearly estimates of the Gini coefficient of household income inequality before taxes, on the basis of its annual *Current Population Survey*. Respondents reported their family income in specified categories, with all incomes in excess of $300,000 treated as the top category. The methodology remained unchanged through 1992, and then, for the 1993 estimates, the ceiling on reportable income was raised to $1,000,000. Not surprisingly, the 1993 Gini jumped upward, and for technical reasons, Census Bureau analysts have declared that "we are unable to determine precisely the proportion of the increase in income inequality between 1992 and 1993 that is attributable to this change." Still, that leaves us with forty-six successive years (1947–92) for which we have

---

FBI homicide data do not include the victims of the September 11, 2001 attacks; if they did, the 2001 rate would be about 20 percent higher. Similarly, the Canadian data do not include the victims of the 1985 Air India bombing; if they did, the 1985 rate would be almost 50 percent higher. The English data for 2002 include 172 deaths that were induced by Dr. Harold Shipman over many years, but were determined to have been homicides only in 2002; without them, the 2002 rate would be reduced from 19.9 to 16.6, and the peak period would appear relatively flat from 2000 through 2004.

[5] The correlation between the Canadian and US homicide rates across the fifty-one years portrayed in Figure 8.1 is 0.854, $p < 0.00001$. Change in the US rate looks smoother, but that probably isn't meaningful: With ten times the population of Canada and thirty times more homicides, the US trajectory has less stochastic "jitter" than Canada's.

Gini estimates and homicide rates that were generated by consistent methods. And over that period, the two were in fact positively associated, albeit only weakly.[6]

Unfortunately, even a statistically significant correlation in data like these is likely to be meaningless. Time series data are especially vulnerable to spurious correlation because trends that have distinct causes often proceed in the same direction, at least for a while, purely by chance. The distance between Halley's comet and the sun has been increasing since February 1986, and so has the population of Brazil; their correlation over the last thirty years is close to 1.0, but it would be lunacy to infer a causal link between the two. If two trends switch direction together, and better yet if they do so repeatedly, we have grounds to suspect some sort of causal connection. But if all that we have is a correlation between two unidirectional (monotonic) trends, we have no such grounds. Granted, the trajectories of the US Gini and homicide rates from 1947 to 1992 weren't strictly monotonic—if they were, their correlation would be higher—but their significant positive association reflects little more than the fact that both measures were at their lowest in the 1950s and at their highest toward the end of the forty-six-year data set. There could be any number of explanations for that.

If you are still attracted to the hypothesis that inequality and homicide ought to rise and fall in synchrony, sorry, but the news is about to get worse. Having gained only weak support, at best, from the 1947–92 data series, that hypothesis is totally at odds with what happened next. In 1993, when the top reportable income was raised, a new series of consistently defined data began, and ever since, the household Gini index has been rising with only minor interruptions, while the homicide rate has been falling. The result of those opposing trends is that over this second period, not only are the two variables now negatively correlated, but the relationship looks to be much stronger than the positive correlation over the previous period. Finally, if we adjust the Gini coefficients to make them as comparable as we can, from that first survey in 1947 through 2013 (the most recent year available), and if we then

---

[6] See Jones and Weinberg (2000) for description and discussion of Gini estimates from *Current Population Survey* data; the quotation about the change in methodology and resultant indeterminacy is from page 1. The correlation between pre-tax household Gini and the homicide rate from 1947 through 1992 was 0.295, p = 0.046.

ask whether inequality and homicide have tended to move in parallel over the entire sixty-seven years, we end up with no association at all.[7]

In sum, we have no basis for suggesting that trends in the homicide rate mirror trends in income inequality, at least not in the United States. The evidence for Canada is only slightly more encouraging: My colleagues and I have reported that although the national Gini was stable and homicide was declining from 1981 through 1996, trends in the separate provincial homicide rates were positively associated with local, but not national, trends in inequality. However, this positive relationship, albeit significant, was small. Certain dramatic changes in other countries, such as the increases in both inequality and violence that attended the fall of the Soviet Union, may also suggest a link, but a skeptic can reasonably protest that any such example has the evidentiary status of an anecdote. As far as I am aware, the ups and downs of income inequality have never been shown to provide strong prediction of simultaneous parallel change in the homicide rate, anywhere.[8]

For some analysts, the observation that inequality and homicide don't move in lockstep is the deal-breaker: the ugly fact that slew the beautiful theory implicating inequality as a causal factor. One such analyst is Harvard psychologist Steven Pinker, the author of *The Better Angels of our Nature*, a 2011 best-seller about "why violence has declined" over the last few centuries and perhaps even over millenia. In this 700-page treatise, drawing from every social science, Pinker cites well over a thousand references, and yet everything that he has to say about economic inequality is contained in one dismissive paragraph:

> Among economic measures, inequality is generally a better predictor of violence than unemployment. But the Gini coefficient, the standard index of income inequality, actually *rose* in the United States from 1990 to 2000, while crime was falling, and it had hit its low point in 1968, when crime was soaring. The problem with invoking inequality to explain changes in violence is that while it correlates with violence across states and countries, it does not correlate with violence over time within a state or country, possibly because the real cause of

---

[7] The correlation between the US homicide rate and the new pre-tax household Gini estimates for 1993 to 2013 is −0.807, p < 0.0001. Accepting the "best guess" from Jones and Weinberg (2000) that one-third of the 1993 Gini jump was artifactual, I estimate the homicide-Gini correlation over the full sixty-seven-year period (1947–2013) at −0.137, p = 0.269.

[8] Daly et al. (2001) reported the Canadian analyses. Regarding homicide in Russia and the former Soviet Union, see, for example, Walberg et al. (1998) and various chapters in Liem and Pridemore (2012).

the differences is not inequality per se but stable features of a state's governance or culture that affect both inequality and violence. (For example, in unequal societies, poor neighborhoods are left without police protection and can become zones of violent anarchy.)[9]

Case closed? Not so fast! According to Pinker's reasoning, my argument that inequality fuels competition and violence is undermined by the observation that homicide rates and the Gini are sometimes seen to be moving in opposite directions. But why should the two move up and down in synchrony? How *could* they? Nobody imagines that potentially violent men recalibrate their willingness to kill in response to the latest survey-based estimate of the Gini coefficient. If inequality affects our behavior, its effects must be mediated by some sort of cumulative influence of our experiences. In other words, any genuine effect of inequality will necessarily be a "lagged" effect: an effect of past inequality on present behavior.

Those who would have us believe that inequality is a harmless bogeyman routinely neglect this point, perhaps wittingly, perhaps not. A study of homicide that appeared, incongruously, in the *Journal of Peace Research*, provides a case in point. Its author, Eric Neumayer of the London School of Economics, analyzed data from 117 countries over a period of eighteen years, and drew two provocative conclusions: first, that "policies aimed at improving equity have no effect on violent crime," and secondly, that "the ... effect of income inequality found in many studies that rely purely on cross-sectional information, is likely to be spurious." If you are wondering what those failed "policies" were, a careful reading will not enlighten you: Neumayer neglects to mention any actual policies, much less to incorporate them into his analyses. Moreover, by his own description, he "wiped out" cross-national variability by statistical means, thereby eliminating from further consideration the great majority of his data set's diversity in policy, in inequality, and in violence. And as for possible lagged effects of inequality, they too were obliterated. The resultant analytic method restricted potential determinants of the homicide rate, *by design*, to measures whose temporal variability within (not between) countries, over a period of less than one generation, was associated with simultaneous (not subsequent) local variability in homicide. The fact that the Gini had no demonstrable effects in such an analysis is neither surprising

---

[9] Quoted from Pinker (2011, 119).

nor informative, and Neumayer's conclusions about ineffectual policies and spurious effects are pure bombast.[10]

Ghosts of Our Pasts

Once we recognize that any genuine effects of inequality will necessarily be effects of inequality experienced in the past, what sorts of delays should we be looking for? Well, that depends. Predictions about the effects of past experience are ideally derived from a combination of knowledge and theory. Without a well-validated theoretical understanding of how inequality affects us, we can only guess that the relevant lags may be several, and some perhaps surprisingly long. In order to predict lagged effects correctly, it would surely help to know how the cumulative experiences of relative deprivation affect ambitions, perceptions of injustice, envy, and anger. We would also want to understand how differential access to unequally distributed opportunities and resources affects children's development, as well as what effects these inequalities exert on the distribution of life course transitions into (and out of) employment, marriage, and parenthood. It would also help to know how effectively the worldviews of parents are transmitted to their children, and it might even be crucial to understand prenatal influences on temperament and how the stresses in a woman's childhood affect the uterine environment experienced by her children. *None* of these things is well enough understood to warrant a quantitative prediction. About all that we can say with confidence is that it's hard to imagine *any* plausible mode of influence that would generate synchronous trajectories of the Gini and the homicide rate from year to year.

If it is not possible to specify, *a priori*, when the most influential experiences should have occurred, could we not just look for whatever lagged effects there may be, without making any predictions? That was the approach taken by Ohio State University sociologist Hui

---

[10] See Neumayer (2003); the two brief quotations are from pages 619 and 633. The "wiping out" of cross-national variability was achieved by including country-specific "fixed effects" among the predictors; in a data set only eighteen years long, most of the variability in both inequality and homicide resides in those obliterated, relatively stable, cross-national differences. Possible lagged effects of Gini were not detectable because the previous period's homicide rate was the only lagged variable included among the predictors.

By contrast, Gini *was* a significant predictor in a conceptually similar analysis by Jacobs and Richardson (2008) that was limited to developed nations and made greater room for lagged effects. Jacobs and Richardson fault Neumayer both for using developing nations data of dubious reliability and for failing to "stipulate moving averages of sufficient length to capture the nontransitory, cumulative effects" (42, footnote 1).

Zheng in a recent study with the eye-catching title "Do People Die from Inequality of a Decade Ago?" What Zheng sought to know was not whether inequality affects homicide, but whether it exerts lagged effects on mortality in general. He began with US *National Health Interview Survey* data on 701,179 Americans, and followed them up to see who died in each year after being surveyed. His question was whether one's chance of dying in a given year would be affected by the current Gini, and by last year's Gini and the previous year's and the year before *that*'s, and so on, over and above the differential chances of dying associated with the individual demographic attributes of age, sex, ethnicity, marital status, employment status, and income.

Zheng's results were intriguing. Current inequality had no demonstrable effect, and neither did the levels of inequality prevailing last year, or two years ago. At a lag of three to five years, however, a significant negative impact of past inequality on present survival began to appear, and it got bigger with each step back in time until reaching its maximum at a lag of seven years. Farther back in time, the effects began to fall, but they remained statistically significant back to a twelve-year lag. Importantly, these lagged effects were additive: The inequality that prevailed seven years ago apparently affected mortality the most, but the levels of inequality that prevailed five years ago, and six, and eight, and nine, and so on back to twelve years in the past, *each* had a significant additional impact. If Zheng's analytic methods are sound, then not only does the inequality that one has experienced in the past exert a lagged effect on one's current risk of death, but the damaging effects of exposure to inequality pile up over a period of years.[11]

No one has conducted the same sort of analysis with homicide as the outcome, and it wouldn't actually make a lot of sense to try. Zheng had very large numbers to work with, and everyone is eventually going to die. By contrast, only a tiny minority of those in an analogous prospective study would eventually kill, and even those who *did* kill someone

---

[11] See Zheng (2013). Whether the most recent Gini to exert significant effects was three or five years ago varied across alternative analytic methods, but all analyses yielded a smooth rising and falling pattern that reached a peak several years in the past. Remarkably, Zheng used only the national Gini, and it would be interesting to know how substituting a more local (e.g., state-level) Gini into the analysis would affect the results.

I hedge by saying "if Zheng's analytic methods are sound" because his approach seems vulnerable to hidden variable confound effects: If a specific historical event elevated US mortality levels across the board, for example, that could create a spurious apparent effect of the particular preceding profile of Gini coefficients.

would not all be identified. Other approaches are therefore required. But even though Zheng's study doesn't provide direct guidance for an investigation of the lagged effects of inequality on homicide, his results are of interest in the present context because of their more general implications. One is that the impact of prolonged exposures to inequality can build up. Another is that experiences in the relatively distant past can sometimes have a bigger impact than more recent ones.

That second point is initially surprising. If your aim is to predict the probable consequences of alternative courses of action, in order to make the best choices, wouldn't the most recent events provide better information about the prospects and threats in your environment than events in the distant past? Yes, they probably would, but evaluating the present environment isn't the only thing that a well-functioning individual needs to do. Behaving with maximum effectiveness requires that you invest time and effort in developing competencies, sometimes over the course of years, and it often requires committing yourself to mastering a particular set of complementary skills, while giving up any hope of becoming a jack-of-all-trades. Self-discipline and certain physical talents might make identical contributions to success in sumo and in ballet, but a young man who trains to be a sumo wrestler will nevertheless have shut the door on pursuing a career as a ballet dancer.[12]

Can a mild-mannered man "break bad" in mid-life, and reinvent himself as an efficacious dangerous dude? In a television series, sure, but in the real world, that's a lot to ask. I certainly couldn't have! I never acquired the sang-froid—or the quickness, or the musculature—that I would have needed to deliver an incapacitating sucker punch, much less to face down an angry antagonist. I am not bragging about my moral superiority here, nor am I even suggesting that in the event of a negative tenure decision, my professorial skills could not have been put to use in the service of exploitative crime. But in a social milieu in which a man must be ready to back up his actions with hands-on violence, I'd have been dead meat. Decades of longitudinal research in criminology—including both retrospective studies of violent criminals' pasts and prospective studies that either start with children or compare delinquents to same-age control groups—are consistent in indicating that if you want to use violence effectively in adulthood, it helps to

---

[12] See Frankenhuis and Panchanathan (2011) and Panchanathan and Frankenhuis (2016) for discussion, examples, and theoretical treatments of how and why specialization in early development is often favored by natural selection.

153

have fought in childhood, ideally quite a lot. According to Washington University's Lee Robins (1922–2009), one of the pioneering researchers and acknowledged leaders in this field, "adult antisocial behavior virtually requires childhood antisocial behavior."[13]

Like the sumo wrestler, the antisocial child makes some early commitments in his physical development as well as in his psychological development. In a recent research report, Joshua Isen and colleagues at the University of Minnesota noted that "Young men with superior upper-body strength typically show a greater proclivity for physical aggression than their weaker male counterparts" and questioned what they called the "traditional interpretation of this phenomenon," namely that "young men calibrate their attitudes and behaviors to their physical formidability." Their longitudinal study instead indicated that the antisociality comes first and predisposes boys to muscle up: "Boys, but not girls, with greater antisocial tendencies in childhood attained larger increases in physical strength between the ages of 11 and 17."[14]

Unfortunately, clear-headed consideration of these developmental issues has been impeded, once again, by an uncritical supposition that all violence, crime, and antisocial behavior are pathological. "Oppositional defiant disorder" is a psychiatric diagnosis that is apt to be inflicted on a child who too strenuously resists the authority of his elders. If he persists in his bolshy ways, he may graduate to "conduct disorder" and then to "antisocial personality disorder." With few exceptions, criminologists who study the life course have bought into this pathologizing of troublemakers. The 1998 prospectus announcing a multimillion dollar longitudinal research Program on Human Development and Criminal Behavior, sponsored by the US Department of Justice and the John D. and Catherine T. MacArthur Foundation, declares on its first page that "an enquiry into the causes of crime is at the same time an inquiry into the causes of general defects in character and behavior."

The trouble, of course, is that being oppositional and defiant and antisocial *cannot* be assumed to reflect "disorder." Many developmental psychologists, especially those with an evolutionary overview, have understood this very well, and have tried hard to communicate it to others. According to Jay Belsky, a prominent professor of Human Development at the University of California and former Director of

---

[13] Farrington and Welsh (2007) list more than thirty major longitudinal studies of the predictors of criminal offending. The quotation is from Robins (1978, 611).

[14] Quotes in this paragraph are from the abstract of Isen et al. (2015).

the Institute for the Study of Children, Families and Social Issues at the University of London,

> From the standpoint of the majority culture—which would include that of families, schools, and law enforcement agencies—it is indisputable that high levels of aggressiveness and disobedience ... are a problem [but] it is also necessary to recognize that externalizing behavior, even in the extreme, is not always maladaptive ... It may well be the case, for example, that the child going to a crime-ridden inner-city school is much better off, in terms of getting along with peers and even surviving, if he or she hits first and asks questions later. The less aggressive child may be a victim sufficiently often that it threatens his or her very survival, to say nothing of his or her psychological well-being.[15]

But while psychologists are increasingly aware of this prejudicial error, criminologists remain vulnerable to it, and it's not hard to see why. Their longitudinal studies have repeatedly shown that major risk factors for criminal offending, including violent offending—apart from social class, which is the best predictor—include low intelligence, a lack of parental supervision, and mistreatment in childhood. These are all readily interpreted as deficiencies. Associated aspects of personality, such as irritability and impatience, are further predictors of crime, and it's easy to spin them as deficits, too. And yet it should be obvious that none of this justifies the characterization of criminal behavior itself as the manifestation of "defects." Even within criminology, the "rational choice" approach recognizes that while exploiting others to your own advantage isn't *nice*, that doesn't make it dysfunctional. "Crime" is prohibited and penalized precisely *because* there are incentives to commit it, and because potential perpetrators who are sufficiently *compos mentis* to respond to crime's costs as well as its benefits can be deterred by raising those costs. And as for those risk factors for criminal offending, most, perhaps all, are readily reinterpreted as signals from the environment to the developing youth, telling him that patiently playing by the rules is unlikely to be a winning strategy. For others, maybe, but for you, in your circumstances, no.[16]

---

[15] The quote is from Belsky (1997, 183).

[16] A few criminologists have recognized and bemoaned the error of pathologizing crime; for eloquent complaints about this prejudice, see. for example, Cohen and Machalek (1988, 1994). For reviews of longitudinal studies of the childhood predictors of adult crime and violence, see, for example, Piquero and Mazerolle (2001) and Farrington and Welsh (2007); all this research has been conducted in rich countries, in which crime and violence are primarily the recourse of the disadvantaged. For a persuasive re-interpretation of certain supposedly pathological effects of childhood stress as adaptive coping processes, see Frankenhuis and de Weerth (2013).

Choosing the Right Path

Salamanders, like frogs and toads, are amphibians whose young develop as aquatic tadpoles before metamorphosing into four-footed, terrestrial adults. In the Arizona Tiger Salamander, tadpoles come in two varieties: a "typical" morph that feeds primarily on invertebrates, and a larger "cannibal" morph whose distinctive anatomy is specialized for catching and eating other tadpoles. Which of these morphs a tiny larva will become depends, in part, on the social environment: The larva is increasingly likely to turn into a cannibal as the local density of tadpoles increases, but is decreasingly likely to do so as the proportion of those neighbors who are close kin increases. The adaptive function of these responses to the social environment is clear: Higher tadpole density means more competition for limited food, which raises the utility of eating your competitors. However, the survival and reproduction of close kin contributes to your indirect fitness, so their local prevalence suggests that maybe you should just stick to a diet of insect larvae. This is not simply some freakish fable. According to evolutionary biologist David Pfennig, who discovered the effect of kinship, this sort of duality is widespread: Two distinct forms, one cannibalistic and one not, co-exist in many other species, including larval toads, nematode worms, rotifers, and protozoa, and "which path an individual takes depends mainly on the environment in which it was raised" in every case that has been investigated. [17]

Pfennig's salamanders illustrate four very general points that I consider essential if we are going to think clearly about criminal careers and the lagged effects of experiences. First, the fact that behavior is nasty—even lethal—is no indication, in and of itself, that there is something wrong with its perpetrator. Second, experiences early in development can have long-lasting effects. Third, there are "switch points" in development, at which heading down one pathway forecloses alternative trajectories. (Consider, for example, the prenatal switch point at which most fetal mammals commit themselves to becoming either a female or a male.) Fourth, these aspects of development are not merely unfortunate constraints, but are often "design features" that improve the adaptive functioning of the resultant creature.

---

[17] Regarding facultative development in Arizona Tiger Salamanders, see Pfennig and Collins (1993) and Pfennig et al. (1999). The quote about similar phenomena in other taxa is from Pfennig and Sherman (1995, 102).

Developmental psychologists and biologists have known for decades that early experience can have large, lasting effects, and that there are "sensitive periods" in which particular experiences have a much greater impact than they would have had if they had occurred earlier or later. Development works this way not simply because it is a cumulative process, but because a commitment of time and tissues is often required to build up so-called "embodied capital": the physique and condition, expertise and skills that enable success. Noting that it often pays to "sample cues to the environmental state early in life and use this information to start constructing a phenotype that is adaptive later in life," evolutionary theorists Willem Frankenhuis and Karthik Panchanathan have explored the conditions under which natural selection should favor sensitive periods in development, and have shown that they are likely to evolve wherever efficacy as an adult depends on physical attributes and/or skills that have to be honed to local conditions through extensive practice. Perhaps because *Homo sapiens* depends so heavily on culturally variable technologies, our species is apparently unique in the extent to which crucial life skills match these conditions; among hunter-gatherers, a typical man's hunting prowess apparently continues to improve into his mid-thirties.[18]

Generations

In the latter decades of the twentieth century, something very odd happened to the age-crime curve in Japan. In the 1950s and 1960s, homicides by Japanese men followed a familiar pattern, rising rapidly after adolescence to a peak rate when men were in their early twenties, followed by an initially steep, and then more gradual, monotonic decline as a function of increasing age. But around 1970, the peak age of offending started to get older, and by the mid- to late-1980s, men in their forties had a higher homicide rate than men in their twenties. The curve was also falling and flattening out as well. By the year 2000, Japanese men ranging in age from their late teens through their fifties were all killing at about the same low per capita rate.[19]

Some things had not changed. According to behavioral ecologist Mariko Hiraiwa-Hasegawa, who reported these remarkable findings,

---

[18] The quote is from Frankenhuis and Panchanathan (2011, 338). Regarding the surprisingly long time that it takes to develop the skills to be an effective hunter-gatherer, see Kaplan et al. (2000) and Bock (2002).

[19] The facts reviewed in this and the ensuing paragraphs were reported by Hiraiwa-Hasegawa (2005).

the majority of the male-male homicides in Japan arose in the context of the same sort of status and face disputes that are familiar to homicide researchers in the west, and this was no less true in the 1990s than it had been in the 1950s. Unemployed men had remained overrepresented as killers down through the decades, and so had relatively uneducated men.

The key to the puzzle was a huge decline in the total numbers of homicides, and especially in those committed by men in their twenties. The age-crime curve hadn't really disappeared. Japanese men who were born in the 1930s had their highest homicide rate when they were in their twenties and became less and less likely to kill as they grew older. The same was true of men born in the 1940s, the 1950s, and the 1960s. In other words, each "age cohort" displayed an age-crime curve of the usual general shape. What had obscured this consistency was the fact that the age-crime curves of succeeding birth cohorts were getting lower and lower so rapidly that by the year 2000, the men born around 1950 had a homicide rate at age 50 that was roughly equal to the contemporaneous rate being perpetrated by the twenty-year-olds who had been born around 1980! And why was that? Hiraiwa-Hasegawa argued persuasively that Japan's rapid post-war economic progress, falling inequality, and increasing access to education had improved the opportunities facing the young much more than was the case for their elders.

Differences in the behavior of successive birth cohorts are seldom so rapid and dramatic as in this example from post-war Japan, but that doesn't mean they're unimportant. One major reason why people born only a few years apart differ is that birth cohorts vary in size, and their sheer numbers affect the opportunities that their members confront. After the Second World War, the United States experienced a "baby boom" that crested in the 1950s and continued into the 1960s. Between 1954 and 1964, more than four million babies were born each year. Then the birth rate began to fall, and even though the population kept growing, the total number of births never surpassed four million again for the next quarter century. The biggest single-year change was a 6.6 percent drop between 1964 and 1965, representing more than a quarter of a million fewer births in 1965 than in the preceding year. But of course, school boards didn't respond by shutting 6.6 percent of first-grade classrooms between one year and the next, nor did universities slash their freshman admissions commensurately. The upshot is that the 1965 cohort confronted smaller average class sizes and more educational opportunities than the 1964 cohort, over and above the effects of any trends in total availability. When cohort size takes a big drop, competition takes a little holiday.

The same logic applies to other markets besides that for education. Economists and sociologists have long been aware that larger birth cohorts face more intense competition for jobs. In a 1979 paper entitled "Effects of cohort size on earnings: the baby boom babies' financial bust," Finis Welch, a prominent American labor economist, concluded that cohort size has had a substantial impact on entry-level salaries, and that the "income-depressant effects of (own) cohort size decline over the career but do not vanish altogether."[20]

Even marriage markets may exhibit analogous effects, depending on the ages at which men and women marry and the trajectories of cohort size over several years. In the late-1980s and early-90s, the average age at first marriage in the United States was twenty-six for men, and twenty-four for women. When the men from that 1964 birth cohort turned twenty-six in 1990, they outnumbered twenty-four-year-old women (from the 1966 cohort) by a ratio of 111:100. Only a year later, when men from the smaller 1965 birth cohort reached the age of twenty-six, the ratio by which they outnumbered twenty-four-year-old women (from the 1967 cohort) had fallen below 107:100.

The consequences are complicated by the fact that competition isn't strictly contained within cohorts. Marriage, in particular, is obviously not confined to couples of any particular age or age disparity, and wife-seeking men born in 1965 obviously had to contend with competitors from preceding, larger cohorts. The same caveat applies, with slightly lesser force, to labor market competition, and with lesser force again, to limited educational opportunities. Nevertheless, it is well established that the vicissitudes of birth rate and cohort size sometimes assuage and at other times aggravate the fierceness of competition among men, over time frames that can extend for many years. It is therefore no surprise that birth cohort size has been found by criminologist Robert O'Brien and his colleagues to be a positive predictor of homicide perpetration in the United States, when the confounding effects of age and gross temporal trends ("period") are appropriately controlled.[21]

---

[20] The quoted sentence is from the abstract of Welch (1979, S65).

[21] Easterlin (1987) has made what is widely acknowledged as the most thorough and forceful case for the pervasive influence of birth cohort size on opportunities and attainments throughout the life course. Cohort size effects on homicide were demonstrated by O'Brien et al. (1991); see also O'Brien and Stockard (2009) and O'Brien (2011).

In addition to relative cohort size and the population's age structure, there can be any number of local, idiosyncratic reasons why the life course of one birth cohort differs systematically from that of another. A new government program could, in principle, enable young adults to build equity in the form of home ownership in a way that was unavailable to their parents, for example, with consequences that affect the rest of their lives. Moreover, if early experience is influential—and it clearly often is—then many sorts of change over time may translate into consequential change in the developmentally relevant experiences of successive cohorts. Early nutrition affects not only growth and eventual stature, but the risk of developing various diseases in adulthood, and the pace and details of cognitive decline in late life.[22]

Social effects of early experience can be subtle. Consider, for example, the effects of birth order. The eldest child in a family typically receives more parental investment than laterborns. The eldest is more likely to attend university than younger siblings, to take but one example, and among those who *do* go to university, firstborns get more financial help from parents, on average, than laterborns. It is therefore unsurprising that a wide range of evidence indicates that firstborns tend to be more supportive of the status quo than their younger brothers and sisters. Moreover, as one of my former PhD students, Catherine Salmon, has shown, it is especially the middleborn children—those with at least one older and at least one younger sibling—who differ from both the firstborn and the last, and that one way in which they differ is that middleborns are relatively detached from their genetic relatives and invest relatively great effort and attention in their social relationships with unrelated friends and acquaintances instead. Relatedly, middleborns tend to be somewhat less conservative and more open to new ideas than either firstborns or lastborns. So what happens when large families become infrequent and a brood of exactly two children becomes a prevalent ideal? Middleborns will necessarily constitute a shrinking proportion of each successive cohort, a trend that could have important effects on the distribution of sociopolitical views.[23]

Of course, early experience isn't the whole story. Things that happen subsequently affect you, too, and these effects can also endure for many

---

[22] For effects of early childhood influences on adult outcomes, see, for example, Bock and Whelan (1991) and, more generally, Kuzawa and Thayer (2011), and del Giudice (2014).
[23] Regarding how middleborns differ from first and lastborns, see, for example, Salmon and Daly (1998) and Salmon (2003); on birth order effects in general, see Sulloway (2007).

years. Paolo Giuliano of UCLA's Anderson School of Management and Antonio Spilimbergo of the International Monetary Fund recently used a wide range of evidence to assemble a strong case that having lived through a recession when one was between the ages of eighteen and twenty-five, for example, makes one relatively likely to believe that luck is a more important determinant of success than effort, and relatively supportive of economic redistribution, and that these attitudes persist for decades.[24]

Cohort Size and Homicide

If there were no baby booms and busts—if birth cohorts didn't vary in size or if they steadily tracked the population growth rate—and if age-specific mortality patterns were stable, too, then a fixed age structure would persist for decades. However, birth rates do in fact go up and down, and age-specific mortality patterns do change. The result is that the age structure of populations can change rapidly, substantially, and consequentially. In 1960, 13.2 percent of the population of the United States consisted of men between the ages of fifteen and thirty-four. But as the post-war baby boomers became teenagers and young adults, things shifted, and by 1980, that same demographic group of men 15–34 constituted 17.5 percent of the populace. Their proportionate share of the total population had grown by over 30 percent in just twenty years! And then it began to fall again. Figure 8.2 portrays these changes.

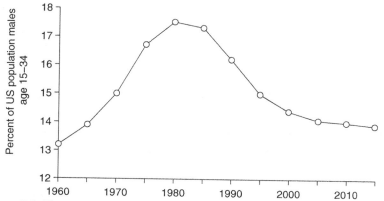

Figure 8.2. The percentage of the population of the United States consisting of young men 15–34 years of age, 1960–2015.

---

[24] For the lasting effects of a recession on attitudes, see Giuliano and Spilimbergo (2014).

Does this curve looks familiar? If so, that may be because it resembles the trajectory of the US homicide rate over the same period, as portrayed in figure 8.1. And could that be more than just a coincidence? Of course it could! This is, after all, the demographic group that is most likely to kill, so it would be strange if the gross homicide rate did *not* depend, in part, on young men's share of the total populace. And in fact, there is a lot of evidence that the proportion consisting of young men indeed makes a difference, both in cross-sectional and in longitudinal analyses. In Chapter 2, for example, you saw that there was a strong positive relationship between income inequality and the homicide rate in 1990, comparing across the fifty US states, so strong that the Gini index could account for half of the variance in homicide. My colleagues and I then looked at a variety of state-level variables to see if any of them could account for a significant proportion of the remaining variance that had *not* been "explained" by inequality, and we were able to identify only one: the proportion of a state's population that consisted of young men.

There is, however, a sense in which I have cheated a little in how I designed figure 8.2. By portraying the range of the young male percentage from only 12 through 18, I made the changes look bigger than if I had instead drawn it with a "true zero." With the range extending from 0 to 18, the rise and fall would look much less impressive, and would not be as visually reminiscent of the homicide curve. This issue of alternative data portrayals may sound like a mere matter of optics or aesthetics, but there is an important substantive question lurking behind it. The US homicide rate doubled between 1963 and 1973, bounced around for a while, and then fell back to that 1963 level fifty years later. *How much* of that roller-coaster ride can be attributed to change in the population's age structure?

A popular answer is "some, but not much." In 2004, Steven Levitt, the economist whose best-selling book *Freakonomics* made him a pop guru, wrote a professional article in the *Journal of Economic Perspectives* entitled "Understanding why crime fell in the 1990s: four factors that explain the decline and six that do not." Changing demographics, Levitt concluded, was one of the "six that do not," although he conceded that "overall changes in the age distribution may have reduced homicide and violent crime by a few percent and property crime by as much as 5–6 percent." This is an old argument, and although Levitt's version is more sophisticated than some earlier ones, it is a specious argument, predicated on the assumption that a "demographic explanation" is necessarily one that attributes fixed tendencies to each demographic group and then formulaically generates an expected magnitude of change from the various groups' new proportionate representations. The real world is more subtle than that. As Margo Wilson and I complained in 1988, with respect to an essentially similar dismissal of demographic change:

> Violence is not simply a "trait" of individuals, but a product of social interactions. The interpersonal violence of young men is a manifestation of competitiveness; if the proportional representation of young men in a population increases, might not the level of competition experienced by *all* men increase? Moreover, if the proportion of men who are in a violence-prone age-class doubles (for example), then even by a simplistic random model, the proportion of all dyadic encounters that will involve *two* such men will *quadruple*; might we not expect a greater than linear increase in violence with each increment in the numbers of violence-prone persons? And how does the number of men in other age classes affect the perceived marital and economic prospects of young men, and hence their risk-prone, violent tendencies? Our point is simply that "demography alone" actually "explains" nothing without some individual-level specification of how demographic and other effects upon violence are mediated.[25]

Much as we might wish to do so, we simply cannot finesse our way around the big social psychological and developmental issues: What aspects of their social environments are people sensitive to, exactly, and how exactly do they respond, both immediately and developmentally? A complete understanding of the effects of cohorts and population age structures will require answers to these questions, as will a complete understanding of the effects of inequality.

I am not suggesting that once we understand how income inequality, age structure, and the varying experiences of cohorts work their magic on the developing human being, these three factors will then suffice to explain the variability in homicide rates. Other things undoubtedly matter, too, perhaps the most important of which is differential access to disinterested third party justice and the resultant variability in people's recourse to self-help justice. We will revisit this issue in Chapter 10.

---

[25] Levitt (2004) deals only with the United States; the quoted sentence dismissing age structure as an important factor is on page 172. The actual analysis on which this dismissal is based is in Levitt (1999), and is more sophisticated than prior pooh-poohings of demographic effects because it allows for nonlinear impacts of cohort size; Levitt still fails, however, to take seriously the question of how a population's age structure might affect the opportunity structure facing young men. The quoted passage concluding the paragraph is from Daly and Wilson (1988, 279).

What I *am* suggesting is that the data on longitudinal trends have not in the slightest undermined the thesis that inequality is a major source of interpersonal competition and violence. What the data on longitudinal trends *have* done is to draw our attention to the importance of questions about the developmental processes by which inequality and other aspects of our social environment leave their marks.

9

Too Much Inequality

[There is] a tentative consensus in the growth literature that inequality can undermine progress in health and education, cause investment-reducing political and economic instability, and undercut the social consensus required to adjust in the face of major shocks, and thus that it tends to reduce the pace and durability of growth.
—Jonathan Ostry, *International Monetary Fund*
Staff Discussion Note, 2014

Dividing the Pie

Economic inequality in modern nation states provokes interpersonal competition, and one extreme manifestation of that competition is homicidal violence. But even those who are persuaded that this is so may still be wondering whether inequality's benefits might exceed its costs.

Imagine that you are a citizen of the United States of America in the year 2005. Your country's economy is generally viewed as healthy, and the immense advantages of "the 1 %" are not yet on the radar of public opinion. You have agreed to participate in a survey, and before answering any questions, you are asked to read the following definition of *wealth*:

> Wealth, also known as net worth, is defined as the total value of everything someone owns minus any debt that he or she owes. A person's net worth includes his or her bank account savings plus the value of other things such as property, stocks, bonds, art, collections, etc., minus the value of things like loans and mortgages.

You are then asked to estimate, to the best of your ability, what percent of the country's wealth is owned by the richest 20 percent of families, by the next richest 20 percent, and so on down to the poorest 20 percent. Having recorded your best guesses, you are finally asked an opinion question: Ideally, what percent of all wealth do you think each of those 20 percent segments of the population ("quintiles") *ought* to possess.

165

Have you picked your answers?

A representative sample of 5522 Americans answered these and other questions in a study conducted in 2005 by psychologists Michael Norton of the Harvard Business School and Dan Ariely of Duke University. The average respondent guessed that the richest quintile owned 59 percent of the country's wealth, and expressed the opinion that such a large share was far too high. Ideally, their cut should only be 32 percent. As for the poorest quintile, the average respondent guessed that they possessed 3 percent of the wealth, and thought that such a meager share wasn't nearly enough. The poorest quintile's share of the total pie ought ideally to be 11 percent.[1]

The true state of affairs was far worse than those survey respondents imagined. In reality, the share of total wealth that was held by the richest 20 percent of American households at the time of the survey wasn't the fat 59 percent that the average person guessed, which would have left 41 percent for everyone else. The richest quintile actually owned 84 percent, leaving a paltry 16 percent for the remaining 80 percent of the population to scramble after. And as for the poorest quintile, the sorry 3 percent of total wealth that was the average guess was *thirty times* too high: Their actual slice of the pie was a microscopically thin one one-thousandth share.

In sum, Americans grossly underestimated the degree to which wealth is concentrated in the hands of a minority in their country, and yet they *still* felt that the concentration of wealth was excessive. Perhaps the most remarkable finding was how similar were the responses of women and men, Democrats and Republicans, and even those with very different personal incomes; the differences between these groups were tiny, both with respect to what they believed to be the reality and with respect to the distribution that they thought would be ideal. Virtually everybody guessed that wealth was much more equitably distributed than is actually the case, and virtually everybody, regardless of their own socioeconomic status or their politics, maintained that the distribution of wealth still wasn't nearly equitable enough.

These survey results raise an obvious question: If a more equitable society is what almost all Americans want, why don't they use their power as voters to make it happen? Why, in other words, do they persist in electing politicians and parties whose policies keep making

---

[1] These survey results were reported by Norton and Ariely (2011).

inequality worse? The responses to the survey questions point to one partial answer: The public simply doesn't know how bad the situation actually is. Another partial answer is that Norton and Ariely's results can hardly be interpreted as a clear call to action; someone who believes that wealth "ought ideally" to be more evenly distributed doesn't necessarily think that *governments* should be doing anything to redistribute money from the rich to the poor.

A further problem with efforts to derive policy implications from surveys is that public opinion depends heavily on exactly how pollsters formulate (or "frame") their questions. Survey responses are often more visceral than reasoned, and when questions include emotionally laden buzzwords, respondents often endorse statements that are logical opposites. One example from the *British Social Attitudes Survey* of 2004 concerned this item: "Government should redistribute income from the better off to those who are less well off." Fifteen percent of those who *disagreed* with this statement nevertheless expressed the view elsewhere in the same survey that the government was not doing *enough* "to redistribute income from the better off to those who are less well off." Self-contradictions like this might, in principle, bespeak mere inattentiveness, but their distribution is not random. A plausible (and testable) hypothesis about the specific example here is that for certain respondents, a knee-jerk antipathy to the word "government" elicits a negative evaluation of government action and government inaction alike.[2]

A popular bogeyman in American political discourse is the "welfare bum": an able-bodied recipient of public assistance who would rather parasitize hard-working tax-payers than work. In reality, welfare dependency is scarcely anyone's preference in the United States, thanks to the meager assistance available, and the humiliation and bureaucratic hurdles that must be overcome to receive it. But this phantom freeloader is a potent rhetorical weapon nonetheless. "Welfare fraud" is a related bogeyman that Ronald Reagan, in particular, exploited brilliantly. The fact that such fraud constitutes a miniscule drain on the public purse has no evident impact on the outrage that it evokes, and sadly, the "reforms" that are justified as responses *to* welfare fraud

---

[2] The *British Social Attitudes* Survey results were reported by Sefton (2005), who documents and discusses this and other examples of self-contradictory responding. Relatedly, support for any government program drops, in the United States and elsewhere, if the question explicitly mentions the use of tax money to implement it.

typically entail little more than slashing benefits for all recipients, worthy or not. There is an ugly, racialized element to this bogus issue: Princeton political scientist Martin Gilens has shown that media on all sides of the US political spectrum disproportionately put a black face on the "undeserving poor," and switch to a white face when the story is instead a sympathetic one about the "deserving poor." According to Gilens, this imagery has contributed to a tendency for poor whites to disparage and resent poor blacks, as well as to a public misperception that poverty itself, especially urban poverty, is almost exclusively an African-American problem.[3]

Dishearteningly, the poor themselves often display a surprisingly harsh attitude toward those who are even worse off. We have seen in previous chapters that hostile competitiveness can be most intense near the bottom of a social hierarchy, and as every union organizer is sadly aware, the utility of solidarity can be a tough sell. Princeton economist Ilyana Kuziemko and her colleagues have proposed that "last place aversion"—a fear among those near the bottom that they might fall even lower—is part of the problem. As regards minimum wages, for example:

> In our surveys, we asked Americans whether they supported an increase to the minimum wage, currently $7.25 per hour. Those making $7.25 or below were very likely to support the increase—after all, they would be immediate beneficiaries. In addition, people making substantially more than $7.25 were also fairly positive towards the increase. Which group was the most opposed? Those making just above the minimum wage, between $7.26 and $8.25. We might expect people who make just below and just above $7.25 to have similar lifestyles and policy attitudes—but in this case, while those making below $7.25 would benefit if the minimum wage were raised to, say, $8.25, those making just above $7.25 would run the risk of falling into a tie for last place.[4]

Is the United States exceptional in these matters? In some ways, perhaps so: The United States seems to be leading the pack in reducing social services and delegitimizing collective action. However, other aspects of the story above are widespread. For example, it is not at all exceptional that Americans should both underestimate inequality and consider it

---

[3] See Gilens (1999).
[4] The quote is from Kuziemko and Norton (2011); for a full report of the research, see Kuziemko et al. (2014).

excessive nonetheless. In a 1999 survey, British respondents estimated the average salary of the "chairman of a large national corporation" at £125,000 and that of an "unskilled factory worker" at £10,000, and their proposals about how much the chairman and the factory worker "should" be paid would have cut that naïve estimate of a 12.5-fold difference in half. In reality, that average chairman's salary was then more than half a million pounds, and he was already earning more than forty times as much as the average unskilled factory worker. The United Kingdom is also like the United States in the fact that public opinion in these matters has had no detectable effect; that British chairman's advantage over the factory worker has ballooned to more than 100-fold today.[5]

Six years after conducting the US survey with which we began this chapter, Norton and Ariely teamed up with researchers in Australia to repeat the study there. Figure 9.1 portrays the results for the two countries, which are in some ways quite different. Inequality in Australia in 2011 was not nearly so extreme as in the United States (even though the US data were six years older and inequality has continued to increase): The richest quintile in Australia held "only" 61 percent of

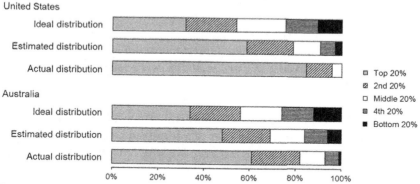

Figure 9.1. Ideal, estimated, and actual distributions of wealth in the United States, 2005, and in Australia, 2011. For each country, the top bar shows the distribution of wealth across quintiles that the average survey respondent considered "ideal," the middle bar shows what those same respondents estimated the true situation to be like, and the bottom bar shows the actual distribution. Redrawn from Norton et al. (2014).

---

[5] The British survey data are from Hills (2004). Regarding the decline of organized labor in the United States and elsewhere, see, for example, Visser (2006).

all wealth, compared to the 84 percent figure in the United States, for example, and the bottom 40 percent of Australians possessed 7 percent of all wealth, compared to a minuscule 0.3 percent in the United States As regards the survey responses, however, the results from the two countries were very much alike. Australians, too, severely underestimated the prevailing inequality, although they were not as far off the mark as their American counterparts. Moreover, despite that misperception, Australians resembled Americans in their belief that the distribution ought to be a great deal more equitable still. Finally, a particularly striking aspect of the data is just how similar the "ideal" distributions favored by survey respondents in the two countries were.[6]

The close similarity of the Australian and American ideals in figure 9.1 suggests that the exceptional degree of inequality in the United States is not indicative of an exceptional tolerance of inequality. Other evidence, however, indicates that Americans really *are* more accepting of inequality than their counterparts in Australia and other developed nations. In a 1987 survey, for example, random samples of the citizenry of several countries were asked what pay they would deem appropriate for each of a number of occupations ranging from an unskilled laborer to the C.E.O. of a major corporation; 34 percent of the US respondents proposed a rate of pay for the highest occupational status that was more than five times what they thought the lowest should receive, compared to 15 to 21 percent of the respondents in Switzerland, West Germany, the Netherlands, and the United Kingdom, and only 8 percent of Australians. But even so, the Americans who were surveyed can hardly be said to have been supportive of the prevailing level of inequality: A large majority believed that top corporate executives should *not* be paid more than five times as much as an unskilled worker, at a time when that pay ratio was already in excess of a hundred to one![7]

More recently, Sorapop Kiatpongsan and Norton extended this sort of survey to a set of forty countries, and found no exceptions to the general pattern that we have seen so far. In *every* country, survey respondents grossly underestimated the ratio by which executive pay exceeds worker pay, but still believed that the pay differential was much

---

[6] The Australian survey results are reported by Norton et al. (2014).

[7] The 1987 international survey results were presented by Kelley and Evans (1993). The same survey was repeated five years later, at which time both the actual and the acceptable or ideal levels of inequality had risen in all the surveyed countries, suggesting that preferences may be shaped in part by the current reality; see Austen (2002).

too high. And again, these generalizations hold across all income levels and political affiliations. The United States didn't even top the table with respect to what respondents thought an appropriate pay ratio would be—Taiwan led in that regard—but among the subset of countries for which the actual pay ratio could be computed, the United States had by far the largest.[8]

And so, we might ask again: If a more equitable society is what Americans want, why don't they use their power as voters to make it happen? But even to ask this question is to presuppose that the electorate *has* that power. Is the *realpolitik* of American democracy even responsive to the will of the majority, anyway? The available evidence is not reassuring. Martin Gilens has summarized his own substantial research thus:

> When Americans with different income levels differ in their policy preferences, actual policy outcomes strongly reflect the preferences of the most affluent but bear virtually no relationship to the preferences of poor or middle income Americans. This vast discrepancy in government responsiveness to citizens with different incomes stands in stark contrast to the ideal of political equality that Americans hold dear.

In a particularly thorough recent analysis of many hundreds of actual policy decisions, Gilens and Benjamin Page assessed whose preferences prevail when those of the majority differ from what one or another type of interest group advocates. Their conclusion:

> Economic elites and organized groups representing business interests have substantial independent impacts on U.S. government policy, while average citizens and mass-based interest groups have little or no independent influence.

How ironic that the insidious influence of demonized "interest groups" is a staple complaint of those conservative interests who are in fact the only groups with any demonstrable influence on their government![9]

---

[8] See Kiatpongsan and Norton (2014).

[9] The "When Americans. . ." quotation is from Gilens's web-page summary description of his 2012 book, *Affluence and Influence*, at http://scholar.princeton.edu/mgilens/pages/research. The more recent analysis addressing the influence exerted by different sorts of interest groups as well as by the rich is that by Gilens and Page (2014); the "economic elites. . ." quotation is from their abstract (564).

Meritocracy, Mobility, and the American Dream

The novelist John Steinbeck supposedly said "Socialism never took root in America because the poor see themselves not as an exploited proletariat, but as temporarily embarrassed millionaires." In a cartoon in the *New Yorker* magazine, two men are sitting in a bar; one is wearing an expensive suit and grinning over his martini at the scruffy beer-drinker three seats away, who proclaims drunkenly to no-one in particular "As a potential lottery winner, I totally support tax cuts for the wealthy." *New York Times* columnist David Brooks cites a survey in which 19 percent of Americans purportedly claimed to be among the top 1 percent of earners, and another 20 percent said that they expected to get there some day; in the United States, says Brooks, "None of us is really poor; we're just pre-rich."[10]

Is that really it? Are Americans opposed to redistributive policies—to things like a social safety net of the sort that Europeans take for granted and the progressive income tax that could pay for it—because they believe that soaking the rich is soaking their future selves? It sounds too facile; the poor are surely not *that* deluded! And yet the citizens of the United States do seem to harbor an exceptionally jaundiced view of taxation and government services, even at the lower rungs of the economic ladder, as well as an exceptional faith in the possibility of moving up. Relentless propagandizing by right-wing media owned by a handful of the über-wealthy surely plays a role in this, but the so-called American Dream is older than that. Wikipedia explains it thus:

> The **American Dream** is a national ethos of the United States, a set of ideals in which freedom includes the opportunity for prosperity and success, and an upward social mobility for the family and children, achieved through hard work in a society with few barriers.[11]

In 1998, a graduate student named Heather Beth Johnson set out to study attitudes to wealth and inequality in the United States, but as she explains in her book *The American Dream and the Power of Wealth*, she got drawn in a slightly different direction. Her interviewees kept singing

[10] Wright (2004, 124) attributed the "temporarily embarrassed millionaires" witticism to Steinbeck, but he apparently never said exactly that; see http://en.wikiquote.org/wiki/John_Steinbeck. The "potential winner" cartoon, by David Sipress, appeared in the *New Yorker* on October 4, 2010. Brooks's column, entitled "The triumph of hope over self-interest" appeared in the January 12, 2003 edition of the *New York* Times.

[11] Downloaded on February 15, 2015, from http://en.wikipedia.org/wiki/American_Dream.

the praises of meritocracy in the United States. Especially remarkable to Johnson were her wealthiest respondents, who would cheerfully acknowledge their lifelong advantages and how much those advantages had helped them get ahead, but then, often in the next breath, insist that they had earned their way by hard work and that any American with gumption could do the same. Intrigued, Johnson devised a more focused set of questions and interviewed another twenty wealthy families in 2003. Would they really defend the claim that the United States is an equal-opportunity meritocracy?

> *Interviewer*: Research has said that the American Dream is the idea that with hard work and desire, individual potential is unconstrained. They say that the American Dream promises that everyone, regardless of background, succeeds through their own actions. It's the idea that we get ahead through individual achievement alone. That our family backgrounds don't matter.

Johnson was gobsmacked by the responses that this definition and her follow-up questions evoked. *Every one* of her interviewees endorsed this characterization of the "dream" not merely as an ideal, but as a valid description of how contemporary American society actually functions. Even when they were challenged about the contradictions in their answers, these affluent, educated respondents held firm. The proposition that the United States is meritocratic—and in the opinion of many, uniquely so—was nonnegotiable.[12]

According to comedian George Carlin, "it's called the American Dream because you have to be asleep to believe it." Should Carlin's zinger be amended to read "asleep *or rich*"? Johnson might demur, because interviewees at *every* socioeconomic level seemed committed to the Dream. After providing numerous striking illustrations from her transcripts, she concludes:

> Just as people with wealth credited themselves for their success, conversely, those who lacked family wealth blamed themselves. Conviction in meritocracy worked both ways, and meritocracy could justify both positions. The themes of "sticking to one's ideals," "being focused" and "motivated," and being "willing to work hard" were as consistent in interviews with working-class and impoverished families as they were in affluent families.

---

[12] See Johnson (2014). The quoted passage is from pages 35–36.

Nevertheless, other evidence indicates that those who are less advantaged have their doubts that the meritocracy is working. In one interview study of workers in Indiana, a very large majority agreed that the American Dream was becoming less attainable; unsurprisingly, this pessimism was especially strong among those who had encountered some form of job insecurity. Moreover, decades of survey studies indicate that higher income, being a member of the dominant white majority, and being a male are all positive predictors of buy-in to the equal opportunity story.[13]

The surveys tell us that faith in the American Dream isn't universal, and that it is to some degree predictable on the basis of relative position. No surprises there, nor in the fact that those who have actually attained some upward mobility can be even noisier advocates of the Dream's validity than those born rich. Consider this "Message from the Association's Officers":

> The Horatio Alger Association of Distinguished Americans was established in 1947 to remind fellow citizens that opportunities continue to abound through the American free-enterprise system and education. Kenneth Beebe, President of the American Schools and Colleges Association, was concerned by the trend of thought among young people that opportunity was a thing of the past. Realizing that this attitude could be countered by focusing attention on individuals who had achieved success in spite of adverse circumstances, he established the Horatio Alger Award. He named the award after the writer of 'rags to riches' novels in the 19th century, Horatio Alger, Jr. This helped to reinforce the values represented by the Award.[14]

Of course, none of this undermines Heather Beth Johnson's central message: Beliefs about opportunity and meritocracy in the United States are often unexamined and self-contradictory, and both rich and poor recite a sloganized American Dream like a mantra, at least out of one side of their mouths. Arguably, the positive glow that surrounds this ideology makes it an effective rhetorical weapon against collective action and social programs.

---

[13] The quoted passage is from Johnson (2014, 162). For survey work indicating that belief in a functioning American meritocracy is predictably associated with advantage, see, for example, Kluegel and Smith (1986) and Bobo (1991). Starks (2003) reported the results of the Indiana survey; it was conducted in 1998, when the state's economy was strong, which makes the general pessimism all the more remarkable.
[14] Downloaded on February 20, 2015, from http:// www.horatioalger.org/letter.cfm.

And yes, the United States *is* exceptional in this regard. The 1999 *European Values Survey* includes four items grouped under the question "In order to be considered 'just', what should a society provide?" Respondents were asked to what extent they agreed with each of the four:

A. Eliminating big inequalities in income between citizens.
B. Guaranteeing that basic needs are met for all, in terms of food, housing, clothes, education, health.
C. Recognizing people on their merits.
D. Giving young people equal opportunity to pursue their education irrespective of family income.

Over thirty thousand respondents from twenty-five countries participated, and most agreed with option A. (Danes were the only nationality whose average response was slightly on the "disagree" side of neutral, perhaps because Denmark doesn't *have* "big inequalities in income" to eliminate.) Moreover, one's level of agreement that justice requires "recognizing people on their merits" stood out as a strong *positive* predictor of one's agreement with the "eliminating big inequalities" item. This seems to be at odds with how Americans invoke merit as a grounds for *not* redistributing income, but the contrast makes sense in the light of evidence that Americans blame the poor for their poverty and Europeans don't. In *World Values Survey* data from 1981 through 1997, 60 percent of Europeans but only 29 percent of Americans agreed that "The poor are trapped in poverty"; 54 percent of Europeans but only 30 percent of Americans agreed that "Luck determines income"; and 26 percent of Europeans agreed that "The poor are lazy" compared to 60 percent of Americans.[15]

Harvard economist Alberto Alesina and his colleagues have posed the question "Why doesn't the United States have a European-style welfare state?," and have analyzed many survey results like those I just described in search of the correlates and probable origins of the underlying attitudes. Echoing Martin Gilens's point about the black face of America's "undeserving poor," these researchers found considerable evidence that racism is part of the story, but only one part. Other beliefs and attitudes seemed to be important, too, whereas simple economic

---

[15] The *European Values Survey* results are from Kaltenthaler et al. (2008). The *Word Values Survey* data for 1981–97 were amalgamated and summarized by Alesina et al. (2001).

"self-interest" explanations fared poorly in their many analyses. Their conclusion:

> Americans redistribute less than Europeans for three reasons: because the majority of Americans believe that redistribution favors racial minorities, because Americans believe that they live in an open and fair society and that if someone is poor it is his or her own fault, and because the political system is geared toward preventing redistribution.

Alesina's point about political system differences warrants elaboration. In a nutshell:

> The formation of the United States as a federation of independent territories led to a structure that often creates obstacles to centralized redistributive policies. The relative political stability of the United States over more than two centuries means that it is still governed by an eighteenth-century constitution designed to protect property. As world war and revolution uprooted the old European monarchies, the twentieth century constitutions that replaced them were more oriented toward majority rule, and less toward protection of private property.[16]

In principle, the majority opinions of Americans and Europeans *could* have both been correct. Maybe poor Europeans really are trapped in poverty, but things are different in meritocratic America, where you can get ahead if you're just willing to work hard enough. That is exactly what many Americans apparently believe, explicitly contrasting their own supposedly classless society where "anyone can make it" with the sclerotic hierarchies of the "Old World." But if you buy that story, you're going to have a hard time explaining the facts about economic and social mobility in different countries.

If you were a boy whose father's earnings placed him in the top 10 percent, how likely is it that you would grow up to be an earner in that same top bracket? In the United States, you would have a 26 percent probability of remaining in the top tenth (or "decile"); in Canada, only 18 percent. And what would be your chances of slipping all the way to the *bottom* decile? The answer is 8 percent in Canada, and less than 3 percent in the United States. So Americans who are born rich tend to stay rich. But what about moving up? The answer is that 16 percent of

---

[16] The quoted passages are from Alesina et al. (2001, 60 and 2). See also Fong (2001), Alesina and Glaeser (2004) and Bonica et al. (2013).

Canadian boys whose fathers were in the *bottom* decile of earners will remain there as adults, *versus* 22 percent of American boys. However you slice it, "intergenerational earnings mobility"—the extent to which the son's income is independent of the father's—is higher in Canada than in the United States and it's higher than in the United States in most of Europe, and in Japan and Australia and New Zealand, too. Among the developed countries, only Great Britain and Italy have levels of intergenerational income mobility that are as low as that in the United States. In my experience, this is a revelation that shocks Americans, with the exception of those who indignantly refuse to believe it. The United States is *the* land of opportunity, damn it! The front cover of the Horatio Alger Association's annual report is emblazoned "ONLY IN AMERICA. Opportunity still knocks."[17]

It's time to introject a word of caution about "mobility." Economic mobility is typically portrayed in the media as an unvarnished good. In a *New York Times* story about recent research on regional differences in intergenerational mobility within the United States, for example, David Leonhardt equates economic mobility with "people's chances of rising beyond the station of their birth," with "climbing the income ladder," and with "the chances that children escape poverty." The trouble with this positive spin is that standard indices of mobility are simply measures of movement between deciles or (more commonly) quintiles. In each generation, 20 percent are still going to be in the top quintile, 20 percent in the bottom quintile, and 20 percent in each of other three, so every move up is necessarily offset by an equal and opposite move down. It follows that there is no logical justification for referring to a raw mobility measure as an indicator of *upward* mobility. You could just as well have said *downward* mobility instead.[18]

There is, of course, no question that social and economic mobility must be *possible* if there is to be fairness in the form of merit-based reward. The problem is that typical indices of mobility cannot simply be assumed to be direct indicators of meritocracy, justice, or an overall upward trend in material well-being. Maybe genuine equality of opportunity typically elevates both mobility and prosperity, but not necessarily. At least in principle, intergenerational earnings mobility

[17] The data on intergenerational mobility are from Corak (2013a). The Horatio Alger Association grants an honorary almost-Americans status to Canadians—Wayne Gretzky has been a recipient of their rags-to-riches award, in spite of his comfortable middle-class background—but it makes no such concessions to Europeans.

[18] Leonhardt's article appeared in the *New York Times* on July 22, 2013.

could be low in an established equal-opportunity meritocracy, if heritable talents were major determinants of outcomes. And perhaps more importantly, mobility can be expected to be high in a bleak world of unpredictable economic shocks and dumb luck, where the outcomes that befall individuals have nothing to do with their efforts or any other meritorious attributes. So an index of mobility, on its own, tells us less than we might imagine. To find out whether high mobility really is associated with prosperity and other good things, we have to consult the real world, and not just our intuitions. It could go either way.

The good news for its boosters is that, by and large, mobility usually *is* associated with good things. According to recent research on the differences among US cities, for example, those that have higher mobility also have better primary schools, less racial segregation, lower levels of income inequality, and greater social capital. That all sounds good, and yet the implications still aren't entirely clear. The association with low income inequality is encouraging, and it matches cross-national findings, but it could, in principle, be largely artifactual because identical random gains or losses of a few thousand dollars will generate more movement across quintile boundaries, and hence more "mobility," where the dispersion of incomes is low than where it is higher. And although "social capital" is conceptualized as civic engagement and connectedness to one's community, it is somewhat clumsily assayed by the mere prevalence of voluntary organizations. The most encouraging finding to emerge from this US city-level study is that greater mobility does indeed seem to be associated with upward absolute movement, and hence with gains.[19]

As far as I am aware, the question of whether economic mobility is predictive of violent crime rates has not yet been investigated. The strong associations of income inequality with both homicide and mobility suggest that the latter two quantities will also tend to be positively correlated, but will mobility retain any apparent connection with homicide when inequality is statistically controlled? Low mobility might even tend to reduce interpersonal violence, if the conditions that most provoke escalated competition include a combination of high inequality, being of low personal social status, *and* seeing that some

---

[19] For correlates of mobility across US cities, see Chetty et al. (2014); this is the same research project that Leonhardt was reporting on in the *New York Times*. Regarding "social capital," see Rupasingha et al. (2006). Cross-national evidence that higher intergenerational mobility is strongly associated with lower income inequality in the OECD countries and more broadly is presented by Corak (2013a, 2013b).

people are nevertheless managing to get ahead. Mobility and *beliefs about* mobility are both potentially potent social forces, and research on the American Dream tells us that they are to some degree dissociable.

For the time being, the only honest conclusion concerning the possible effects of mobility on violence is a regrettably lame one: More research is required.

Costs of Inequality

The costs that economic immobility imposes on society remain to be elucidated. But the costs imposed by economic inequality are much clearer, and they extend far beyond the effects on homicide that have been my primary focus. Apparent costs of inequality in the domain of health were brought to the fore by the famous *Whitehall Studies* of disease and mortality among British civil servants, which were launched by the Scottish medical epidemiologist Donald Reid (1914–77) in 1967, and which continue to this day.

The basic idea behind *Whitehall I* was brilliant. By studying government employees, the investigators were able to ensure the unanimous participation of many thousands of workers, in relatively stable jobs, at a wide range of occupational statuses. The main findings were—and continue to be—that there is a "gradient" such that lower status is associated with higher rates of death from a wide range of diseases. Not surprisingly, various physical and lifestyle factors that are known risk factors for disease are also associated with occupational status, but the large numbers enabled the researchers to isolate their effects. A typical result was the following:

> Men in the lower employment grades were shorter, heavier for their height, had higher blood pressure, higher plasma glucose, smoked more, and reported less leisure-time physical activity than men in the higher grades. Yet when allowance was made for the influence on mortality of all of these factors plus plasma cholesterol, the inverse association between grade of employment and CHD [coronary heart disease] mortality was still strong.[20]

The ongoing *Whitehall II* study continues to produce new findings on a wide range of medical issues, only some of which are linked to status. But relative position in the occupational status hierarchy is my focus here, and the story hasn't changed. For present purposes,

---

[20] The quoted results are from the abstract of Marmot *et al.* (1978, 244).

179

the most striking thing about the results from both Whitehall studies is that health and life expectancy improve steadily all the way up the hierarchy. Considerable evidence points to stress as a mediator of these effects, and one salutory effect of *Whitehall I* has been its debunking of the myth that the burden of responsibility makes top-level decision makers uniquely vulnerable to stress-related disease. The evidence indicates precisely the opposite: The burden of stress is lightened by each step up the hierarchy.[21]

There is now an immense literature on the negative health consequences of inequality. There is also an immense body of critique. The critics generally acknowledge that inequality is a ubiquitous correlate of morbidity and mortality, but they remain skeptical that it is a cause. As we have already seen with violence, many potentially relevant variables are correlated with one another, and no causal model that purports to explain the findings is immune to criticism. Others have reviewed this literature, and I will not do so here.[22]

When I first heard about the *Whitehall Studies*, they were epitomized for me in the form of a fable. If Clive and Nigel have identical civil service jobs in London, at the same £40,000 salary, but Clive works in a cubicle where the colleagues to his left and his right also make £40K, whereas Nigel's cubicle is flanked by one co-worker earning £30K and another earning £50K, then Nigel will be the more likely of the two to contract various diseases and to die.

That sounded about as close to a smoking gun as one could hope for, but the fable was a little too good to be true. The *Whitehall Studies* permit no such analyses and have produced no such findings. That said, it seems to me scarcely plausible that the findings reflect *nothing* about relative position, such that everything can be explained purely in terms of individual-level variables that happen to be correlated with occupational status. The gradient of improved health and longevity that differentiates each level of the hierarchy, from the lowest minions through middle and managerial positions all the way to the top, may not quite qualify as a smoking gun, but it definitively transfers the burden of proof to the nay-sayers.

In 2009, a best-seller by two English epidemiologists, Richard Wilkinson and Kate Pickett, brought the apparent effects of inequality on

---

[21] For other results of the *Whitehall Studies*, see Marmot (2004).

[22] For reviews of this literature and the controversies about whether inequality is really causal, see, for example, Lynch et al. (2004), Subramanian and Kawachi (2004), Babones (2008), Wilkinson and Pickett (2009), and Rowlingson (2011).

health into the public eye. "*The Spirit Level: Why More Equal Societies Almost Always do Better*" presented an immense amount of data—from the Whitehall studies, the authors' own research, and many other sources—in the service of an argument that excessive inequality is to blame for a panoply of ills. The book begins with a proposal that the improvements in the citizenry's well-being that can be derived purely from economic growth have topped out in the developed world: In cross-national comparisons, health, happiness and longevity are all shown to exhibit steep improvements with gross domestic product (GDP) at the low end, but the gains diminish, and beyond about US$20K per capita per annum (a rough threshold for being deemed a developed economy), there is no remaining relationship between a nation's GDP and these indicators of well-being. Nevertheless, *within* each rich country, steep gradients continue to be apparent: Life expectancy, health and happiness all increase steadily as you ascend the hierarchy of status and wealth.

From this starting point, Wilkinson and Pickett develop two linked arguments, both of which they support with many data portrayals. One thread—backed mainly by comparisons among rich countries and across the US states.—is that an extremely broad range of social and health problems are highly correlated with income inequality, but not with average income. The other line of argument is that inequality probably causes these ills, primarily through the damage done by chronic social stress and anxiety, which in turn derive from low levels of trust and fraught social comparisons. Wilkinson and Pickett's review and synthesis of disparate scientific literatures in the service of these two interwoven strands was a *tour de force*.

Business-friendly media were horrified, and rushed to set the record straight. A review in the *Wall Street Journal* dismissed fans of the book as "socialist ideologues." The review's four authors—three members of a right-wing think-tank, plus a smoker's rights lobbyist—asserted (without deigning to offer any evidence) that although inequality is indeed correlated with social problems, it is the social problems that cause the inequality, rather than the reverse. They then mockingly suggested that where neighborhoods have crime, gangs, and drug problems, then "by the Wilkinson-Pickett reckoning . . . societal malaise can be alleviated by reducing income in the surrounding neighborhoods."[23]

---

[23] The *Wall Street Journal* review appeared on July 9, 2010 (see http://online.wsj.com/news/ articles/SB127862421912914915).

The Toronto *Globe & Mail* styles itself "Canada's national newspaper" and centrist in its politics. As a subscriber to the Saturday edition, I was unsurprised when international affairs columnist Doug Saunders lectured his readers, with characteristic condescension, as follows:

> Inequality is a badly misunderstood topic, and recent books like Richard Wilkinson and Kate Pickett's *The Spirit Level* don't help—they argue rightly that more equal societies are often better, but create the false perception that a change in equality means an improvement in life. If that were the case, then governments should never pursue economic growth, because it almost always causes a rise in measured inequality.[24]

Eight weeks later, I *was* surprised to see *The Spirit Level* on the *Globe*'s op-ed page again. It had apparently struck a nerve. Another regular columnist, Margaret Wente, correctly characterized the book as maintaining that relatively unequal societies "have more crime, more drug abuse, more heart disease, more prisons and more of every social pathology than equal ones." And then she continued thus:

> But it isn't hard to fire a cannonball through [this] thesis. Take Japan. It is extremely equal. But Japan is heading toward catastrophe, both demographic and financial. Japan is so xenophobic that immigrants are not welcome, full stop. Nobody has children any more, and Japan remains the most sexist country in the developed world. If Japan were a person, it would be diagnosed as morbidly depressed.

Kapow! Take *that*, socialist ideologues![25]

Not every attack on *The Spirit Level* was as fatuous as the three that I have quoted, but few, if any, were even-handed. Or seriously damaging. A recurrent complaint was that Wilkinson and Pickett present their evidence primarily in the form of bivariate scatter plots, often failing to provide a thorough explanation of the measures or to dispose convincingly of third-variable (confound) explanations for the observed relationships between inequality and various social ills. This was not altogether unfair. Striving for a broadly accessible style, the two epidemiologists opted for readily grasped data portrayals, and

---

[24] Saunders's op-ed column in the *Globe & Mail* appeared on November 13, 2010 (see http://www.theglobeandmail.com/globe-debate/in-solving-the-financial-crisis-lets-not-resort-to-social-cleansing/article4346662/).

[25] Wente's op-ed column in the *Globe & Mail* appeared on January 8, 2011 (see http://www.theglobeandmail.com/globe-debate/does-inequality-matter/article621591/).

they consigned the primary research literature containing the details of variable construction and the relevant multivariate analyses and statistical controls to a foot-noted reference list. Perhaps they should have tried harder to communicate these subtleties, but any conscientious reviewer would have checked the research literature that the book cites before declaring that the supporting evidence contained therein doesn't exist!

Strong associations between inequality and a variety of social and health problems are undeniable facts. The only real controversies concern whether inequality plays a direct causal role or is itself another sorry consequence of the real culprits. Wilkinson, Pickett, and the many others who have indicted inequality as an evil have identified plausible pathways by which it *could* play a causal role, and have amassed substantial evidence for the reality and potency of component links in those pathways. Some lingering skepticism about the indictment may or may not be warranted, but confident claims that inequality is blameless have no empirical foundation, and are hard to explain as anything other than faith-based free-market ideology.[26]

The Big Lie

Regardless of whether you get your news from the internet, television, or an old-fashioned newspaper like the Toronto *Globe & Mail*, you are likely to have encountered views like those displayed by the business press in its attacks on *The Spirit Level*. We don't believe a word of it, they snort, and anyway, even if it's true, inequality is an essential aspect of the capitalist system that makes us all better off. If you mess with financial incentives, you'll kill the goose that lays the golden eggs. As John F. Kennedy was fond of saying, "A rising tide lifts all boats."[27]

The apologia for inequality can be stated in four sentences that make it sound almost like a piece of deductive logic:

(1) The requisites for growth and prosperity include innovation, entrepreneurial risk-taking, and a widespread willingness to work hard.
(2) The incentives for each of these requisites are largely or entirely financial.

---

[26] For a relatively recent, thorough, and even-handed review of the controversies, see Rowlingson (2011).

[27] According to Sorensen (2008, 227), Kennedy got the "rising tide" aphorism from the New England regional Chamber of Commerce.

(3) Reducing inequality entails redistributing financial rewards from the winners to the losers.
(4) Therefore, efforts to reduce inequality necessarily undermine incentives and impede productivity and growth.

Q.E.D.

It may come as a bit of a surprise, then, to learn that the evidence has been running against this argument for decades, and that few economists still buy it.

Joseph Stiglitz is a former chief economist of the World Bank and a recipient of the 2001 Nobel Prize in economics for his role in "laying the foundations for the theory of markets with asymmetric information." In the preface to his 2012 best-seller *The Price of Inequality*, a dense but accessible critique of growing inequality's dark side, Stiglitz recalls that when he was a Fulbright scholar in the 1960s, "it was still thought that there were major trade-offs between inequality and growth." Even readers who were totally on board with Stiglitz's progressive arguments may have smiled at his chutzpah, since a half century has passed and exactly the same thing is "still thought" by politicians and pundits today. But Stiglitz wasn't playing a rhetorical trick. The science of economics really has discarded that old, failed conventional wisdom.[28]

A strong case can be made that "growth," which cannot continue indefinitely in a finite world, is not a suitable criterion of progress anyway. Wilkinson and Pickett make precisely that argument after presenting their evidence that although gains in GDP are associated with gains in health, happiness, and longevity in the developing world, that's no longer the case in richer nations, from which they infer that we must now look elsewhere for further progress in human well-being. For present purposes, however, we don't even need to go there. The business press's defense of inequality is wrong even on its own terms. When moneyed interests assert that redistributive policies inhibit economic growth and dismiss those policies' proponents as naïve, they are promulgating a classic "big lie." The weight of the evidence swung away from this claim long ago. Inequality of the magnitude that now prevails in the United States and some other rich countries doesn't facilitate economic activity, growth, and prosperity. It *undermines* these goals. This has been the new, evidence-based, conventional wisdom in economics since the 1990s, and research has identified several reasons *why* inequality is counterproductive.

---

[28] The quote is from page xxvii in the prefatory acknowledgments section of Stiglitz (2012).

Economists were a little slow to figure out the relationship between income inequality and economic performance for the same reason that criminologists were a little slow to figure out the relationship between income inequality and homicide: a shortage of high-quality data. Until the late twentieth century, the study of these issues was hampered by the fact that different nations collected economic survey data in different ways, if they did so at all, and there was no sound basis for comparing income distributions across countries. When the *Luxembourg Income Study* (*LIS*), a nonprofit project aimed at collecting and disseminating comparable data that would permit cross-national comparisons, was launched in 1983, suitable survey data could be gathered from only about a dozen industrialized democracies. Over the ensuing decades, the *LIS* and other analogous efforts have painstakingly added a much wider range of countries, but analysts still struggle to overcome the complications that arise from local variations in survey practices.

Economists advising the United Nations Development Agency, the World Bank, and the International Monetary Fund wanted access to these international data in order to figure out why prosperity was rising in some countries but not others, and once they got the data, one of the first questions they tackled was how the distribution of income affects economic growth. "Working papers" on this question began to circulate soon after the first *LIS* data became available, and by the mid-1990s, several published studies pointed to a possibly surprising conclusion: The countries in which incomes were relatively equitable at a given time tended to be the ones that enjoyed the most economic growth in the years to follow. The studies that reached this conclusion used a variety of measures and analytic techniques, different inclusion criteria, and a diversity of "control variables" chosen to eliminate potential confounds and increase the likelihood that observed relationships within the data reflected real causal links. But despite this diversity of approaches, the results kept coming up the same. In 1996, a prominent Franco-American economist, Roland Bénabou, summed up an already burgeoning research literature as follows: "These regressions, run over a variety of data sets and periods with many different measures of income distribution, deliver a consistent message: Initial inequality is detrimental to long-run growth."[29]

---

[29] Early studies indicating that inequality hampers economic growth include Alesina and Rodrik (1994), Clarke (1995), Perotti (1996), Deininger and Squire (1998), and Persson and Tabellini (1994). The quote is from Bénabou (1996, 13). More recent studies reinforcing the point include Berg et al. (2012) and Herzer and Vollmer (2012).

A consistent message it was, but not quite unanimous. As with any generalization in the social sciences, there has been some dissent. A particularly prominent and forceful dissenting analysis by the Sloan School of Management's Kristin Forbes was published in 2000 in the *American Economic Review*. Confining her study to within-country trends and to shorter time periods than prior analysts, Forbes got an exceptional result: "in the short and medium term, an increase in a country's level of income inequality has a significant positive relationship with subsequent economic growth." However, there are several reasons to be skeptical of even this limited conclusion. One big limitation is that Forbes's narrowed analytic focus ruled out cross-national variation and long-run effects by fiat. Criticisms can also be leveled at her choice of which variables to control: A problem with her approach— and, to be fair, with some analyses that have produced contrary results, as well—is that statistically controlling third variables can be a two-edged sword, removing not only spurious associations due to confounds, but also genuine effects mediated by the controlled variable. Forbes proposes, for example, that cross-national studies may have been misleading because of failures to include statistical controls for corruption which "tends to be positively correlated with inequality and negatively correlated with growth." The problem with this suggestion is that corruption can itself be a result of inequality, as for example when poorly paid police and bureaucrats are expected to generate their own incomes in the form of bribes. Introducing statistical controls for corruption is therefore likely to obliterate a genuine causal chain running from inequality through corruption to low growth.[30]

In any event, quibbles about the merits of Forbes's analysis were rendered moot in 2009, when David Roodman, an economist at the Washington Center for Global Development, dissected her study as a case in point of the misuse of a statistical method—the "generalized method of moments" (GMM) technique—in such a way as to artificially inflate the number of "instrumental variables" and thus produce invalid results. Roodman himself had played a big role in making the GMM statistical technique accessible and popular: He wrote the software for implementing it. He was therefore well positioned to understand its uses and abuses, and he was alarmed and somewhat embarrassed by the ensuing proliferation of analyses like Forbes's.[31]

[30] The quote is from Forbes (2000, 869). Her claim that corruption is an uncontrolled confound in cross-national analyses appears on page 870.

[31] For a full explication of why Forbes's analysis is statistically flawed and invalid, see Roodman (2009).

Of course, analyses indicating that inequality inhibits growth aren't flawless either, but they have held up to scrutiny much better. In retrospect, what remains illuminating about Forbes's paper is that she saw fit to portray herself as a maverick, because her paper "challenges the current belief that income inequality has a negative relationship with economic growth," a conclusion she correctly characterized as "widely accepted" by "most economists." Think about it: In the year 2000, an economist, writing in a leading economics journal, tries to prove that inequality is not always antithetical to growth, and she finds it necessary to acknowledge that her argument flies in the face of economic orthodoxy! That in itself should give pause to anyone who has been taken in by right-wing media promulgation of the Big Lie.

The twenty-first century evidence has only strengthened the orthodoxy from which Forbes dissented. In April 2014, the International Monetary Fund distributed a 30-page discussion paper entitled "Redistribution, inequality, and growth" for staff discussion. The paper reviews relevant prior work and presents new international analyses that distinguish pre-tax "market" income inequality from the net inequality that remains after taxes and redistributive transfers, all of which lead its authors to strong, clear conclusions, first that lower inequality (whether market or net inequality) is predictive of faster and more durable growth, and second that the effects of redistribution itself "are on average pro-growth." Coincidentally, in that same month of April, the rich countries' club known as the OECD (Organization for Economic Cooperation and Development) released a video entitled "Income inequality undermines growth" making a similar argument more accessibly and less technically. You can watch it on YouTube.[32]

The IMF and the OECD are hardly the sort of organizations that could reasonably be called radical, or even left-leaning, as witness the consideration that they have scarcely begun to take seriously the fact that there are limits to growth. So why are they circulating materials which maintain that inequality has damaging effects on economic performance? The answer is that this is the conclusion that most pro-business, pro-growth, mainstream economists have been compelled by the evidence to accept. And that is why pretending otherwise is a Big Lie.

---

[32] The IMF report is by Ostry, Berg, and Tsangarides (2014), and is available at http://www.imf.org/external/pubs/ft/sdn/2014/sdn1402.pdf. The OECD video can be seen at https://www.youtube.com/watch?v=hjD6Qlr1eMM.

Why Inequality Hurts the Economy, Too

So economists have discovered that income inequality damages the economy's health as well as that of the citizenry. But why is that? Researchers whose analyses first pointed to this conclusion were so steeped in the old logic that they initially tried to explain their results by positing that inequality creates political pressure for redistribution, and that the resultant redistribution then dampens incentives and inhibits growth. This interpretation has been laid to rest by the latest IMF analyses, but it never really fit the facts very well. The sluggish growth of initially inequitable countries was not associated with implementation of higher marginal tax rates or other redistributive policies. Quite the contrary in fact: The more equitable countries whose economies performed better were more equitable primarily *because* of more progressive taxation regimes and social welfare policies, and the relatively inequitable countries did not, in general, move to mimic them.

Trends over time within a single country like the United States are embarrassing for trickle-down theorists railing against "confiscatory" marginal tax rates. From 1946 through 1963, US citizens paid income tax at a rate of 91 percent on earnings over $200,000. This top marginal tax rate was reduced to 70 percent in 1965, and remained there until Ronald Reagan's presidency, when it was reduced to 50 percent in his first term and 28 percent in his second. It has remained under 40 percent ever since. Since President Kennedy first lowered the top tax rate in 1963, every cut has been justified partly on the grounds that leaving more money in the pockets of the rich will create a "rising tide" of investment and innovation that will "raise all boats." So what happened to economic growth as the top marginal tax rate was slashed to a level that is now much less than half its post-war value? Figure 9.2 overlays the trends in US economic growth and in the top tax rate since 1960. You don't have to be a socialist ideologue to have difficulty detecting the rising tide.

These US data are not exceptional. But again, why is that? Why is there no sign of the stimulus effects that are always invoked to justify tax cuts for the rich? Well, for one thing, innovation is *not* driven by dreams of fabulous wealth. The transformative discoveries of the 20th century were motivated not by the pursuit of money, but by curiosity and by the pursuit of esteem. The creative people who did the foundational work that brought you antibiotics and open-heart surgery, home computers and the internet, never got rich and weren't trying to get rich.

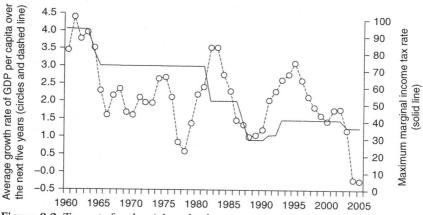

Figure 9.2. Tax cuts for the rich and subsequent growth in the United States. The solid line portrays the top marginal personal income tax rate in the United States for the years 1960–2005. The circles and dashed line portray the average growth rate of the Gross Domestic Product (GDP) in the ensuing five years (e.g., the data point at 2005 is the average growth rate from 2006 through 2010.[33]

Solving scientific and technological problems is intrinsically satisfying for scientists and engineers. Nerds don't respond to an increase in the top marginal income tax rate by cutting back on tinkering in their garages. Many thousands of unpaid volunteers plug away at expanding and improving the information available through *Wikipedia*, providing many millions of others with tangible and intangible benefits.

This is not to say that competitive motives are irrelevant. But competitive success is relative, not absolute, and its rewards are primarily social and positional. *The Double Helix*, James Watson's account of his and Francis Crick's role in elucidating the structure and function of DNA, provides a compelling example of just how competitive scientists can be. Watson doesn't come across as an altruist, nor even as likeable, but it was neither patents nor cash that he was pursuing. He wanted to beat others to a goal and, above all else, he wanted to be recognized as having done so. For other great scientists, even these social payoffs aren't always major motivating factors. Discovery is often its own reward.

---

[33] The top marginal income tax rates are from http://en.wikipedia.org/wiki/Income_tax_in_the_United_States. Ensuing growth is from the *Groningen Growth & Development Centre* database; see http://www.ggdc.net/maddison/maddison-project/home.htm.

Okay, you may be saying, even if scientific discovery isn't driven by financial ambition, the pursuit of profits is surely what motivates the entrepreneurs who translate innovation into something accessible and useful. But even this is at best a partial truth. Entrepreneurs are people, too. Read their autobiographies, and you won't find them wallowing, like Scrooge McDuck, in ever-growing piles of cash. The narratives they delight in telling are mythologized accounts of their achievements: their management strategies and shrewd decisions, how they recognized an opportunity before others, how they wrested control of a company from rivals. Granted, the rich will hide their money in tax havens when they can, and they lobby hard to keep taxes down, but it's only in Ayn Rand's fantasy world that entrepreneurs spitefully go on strike. To a billionaire, the marginal utility of an extra few million is negligible. What never loses its sheen is being widely acknowledged as someone who made exceptional decisions, trounced the competition, and emerged a winner.[34]

The myth from the right is that those who are fabulously wealthy "created" their wealth by translating innovation into something accessible and useful. The truth is very different. As of May, 2015, the four surviving children of the late Walmart magnate, Sam Walton, each had a total net worth in excess of 35 billion dollars, ranking them 10th, 13th, 16th, and 18th on the *Bloomberg Billionaires* list of the world's richest individuals. The total wealth of the Walmart heirs exceeds the total wealth of the poorest 100 million Americans, whose relevant moral failing is having chosen the wrong parents.[35]

Even "self-made" billionaires haven't necessarily earned their fortunes by providing value. In 2010, the Mexican telephone magnate Carlos Slim temporarily overtook Microsoft's Bill Gates as the world's richest man, not because of innovations or the provision of high-quality service, but because his company Telmex enjoyed a virtual monopoly. Slim takes a cut whenever a Mexican makes a phone call, and a hundred million Mexicans make a lot of phone calls. This route to fortune

---

[34] With apparently unintentional irony, Walmart magnate Sam Walton entitled his autobiography *Made in America* (Walton and Huey 1992). For another exemplary billionaire autobiography, see Branson (1998).

[35] The Walton heirs' positions among the world's billionaires were retrieved on May 20, 2015 from http://www.bloomberg.com/billionaires/2015-05-19/cya. Regarding their assets relative to those of the rest of the US population, see Bivens (2012); the conclusion that their assets exceed those of the bottom hundred million Americans still holds even if all negative net worth values (where debts exceed assets) are recoded as zero.

is what economists refer to as "rent seeking": making money not by creating value, but by having somehow positioned oneself to skim off a share of the value created by others. Monopolists routinely do this, and so of course does the financial sector. Why? The answer is the same as the answer to the old joke "Why do dogs spend so much time licking their genitals?" Because they can.[36]

A widely recognized reason why the levels of inequality that prevail today are impeding further economic development is that stagnating or shrinking working-class and middle-class incomes reduce demand. Even the advocates of tax cuts like to say that their policy prescriptions will "jump-start the economy" by putting more disposable income in the hands of consumers. But there are subtler issues. In addition to its effects on consumer demand, a high level of inequality ensures that many people with worthy small business dreams are unable to realize them, even in rich countries. In a classic study in Great Britain, economists David Blanchflower and Andrew Oswald attempted to determine "What makes an entrepreneur?" The answer was not to be found in childhood personality tests, nor in some exceptional urge to be self-employed. The critical factor was adequate start-up funds. Receiving even a small inheritance greatly increased the likelihood that a young adult would start his own business. This isn't solely, nor even primarily, because people who don't already control substantial assets are rationally risk-averse. It's because they usually can't borrow the sums they would need to do it right.[37]

Economists David Evans and Boyan Jovanovic studied a sample of American men, all of whom had been wage workers in 1976 and some of whom had become self-employed by 1978, to see what factors affected the transition to self-employment. One striking finding was that the capitalization of new businesses was limited to about one and a half times the business owner's prior wealth, and from this and other results, the analysts concluded that "Most individuals who enter self-employment face a binding liquidity constraint and as a result use a suboptimal amount of capital to start up their businesses." In plain English, the point is that new businesses often fail because they were never adequately funded to operate at a scale that would have made them efficient. Moreover, a perverse consequence of differential access

---

[36] Regarding the many forms that rent seeking takes in modern economies, and its role in the accumulation of wealth at the top of the US income distribution, see Stiglitz (2012).
[37] For what makes an entrepreneur, see Blanchflower and Oswald (1998).

to start-up funds has been documented by Samuel Bowles of the Santa Fe Institute and the University of Siena: Wealthy entrepreneurs can succeed with shoddier products and lower-quality business plans than would be required for their asset-poor rivals to stay afloat, and this asymmetry has negative effects on efficiency and on average product quality in the economy as a whole.[38]

Yet another reason why inequality hampers economic performance is that inequality has a corrosive effect on trust. Since Adam Smith, economists have understood that transactions of any sort are facilitated by mutual trust, and that a shortfall of trust raises costs. In the words of the Nobel Prize winning economist Kenneth Arrow:

> Trust is an important lubricant of a social system. It is extremely effi-
> cient; it saves a lot of trouble to have a fair degree of reliance on other
> people's word . . . Trust and similar values, loyalty or truth-telling,
> are examples of what the economist would call "externalities." They
> are goods, they are commodities; they have real, practical, economic
> value; they increase the efficiency of the system, enable you to produce
> more goods or more of whatever values you hold in high esteem.
> But they are not commodities for which trade on the open market is
> technically possible or even meaningful.[39]

Figure 9.3 presents an example of the association between distrust and income inequality.

Trust reduces expenditures on contractual guarantees and safe-guards, and on the machinery required to enforce them. Opinions differ on whether lawyers should be considered "rent seeking" parasites on those who actually produce things of value, but everyone would prefer to economize on legal expenses. It is no coincidence that the number of lawyers per capita tends to be higher in the more unequal OECD countries, and the differences are not small: There are an estimated 39 lawyers per 10,000 people in the United States, 25 in England, and 2 in Japan.[40]

The legal expenses that inequality imposes aren't confined to contract law and litigation. Where some are very rich and many others are very

---

[38] Regarding the undercapitalization of new businesses, see Evans and Jovanovic (1989), Bowles (2012), and Stiglitz (2012).

[39] Quoted from Arrow (1974, 23).

[40] Estimated numbers of lawyers are from Ramseyer and Rasmusen (2010). For a defense of the proposition that lawyers are indeed rent seekers and a major drain on the US economy, see Magee (2013).

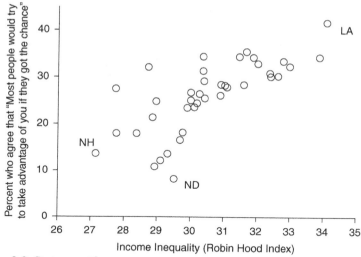

Figure 9.3. State-specific responses to a question in the *U.S. General Social Survey* (1986–90) on whether "most people" are untrustworthy, in relation to income inequality. The "Robin Hood Index" is a closely related alternative to the Gini Index and is highly correlated therewith. Redrawn from Kawachi *et al.* (1997).

poor, the latter have incentives to take from the former, by stealth and by force. Relatively unequal countries therefore spend more on police, jails, and the criminal justice system than their more egalitarian counterparts, and they spend more on extra-legal defenses such as private security guards and locks and burglar alarms and gated communities. Samuel Bowles and Arjun Jayadev refer to this general issue as one of expenditures on "guard labor." Some workers are engaged in producing the goods that people value, others in attempting to usurp them, and still others in protecting them from usurpation. As John Stuart Mill (1806–1873) mused almost 170 years ago:

> It is lamentable to think how a great proportion of all efforts and talents in the world are employed in merely neutralizing one another. It is the proper end of government to reduce this wretched waste to the smallest possible amount, by taking such measures as shall cause the energies now spent by mankind in injuring one another, or in protecting themselves against injury, to be turned to the legitimate employment of the human faculties.[41]

---

[41] Concerning guard labor, see Jayadev and Bowles (2006), Bowles and Jayadev (2012). The quotation is from Mill (1848, 979).

These distinctions are intuitive, but defining what counts as productive labor versus guard labor is tricky. Bowles and Jayadev note with evident dismay that 2012 was the year in which the number of persons employed as private security guards in the United States surpassed the number employed as high school teachers, but they also note that even teachers not only "instruct the next generation in essential productive skills" but also "socialize them to internalize the norms contributing to conformity to the society's institutions," Are even teachers to be considered guard labor, then? The obvious solution is to first define guard labor narrowly—police, security guards, and the like—and then expand the definition to encompass supervisors (who ensure that production workers don't shirk), the criminal justice system, those who make locks and alarms and defensive weapons, those in jail (who are not only removed from the labor pool, but arguably serve as deterrent examples), and even the unemployed (whose existence "disciplines" labor). Then see what you get with your various definitions.[42]

The answer is that pretty much however broadly you define guard labor, certain patterns emerge. One is that guard labor has for some time been consuming an ever-growing percentage of the labor force in the United States and elsewhere. Another is that the more unequal the society, the larger is that percentage. The following example illustrates this point using city-level data and a narrow definition of guard labor:

> Across the U.S. cities with high levels of income inequality—for example, Miami and New York—employ twice as many private security personnel (as a fraction of their labor force) as do less unequal cities like Greensboro and Kansas City. Across the largest 40 urban areas, the correlation between city inequality and private security personnel is a whopping 0.69.

But regardless of whether analysis is based on a broad or a narrow definition of guard labor, and regardless of whether comparison is made across cities, states or nations, the story is similar. The greater the level of economic inequality, the more labor we see diverted from what Mill called "the legitimate employment of the human faculties."[43]

---

[42] Regarding supervisors as guard labor, see Gordon (1994, 1996, 1998) who finds that less egalitarian production systems incur higher supervision costs, but questions whether worker buy-in and alignment of interests might be more the point than inequality itself.
[43] The cross-city correlation quotation is from Bowles and Jayadev (2012).

A Stoppable Juggernaut?

I have argued the case in previous chapters that the levels of economic inequality that prevail in developed nations contribute to interpersonal violence. Others have assembled a strong case that those same levels of inequality damage health and shorten lives all the way up and down the socio-economic hierarchy. The only justification that anyone had to offer for the growing inequality of income and wealth that plagues modern democracies was economic, and now we have seen that economists themselves have demolished the myth that for all its faults, inequality at least stimulates growth.

In September 2011, the Occupy Wall Street protests in New York City brought economic inequality in the United States and other wealthy countries into the spotlight. The ingenious rallying cry "We are the 99%" outflanked those who would dismiss the protestors as a radical minority, simplified confusing economic data, and identified a villain: "the 1%" who had pocketed virtually all of the so-called "recovery" gains after the recession of 2008–2009. Four years later, many are wondering what, if anything, the Occupy movement accomplished. The growth of income inequality in the rich nations continues apace, and the historical analysis of capitalism by the French economist Thomas Piketty in his 2014 surprise bestseller, *Capital in the Twenty-first Century*, has been gloomily interpreted as indicating that we are all on board an unstoppable inequality escalator to hell.[44]

Well, that's nonsense, and Piketty himself never said any such thing. He maintains that remedies are available, and that they are political. There are many reasons why effective political action won't be easy, the most important of which are surely well-financed campaigns of obfuscation designed to misdirect resentment of "the system" at its fellow victims, and to trick voters into voting against their interests. Nevertheless, ordinary people everywhere recognize that there is too much inequality right now, and that is the consensus among health professionals and economists as well. Is political action really impossible?

---

[44] Stiglitz (2012, 3), cites evidence that "the 1%" pocketed 93% of all income gains in the US from 2009 to 2010. Piketty (2014) makes a strong case that in an unfettered capitalist economy, returns on capital ordinarily surpass economic growth, dictating that inequality will continue to grow unless countered either by capital-destroying disruptions such as world wars or by governmental interventions.

10

What Keeps Competitive Violence in Check?

> *Egalitarianism in bands is by no means due to a human nature that is so noncompetitive that we are just "naturally" egalitarian. Rather, egalitarianism involves a deep political tension between individuals who are motivated to dominate, and a rank and file that decides it simply will not be dominated.*
> —Christopher Boehm, "Global Conflict Resolution: An Anthropological Diagnosis of Problems with World Governance," 2003

Are People, by Nature, Nasty or Nice?

Economic inequality has been indicted for a variety of crimes against humanity. My primary focus has been just one of those accusations: that inequality incites violence. Three ostensibly factual arguments for acquitting inequality of this particular charge have been put forward. The first is that "absolute poverty" is the real culprit and that inequality (or "relative poverty") is just an innocent bystander that had the misfortune to be in the wrong place at the wrong time. The second argument is that because temporal trends in inequality and violence don't always proceed in lockstep, they must be mutually irrelevant. The third is that simple, small-scale, band-level societies are the most egalitarian societies in the world, but are nevertheless some of the most lethal societies.

We saw in Chapter 4 that the first of these three arguments is simply false: The evidence implicating inequality survives statistical controls for effects of "absolute poverty," and the evidence for the relevance of the latter is actually much shakier than the evidence pointing at inequality. In Chapter 8, we considered the second empirical argument against inequality's role in causing violence, and concluded that its logic is untenable: Any effects of inequality on violence are necessarily going to be delayed effects, so there was never any reason to *expect* a tight

197

synchrony in the short-run ups and downs of homicide and income inequality. In this final chapter, we will consider the third and final argument that the defenders of inequality have put forward.

In efforts to understand the human capacity for violence, "simple" societies, especially those of hunter-gatherers, are regularly press-ganged into service on behalf of one of two opposing caricatures of life before governments. The first caricature is that which Thomas Hobbes imagined: the "Warre Of Every One Against Every One." The second is that of a peaceful Eden peopled by "Noble Savages," stock characters in jeremiads against the evils of modernity. The central conceit of this second morality tale is that people are virtuous creatures by nature, and their manifest nastiness must therefore be understood as the artificial consequence of some venal innovation, be it patriarchy, colonialism, capitalism, or whatever. Earlier romantics blamed "civilization."

Plenty of ethnographic evidence can be mustered as support for these diametrically opposed visions. Advocates of the misanthropic alternative recount lurid tales of lethal raiding, the abduction of women, and opportunistic massacres. Advocates of the pollyannaish alternative prefer portraits of democratic, egalitarian, even leisurely, tribal life around the campfire. The stories that support both sides of the argument are well documented. Both parables are, at best, half-truths.

Throughout this book, I have maintained that human beings, especially men, possess an evolved capacity for self-interested violence in competitive situations, and that interpreting that capacity as pathological is misguided and ultimately unhelpful. I know that in the eyes of some readers, this will brand me a Hobbesian misanthrope: one of those benighted "social Darwinists" who mistakenly believe that human nature is, at its core, nasty rather than nice. Well, sorry, but I am no such thing, and I don't know anyone else who is, either. Human nature is *both* nasty *and* nice. If it were not, we would have very little to talk about.

My subject has been inequality, competition, and interpersonal violence, and the reasons why these phenomena are apparently intertwined. I have not said a great deal about egalitarianism, cooperation, and the peaceful resolution of differences—the antitheses of inequality, competition, and violence—partly because plenty of other people have written about those phenomena and their evolution. But although I have said little about these prosocial "flip sides" of the evils that have been my focus, I hope it is obvious that when I decry those evils and seek to identify their determinants, I am implicitly assuming that equality, cooperation, and nonviolence are attainable alternatives.[1]

In short, the question with which I began this section—whether human beings are by nature murderous or conciliatory, warlike or peaceful, nasty or nice—is inane. We possess complex, specialized, evolved capacities for a range of prosocial and antisocial behavior. Which of those capacities will be expressed is *conditional*, and all the meaningful questions whose answers might help alleviate human suffering are variants on one big question: "Conditional on what?" One big piece of the answer is that nasty-or-nice is conditional on inequality in wealth and opportunity.

Egalitarianism and Violence in "Simple Societies"

When criminologists ask why homicide rates vary, they attend primarily to modern nation states, and secondarily to historical records. They have paid scant attention to the nonstate, face-to-face societies that anthropologists study and that best reflect the social milieus of human evolution. One exception was a 1991 study by two well-known homicide researchers, Rick Rosenfeld and Steven Messner, who wondered if the relevant variables might be different in such societies, and concluded that they are indeed different, summarizing their investigation as follows:

> A consistent finding to emerge from cross-national studies of crime is a positive relationship between the degree of social inequality and levels of homicide. This finding contrasts with the results of anthropological case studies that reveal high rates of homicide in some extremely egalitarian societies. Viewed together, these two sets of findings raise the question of whether the patterns observed in cross-national research on homicide are generalizable to the typically small, nonindustrial "simple societies" studied by anthropologists, but generally neglected by comparative sociologists. We address this issue in an analysis of homicide for a sample of small, nonindustrial societies. Our findings indicate that the degree of inequality in such societies is not significantly associated with the level of homicide.

[1] The evolution of cooperation has been a central issue in biology for decades; see, e.g., Bourke (2011). De Waal (1989) has made the case for evolved "peacemaking" adaptations that are as complex and specialized as those for violence. Boehm (1999, 2012) argues with extensive ethnographic backing that band-level societies achieve egalitarianism as a compromise outcome between evolved motives to dominate and to avoid being dominated, with the latter able to prevail because of our exceptional evolved cooperative capabilities.

As far as I know, criminologists have never again tried to incorporate such societies into cross-cultural homicide analyses, and citations of this one study have been uncritically accepting of its non-result. That is unfortunate. The conclusion that inequality and homicide are unrelated in "simple societies" was certainly premature, and almost certainly wrong.[2]

The analyses in the Rosenfeld and Messner study included just thirty-two societies. And what made them "simple"? The two criminologists acknowledge that some societies in their sample had "highly complex kin, religious, or other institutions," but decreed that they qualified as "simple" by virtue of being societies with "less complex political and economic organizations, and typically smaller in size, than state-level industrial or industrializing societies." Most of the thirty-two societies had little stratification or role differentiation other than that between the sexes, so that each individual had to be something of a jack-of-all-(gender-appropriate)-trades. But there are a couple of odd exceptions, such as the relatively modern and role-differentiated society of the Serbs (before there was a Serbian nation state) and the highly stratified and complex Wolof society of West Africa. The predominant mode of subsistence among the thirty-two societies was by farming lands held and inherited familially, but the sample also included some full- or part-time hunter-gatherers, nomadic herders, and slash-and-burn horticulturalists. What all thirty-two actually seem to have had in common is that each had a language of its own, and yet had no recognized state.

So what is the nature of the evidence that inequality and violence varied independently of one another in this sample? First, each society was classified on the basis of non-quantitative ethnographic descriptions as exhibiting either "frequent" (n = 21) or "infrequent" (n = 11) acts of "defiant homicide". Whether this binary classification even succeeded in creating two groups with different mean homicide rates, let alone split them cleanly into two non-overlapping groups, is unknown, but this is the sole outcome variable on which all conclusions were based. Four other variables, borrowed from an unpublished PhD thesis on religious movements, were treated as proxies for inequality, and as such, these have even lower face validity than the homicide codes: None of the four

---

[2] The long quote is from the abstract of Rosenfeld and Messner (1991, 51). An example of uncritical acceptance of their non-result is Chamlin and Cochran (2005), who cite it as showing "that inequality is unrelated to homicide in simple, undifferentiated societies" (22) and hence that theory linking inequality and homicide must focus on the peculiarities of "modern societies".

putative indices of inequality had any quantitative basis, nor was any of them even conceptually akin to an index of the distribution of desired goods like the Gini. The fact that these crude and largely irrelevant predictors were not demonstrably associated with the equally crude "defiant homicide" classification, within this small sample, provides the basis for Rosenfeld and Messner's negative conclusion.[3]

So let's start over. A useful first-pass distinction is that between peoples whose diets derive from domesticated animals and/or cultivated plants, on the one hand, and those who subsist on foraged wild foods, on the other. The latter life style, that of hunting and gathering, was how all humans lived until about the last ten thousand years, and it rarely if ever provided an economic basis for the sort of extreme inequality that began to appear as people began to amass large herds and agricultural surpluses. Agriculture also permitted a less nomadic way of life that allowed political differentiation to emerge within settled communities with shared defensive needs, even when it did not entail large surpluses or herds.[4]

Did the transition to agriculture, with its attendant tendency toward elevated inequality, lead to higher levels of lethal conflict? The available evidence suggests that it did. Surprisingly high violent death rates at the hands of fellow tribesmen have characterized some hunter-gatherer societies, and we will come back to this shortly, but it appears that those rates were in general even higher among more settled farmers. Anthropologists Luke Glowacki and Richard Wrangham compiled the best available data on death rates due to "simple warfare" in twenty "acephalous" (headless) nonstate societies, ten farmers, and ten

---

[3] A "defiant homicide" is defined as one that is deemed illegitimate by the larger society *and* by a majority of the killer's own kin; if taken literally, this criterion would eliminate (among many others) all killings to avenge slain kinsmen, which comprise the majority of *all* homicides in some of the societies in Rosenfeld and Messner's sample.

The "inequality" measures are from an unpublished PhD thesis (Justinger 1978); the coding rules can be found at http://huberb.people.cofc.edu/www/Cross%20Cultural%20Data/ANTH%20 491%20PSF%2060%20Variable%20List%20Fall%202011.pdf. The only one of these four variables with an explicit link to wealth was labeled "relative deprivation," and it was constructed not with the aim of representing actual inequality, even crudely, but as an index of mismatches between normative aspirations and the attainable.

[4] Regarding the relationship between inequality by various criteria and mode of subsistence, see Nielsen (2004).

Native Americans on the west coast of Canada and adjacent USA had a sufficiently reliable and abundant food source (salmon) that they could be non-nomadic hunter-gatherers in large settled communities with social role differentiation, stratification, and warfare similar to what is more typical of communities growing staple crops; see, e.g., Ruyle (1973).

hunter-gatherers, all of whom lacked formal chiefly offices or other statuses that bestow authority.

> Simple warfare is distinguished from modern warfare by a lack of clear military leaders, an absence of explicit punitive sanctions for non-participation, and infrequent occurrences of battles and larger conflicts. It consists of surprise raids, ambushes, feuding, chance encounters, and arranged conflicts between individuals of different communities.

Mortality in such contexts varied widely across cultures, with the rates for hunter-gatherers overlapping those for farmers, but on average, the farmers incurred violent death rates that were approximately twice those of hunter-gatherers, a significant difference.[5]

A tricky issue here is the distinction between "homicide," which has been our focus in earlier chapters, and "warfare." When war is conducted by nation states ruled by governments with a degree of legitimacy, then killing enemy combatants is itself legitimized, and is not typically counted as homicide; even killings of *non*-combatant members of the enemy polity are legitimized more often than not, although they are less often glorified. The distinction between an illegitimate ("criminal" or "defiant") homicide and a legitimate act of war gets murkier in the sort of warfare considered by Glowacki and Wrangham. Here, enemies were often personally acquainted, the "different communities" were often products of the fissioning of a larger village within living memory, and participation was voluntary, depending on the individual warrior's personal motives, such as his desire to avenge a wrong perpetrated by one or more individuals in the village being attacked or his ambition to abduct a wife.

Rob Walker and Drew Bailey have amassed cause of death data for eleven well-studied lowland South American tribal groups, almost all of whom both hunted and gardened, and estimate that an average of 30 percent of all deaths after infancy (and a much higher proportion of the deaths of men) resulted from lethal attacks. Approximately half of those killings occurred in the course of "external warfare" with non-tribal enemies, with the other half comprising both "internal warfare" (raids between villages, conducted mainly in order to abduct women or avenge prior deaths) and homicides in which the killer and victim were residents of the same village.[6]

---

[5] The quote is from Glowacki and Wrangham (2013, 444). See also Wrangham et al. (2006).
[6] See Walker and Bailey (2013).

Most of the societies in the cross-cultural studies discussed above have been referred to in the anthropological literature, at one time or another, as "egalitarian." With no widely recognized official leaders, and with individuals free to opt out of raids or other costly collective activities, these societies certainly appear to be egalitarian with respect to decision-making authority, and in most of them, there are few material possessions, limiting important differences in what we would ordinarily think of as wealth. But how we should think about wealth and its distribution is not necessarily straightforward. Even in a society with the simplest technology and very few material possessions, some individuals may be well endowed in some sense while others are destitute.

An interdisciplinary group of anthropologists and economists has recently proposed that in addition to "material wealth," there are two other categories of wealth that can be amassed, inherited by one's offspring, and more or less equitably distributed. "Embodied wealth" refers to both physical attributes and skills that have value, and which may be transmitted from parents to their children by various routes, of which genetic inheritance is just one. "Relational wealth" is more or less the same thing as what sociologists call "social capital": the social positions and connections that affect one's capacity to recruit assistance from other community members. The research team, headed by anthropologist Monique Borgerhoff Mulder, attempted to quantify both the degree to which each of the three types of wealth is transmitted across generations and the extent to which it is inequitably distributed, in each of twenty-one well-studied small-scale societies. Their conclusion:

> Intergenerational transmission of wealth and wealth inequality are substantial among pastoral and small-scale agricultural societies (on a par with or even exceeding the most unequal modern industrial economies) but are limited among horticultural and foraging peoples (equivalent to the most egalitarian of modern industrial populations). Differences in the technology by which a people derive their livelihood and in the institutions and norms making up the economic system jointly contribute to this pattern.[7]

Borgerhoff Mulder and her collaborators found that the inheritance of wealth and its unequal distribution go hand in hand, and persuasively argued that this is so because intergenerational transmission

---

[7] See Borgerhoff Mulder et al. (2009); the quoted conclusion is from their abstract (682).

is largely responsible for generating the inequality. Their conclusion that inequality is more extreme among pastoralists and agriculturalists than among hunter-gatherers is based on a very small sample, but I am persuaded of its soundness because plenty of other ethnographic evidence supports it. What I find least convincing is their conclusion that horticulturalists—whose gardening without the plow distinguishes them from agriculturalists—have low levels of inequality similar to those among hunter-gatherers. A curious aspect of the analysis was that reproductive success was treated as one measure of "embodied wealth," on a par with body weight, grip strength, and various measured skills. Inequality in reproductive success was computed for only two unusual hunter-gatherer societies—Lamalera and Meriam—both of which were settled village-dwelling hunters of large marine animals, and for three horticulturalists, of which the lone South American society—the Tsimane—had far and away the lowest violent death rate of the "hunter-farmers" in Walker and Bailey's study. These considerations suggest that inequality may have been atypically high in Borgerhoff Mulder et al.'s small sample of hunter-gatherers and atypically low in their small sample of horticulturalists, masking differences that would become apparent in a larger and more representative sample of societies.

One tribal society that was not included in their study is that of the Yanomamö, hunter-horticulturalists who occupy the Amazonian borderlands of Venezuela and Brazil. Yanomamö society is frequently called "egalitarian" because there are no recognized chiefs or social strata and little in the way of differential material wealth. In terms of the crucial currency of access to women and to reproductive opportunity, however, the Yanomamö are not at all egalitarian! When Napoleon Chagnon began his studies of these people in 1964, he met several of the adult offspring of a prolific reproducer named Matakuwä ("Shinbone") who had died a quarter century earlier. Shinbone's eleven wives had borne him twenty sons and twenty-three daughters, and they in turn had given him 231 grandchildren. A few other Yanomamö men, including two of Shinbone's brothers, also had large numbers of wives, children, and grandchildren. It follows that a great many Yanomamö boys and men must have died childless.[8]

Might the Yanomamö be exceptional among acephalous hunter-horticulturalists? There is no reason to believe that they are. Although Chagnon famously (and controversially) dubbed them "the fierce

---

[8] Chagnon (1997) details the career of "Shinbone," among others.

people," in recognition of men's pride in warriorship, and although he has demonstrated that *unokais*—men who have performed the ritual purification that is required of those who have killed—had more wives and children than nonkillers, there is no evidence that the Yanomamö society he described was an exceptionally bloody one. According to Walker and Bailey, their violent death rate was actually below average for Amazonian lowland societies: Violent deaths made up an estimated 22 percent of all Yanomamö deaths, a proportion that was surpassed by seven of the other ten societies for which comparable estimates could be derived. That 22 percent value would also be surpassed by various New Guinea horticulturalists, not all of whom engage in "warfare."[9]

As regards polygyny and differential reproduction, there is again no reason to suppose that the Yanomamö were exceptional among acephalous hunter-farmers. Shinbone's reproductive career was remarkable, to be sure, but prolific breeding by a handful of men has been noted in other similar societies. The Xavante Indians of western Brazil, for example, are somewhat more dependent on hunting wild foods than the Yanomamö, and somewhat less polygynous, but when the medical anthropologist James Neel and collaborators visited a Xavante village in 1962, its ninety-one inhabitants included twenty-three living children of one man, Apewe, who was the so-called village "chief" in the sense that he was the senior man in the largest patrilineage. Furthermore, it is worth remarking that what provokes most of the lethal violence within Yanomamö and other horticulturalist villages is either immediate competition over women or revenge for prior abductions and killings that were thus motivated.[10]

In nomadic hunter-gatherer societies, by contrast, nothing remotely like Shinbone's cascade of descendants has ever been documented. In Nancy Howell's study of the Kalahari !Kung San (the basis for figure 3.2), one man sired twelve children and the second most prolific sired nine. Other hunter-gatherers for whom we have exceptionally good census and demographic data are the Hadza of Tanzania and the Ache of Paraguay;

---

[9] Regarding the marital and reproductive advantages of unokais, see Chagnon (1988). The 22 percent violent death rate and the comparative claim are based on Walker and Bailey (2013), Table 1. Regarding violent death rates in horticultural societies in New Guinea, see, e.g., Knauft (1987) and Keeley (1996).

[10] The Xavante information is from Neel et al. (1964). Regarding the relevance of competition over women to lethal conflicts, see Chagnon (1987, 1988). Regarding competition over women as the primary provocation for violence within villages, see Chagnon (1997).

their respective paternity maxima are sixteen and thirteen (of whom ten survived to five years of age).[11]

The societies of Australian aborigines stand out among hunter-gatherers for their exceptional levels of marital polygyny, and it is here that we might expect to see the greatest variability in reproductive success. But having many wives doesn't necessarily translate into having exceptional numbers of children. A revealing case history is that of Ki-in-kumi, "the most influential man in Malau and the head of the biggest household" in C.W.M. Hart and Arnold Pilling's classic ethnography of the Tiwi of Melville and Bathurst Islands off Australia's north coast. The Tiwi marriage system was gerontocratic: Older men monopolized young brides and gave their daughters in marriage, for political reasons, to other old men, while younger men could initially marry only widows much older than themselves. At the time of Hart and Pilling's study, Ki-in-kumi was sixty-six years old and had run up a formidable list of twenty-one wives. Looking more closely, however, we discover that six of these were elderly widows when he married them, and an additional five who had been bestowed upon him by their fathers had died before attaining puberty. Yet another was still only nine years old, and was still living in her natal home. So the twenty-one wives actually included only nine with whom Ki-in-kumi could possibly have reproduced, and in fact, he had just eight living offspring. According to Hart and Pilling, other highly successful men had similar marital and reproductive careers.[12]

In short, hunter-gatherers were relatively egalitarian in the crucial currency of male reproductive opportunity. But with the advent of settled agriculture, that changed. Evolutionary anthropologist Laura Betzig has reviewed the available evidence on differential reproduction in traditional societies, and summarized her findings as follows:

> Data on reproductive success in traditional cultures suggest that for men, but not for women, range and variance rise as subsistence intensifies. For hunter-gatherers, ranges and variances tend to cluster in single digits: they reach 15 or 16, at the high end. For herder-gardeners, ranges and variances are more consistently in double digits: they get as high as 80 or 85. And for full-time agriculturalists in the first civilizations, ranges consistently ran to triple

---

[11] These maximum numbers of progeny come from Howell (1979) for the !Kung, Marlowe (2010) for the Hadza, and Hill and Hurtado (1996) for the Ache.
[12] See Hart and Pilling (1960); the quoted line is from page 63.

digits: emperors from Mesopotamia to Peru were the fathers of hundreds of children.[13]

Finally, the evidence that inequality is in fact predictive of violence in "simple" societies is not limited to comparisons across modes of subsistence, such as the distinction between hunter-gatherers and farmers. If we narrow our focus to hunter-gatherers alone, there is still fairly strong evidence that greater inequality, as manifested in a higher incidence of polygyny, is associated with greater competition and violence among men. Cambridge anthropologist Frank Marlowe has analyzed the associations among various cultural practices and other attributes in a sample consisting of the thirty-six societies that meet the rather stringent definitional criteria for being called hunter-gatherers within the larger 186-society "Standard Cross-cultural Sample." He found that the prevalence of polygynous marriage is significantly associated with measures of both assaults within the community and internal (but not external) warfare. His analyses furthermore suggest that the causal links run primarily from the inequality to the violence, rather than the reverse, although effects in both directions remain plausible.[14]

The measurement and comparison of inequality in small-scale non-state societies is still in its infancy, and estimates of violent death rates in small populations will always be inherently noisy. But with those caveats, the evidence that is presently available strongly suggests that the conclusions reached by Rosenfeld and Messner were wrong, and that the level of inequality is in fact a predictor and a determinant of the corresponding level of violence in simple societies, much as it is in more complex ones such as modern nation states.

What Else Makes a Difference?

In the opening section of this final chapter, I stated my central thesis thus: The evolved human capacity for violence is expressed conditionally, and a big part of what lethal violence is conditional *on* is inequality in wealth and opportunity. But inequality is assuredly not the only relevant factor. What else might violence be conditional upon?

Strong cases grounded in an evolutionary perspective on human nature have been made for at least four additional considerations that influence whether individuals will resort to violence to settle

---

[13] Quoted from Betzig (2012, 309). See also Nielsen (2004).
[14] These analyses were reported by Marlowe (2003).

their disputes: the availability of disinterested third-party justice, the effectiveness of policing, attitudes toward the government, and the prevailing cultural norms about various things including violence itself and the consideration due to others. None of these is altogether independent of the others, nor, for that matter, of inequality.

Let's consider each of these four additional factors briefly, beginning with impartial third-party justice. Unbiased nonviolent dispute resolution procedures are strongly institutionalized and widely available in some settings, virtually nonexistent in others. If there is no justice system to which the parties to a dispute can entrust its resolution, then every man has to be prepared to enforce "self-help" justice, which boils down to defending his interests—with whatever backing he can muster from his kinsmen and other allies—by threat of violence. This is the ethos of the lawless frontier, which has been particularly well described and analyzed by University of North Florida historian David Courtwright. It is also the situation of most of the small-scale societies discussed above, especially those hunter-gatherers and pastoralists who had no fixed home base and were therefore highly vulnerable to attack by rivals bent on expropriating their wives or livestock. And as Courtwright aptly details, it remains the situation for a large underclass in contemporary urban environments.[15]

Policing is obviously a closely linked issue. It's all very well to have an impartial third party rule on how disputes ought fairly to be resolved, but what is to prevent those who are ruled against from reverting to self-help? The answer is surely deterrence, and if we don't want to find ourselves back on a lawless frontier where the third-party judge is powerless and superfluous, that deterrence must also be provided by someone other than the principals to the dispute. There is some evidence that police numbers and police presence have a dampening effect on rates of crime, including homicide, and it would be surprising if they did not. Like every other animal with a brain, *Homo sapiens* has, after all, evolved to let indicators of the probable costs and benefits of alternative courses of action influence decision-making.[16]

Of course, not all "policing" is provided by professional police. Civilian bystanders can be important enforcers. Christopher Boehm has argued that a sort of collective police action against those who are

---

[15] Regarding self-help justice in "frontier" and modern urban societies, see Courtwright (1996).
[16] For evidence that police affect rates of crime including homicide, see Marvell and Moody (1996), Paré (2014).

excessively self-interested characterized the social environments of human evolution, and that "leveling" practices of mockery, derision, ostracism, and other punishments imposed upon unduly ambitious men continue to generate the relative egalitarianism of acephalous band societies today. Indeed, Boehm has amassed considerable evidence that in many hunter-gatherer societies, many of the killings that make their rates of violence surprisingly high are themselves part of this leveling process: the consensual executions of men whose ambitions and anti-social behavior could not otherwise be contained. More generally, Boehm proposes that the egalitarianism of small-scale societies must not be misunderstood as the antithesis of competitive rivalry, but is instead such competition's consequence and its remedy:

> Humans deliberately create and carefully maintain "reverse dominance hierarchies" whereby the potentially subordinate adult males— the rank and file—band together *assertively* to limit the dominance of more aggressive or otherwise outstanding individuals. I have surveyed a large number of egalitarian societies (simple foragers, complex foragers, and many others) from various cultural areas and found evidence of such behavior. The result is far from an absence of male rivalry or inequality, but there is a sharply negative response if someone behaves too assertively or tries to control other males. This syndrome relates to personal autonomy: males will not countenance being "bossed around".[17]

Exactly what it is that motivates third parties to punish transgressors, even in contemporary mass society, has become a lively area of research in experimental economics and social psychology. Some researchers contend that "inequality aversion" or some other explicitly egalitarian motive explains the surprising willingness of many experimental subjects to incur costs in order to right witnessed wrongs that have no direct effects on themselves. Other investigators counter with studies designed to show that equitable outcomes are not important objectives in their own right, but emerge as byproducts of urges to advertise unwillingness to be subordinated, to punish cheats, or to "cut down tall poppies." Either way, we have circled back to the issue of human preferences, tastes, and motives that are egalitarian in their consequences.[18]

---

[17] The quote is from Boehm (1991, 411). See Boehm (1999, 2012) for fuller accounts of the effectively egalitarian leveling practices of hunter-gatherers.

[18] For various perspectives on the motives and objectives that generate egalitarian or leveling effects, see, e.g., Bolton and Ockenfels (2000), Dawes et al. (2007), Yamagishi et al. (2009), and Gavrilets (2012).

Do attitudes toward governments affect rates of violent crime? In his 2009 book *American Homicide*, Ohio State University historian Randolph Roth makes the case that the variability in homicide rates within the United States—both over time and across regions—has closely tracked the citizenry's acceptance of their government as legitimate. In a more recent article, he has summarized his thesis and extended its compass beyond the United States:

> There have been four correlates of low [homicide] rates in North America and Western Europe over the past 450 years:

> (1) the belief that government is stable and that its legal and judicial institutions are unbiased and will redress wrongs and protect lives and property;
> (2) a feeling of trust in government and the officials who run it, and a belief in their legitimacy;
> (3) patriotism, empathy, and fellow feeling arising from racial, religious, or political solidarity;
> (4) the belief that the social hierarchy is legitimate, that one's position in society is or can be satisfactory and that one can command the respect of others without resorting to violence.

These are interpretive claims, not straightforward empirical observations. All these putative correlates had to be inferred indirectly from a mishmash of sources—no pollster has asked standardized questions about these matters at standard intervals—and Roth furthermore concedes that his homicide rate estimates are often far from air-tight. I have trouble crediting the notion that attitudes toward government are major determinants of swings in the homicide rate, given that those swings primarily reflect changes in the behavior of an underclass for whom governments are scarcely visible. But insofar as Roth's conclusions are valid, it is easy to interpret them as additional twists on the factors that we have just been discussing, rather than as an additional, distinct influence on homicide. The "legitimacy" that Roth sees as a suppressor of violence is evidently more or less synonymous with the extent to which individuals believe that the government, police, and judicial system defend their interests and make their aspirations realistic.[19]

The issue of what role "legitimacy" might play in causing violence brings us to the fourth and final item on my list of factors other than inequality that have been proposed to affect the statistical incidence of violence in

---

[19] See Roth (2009, 2011). The quotation about four correlates of homicide is from Roth (2011, 544).

a given society: that society's prevailing norms. In Chapter 7, I explained my reservations about the proposition that violent values explain violent behavior, but it was not my conclusion that the idea is utterly wrong. People clearly respond to the reactions that their behavior elicits, and that being so, violent aggression must be relatively likely where it will elicit admiration and relatively unlikely where it will be abhorred, all else equal. Moreover, social responsiveness isn't merely a matter of sensitivity to the audience at hand. It extends to the socialization of children and hence to the values that they internalize, with potential life-long effects. Cultural norms and values undeniably affect behavior. My primary criticism of theories that give them a leading role in the explanation of violence rests on the observation that people are not culture's puppets: They rebel, questioning the wisdom that their elders try to impart, especially during adolescence, and norms are therefore unstable on a generational time scale, *unless* they are backed up by ecological and institutional factors that maintain their utility as guides about how to behave.[20]

The Power of Ideas

What we have just been revisiting is an ancient debate between *materialism* and *idealism*. Are cultural differences primarily to be understood as responses evoked by the incentive structure of the environment, or as the consequences of the social transmission of different ways of thinking? The proposition that cultural phenomena are "evoked" is a materialist claim that they constitute the responses of a universal human nature to ecological and economic determinants. The contrary proposition that cultural phenomena are "transmitted" implies an idealist claim that the attitudes, values, and construals of reality that one learns from others are the causes of one's behavior. There is, of course, truth in both of these positions, which ensures that the debate never dies. The question of how *much* truth each of these alternative perspectives contains arises with reference to each specific cultural phenomenon under investigation.[21]

---

[20] Humans possess a unique reliance on the wisdom of prior generations, but the benefits of culture's cumulative capacity haven't come for free. Learning from others creates vulnerabilities: Much of what other people (even parents) want young to do and to believe serves their parental interests, not the young's, and these conflicts of interest are selection pressures favoring a nuanced skepticism; see Trivers (1985). Targets of socialization efforts therefore take it all in with a considerable grain of salt, and may reject local norms and values wholesale.

[21] Regarding the history of quarrels between idealists and materialists in the social sciences, see, e.g., Harris (1968), Gangestad et al. (2006), Daly and Wilson (2010).

The Better Angels of our Nature, Steven Pinker's 2011 tome on "why violence has declined" can be read as a spirited defense of the idealist position, since Pinker, following the German sociologist Norbert Elias (1897–1990), stresses the civilizing effects of the spread of enlightenment values. But Pinker's argument is more subtle and multi-faceted than just that. He suggests that "five historical forces" have played causal roles in the downward trend in violence over recent centuries, and explains at least a couple of them in terms that have a strongly materialistic element:

> *The Leviathan*, a state and judiciary with a monopoly on the legitimate use of force, can defuse the temptation of exploitative attack, inhibit the impulse for revenge, and circumvent the self-serving biases that make all parties believe they are on the side of the angels. *Commerce* is a positive-sum game in which everyone can win; as technological progress allows the exchange of goods and ideas over longer distances and among larger groups of trading partners, other people become more valuable alive than dead, and they are less likely to become targets of demonization and dehumanization.[22]

Pinker has been accused by the historian Gregory Hanlon of playing fast and loose with historical data in order to tell a smoother tale of progress in human affairs than the evidence warrants. But regardless of the merits of Hanlon's critique, there is no question that the overall trend in homicide rates in the western world over recent centuries has been dramatically downward, and there can be little doubt that the forces that Pinker calls *Leviathan* and *Commerce* played major roles. My only significant quarrel with Pinker concerns his casual dismissal—which I refuted in Chapter 8—of the importance of inequality. Ironically, the historical tale that Pinker tells is a tale of a long, stuttering decline in various sorts of inequality and in various sorts of violence.[23]

The materialism–idealism opposition has a distinct odor of the ivory tower, but it is not inconsequential. To the extent that culture is an "evoked" response to incentives, it can be changed by manipulating those incentives. But if it is more a matter of attitudes and values that cohere in a socially valued belief system, then the required remedies

---

[22] The quoted passage is from Pinker (2011, xxvi).
[23] See Hanlon (2013) for a detailed and rather scathing critique of Pinker's historical scholarship, a critique that is then leavened by an appreciation of other aspects of Pinker's book, as well as by even sharper critiques of historical treatments of the subject that lack Pinker's evolution-based understanding of human nature.

may be different. People's positions in these controversies, which are not independent of their politics, have policy implications. Idealists tend to favor educational and "consciousness-raising" remedies for social problems. Those with more materialist views favor attacking economic "root causes."

I am more of a materialist than an idealist. I see little evidence that violence can be effectively countered by the intrinsic rectitude or persuasive power of humane, civilized values. Those values have been effectual only when they take the concrete and consequential form of hard-won, vigilantly maintained institutions. Nonviolent beliefs and values are most readily subscribed to and adhered to when realistic ambitions for a better life do not require violence. In other words, nonviolent beliefs and values are able to counteract violence if and only if they are backed up by institutions that effectively counter excessive, unjust inequality.

References

Agnew, R. 1992. "Foundation for a General Strain Theory of Crime and Delinquency." *Criminology* 30:47–87.

Alberts, S., J. C. Buchan, and J. Altmann. 2006. "Sexual Selection in Wild Baboons: From Mating Opportunities to Paternity Success." *Animal Behaviour* 72:1177–96.

Alesina, A., and E. Glaeser. 2004. *Fighting Poverty in the U.S. and Europe: A World of Difference.* Oxford: Oxford University Press.

Alesina, A., E. Glaeser, and B. Sacerdote. 2001. "Why Doesn't the United States have a European-style Welfare State?" *Brookings Papers on Economic Activity* 2:1–69.

Alesina, A., and D. Rodrik. 1994. "Distributive Politics and Economic Growth." *Quarterly Journal of Economics* 109:465–90.

Alexander, G., and M. Hines. 2002. "Sex Differences in Response to Children's Toys in Nonhuman Primates (*Cercopithecus aethiops sabaeus*)." *Evolution & Human Behavior* 23:467–79.

Alexander, R. D. 1987. *The Biology of Moral Systems.* Hawthorne, NY: Aldine de Gruyter.

Alexander, R. D., J. L. Hoogland, R. D. Howard, K. M. Noonan, and P. W. Sherman. 1979. "Sexual Dimorphisms and Breeding Systems in Pinnipeds, Ungulates, Primates, and Humans." In Evolutionary Biology and Human Social Behavior, edited by N. A. Chagnon, W. Irons, 402–35. North Scituate, MA: Duxbury Press.

Alvard, M. S. 2003. "The Adaptive Nature of Culture." *Evolutionary Anthropology* 12:136–49.

Anazawa, M. 2011. "Bottom-up Derivation of Population Models for Competition Involving Multiple Resources." *Theoretical Population Biology* 81:158–67.

Anderson, E. 1994. "The Code of the Streets." *The Atlantic Monthly* May:81–94.

Anderson, E. 1999. *Code of the Street: Decency, Violence, and the Moral Life of the Inner City.* New York: W. W. Norton.

Archer, J. 2006. "Testosterone and Human Aggression: An Evaluation of the Challenge Hypothesis." *Neuroscience & Biobehavioral Reviews* 30:319–45.

Arciero, P. J., M. I. Goran, and E. T. Poehlman. 1993. "Resting Metabolic Rate is Lower in Women than in Men." *Journal of Applied Physiology* 75:2514–20.

Arlacchi, P. 1983. *Mafia, Peasants and Great Estates. Society in Traditional Calabria.* Cambridge, UK: Cambridge University Press.

Arnett, J. 2008. "The Neglected 95%: Why American Psychology Needs to Become Less American." *American Psychologist* 63:602–14.

Arrow, K. J. 1974. *The Limits of Organization.* New York: Norton.

Atkinson, A. B., and A. Brandolini. 2009. "On Data: A Case Study of the Evolution of Income Inequality Across Time and Across Countries." *Cambridge Journal of Economics* 33:381–404.

Atkinson, A. B., T. Piketty, and E. Saez. 2011. "Top Incomes in the Long Run of History." *Journal of Economic Literature* 49:3–71.

Austen, S. 2002. "An International Comparison of Attitudes to Inequality." *International Journal of Social Economics* 29:218–37.

Babones, S. 2008. "Income Inequality and Population Health. Correlation and causality." *Social Science & Medicine* 66:1614–26.

Babones, S. J., and M. J. Alvarez-Rivadulla. 2007. "Standardized Income Inequality Data for Use in Cross-national Research." *Sociological Inquiry* 77:3–22.

Ball-Rokeach, S. J. 1973. "Values and Violence: A Test of the Subculture of Violence Thesis." *American Sociological Review* 38:736–49.

Bateman, A. J. 1948. "Intrasexual Selection in *Drosophila*." *Heredity* 2:340–68.

Bee, H. L., S. K. Mitchell, K. E. Barnard, S. J. Eyres, and M. A. Hammond. 1984. "Predicting Intellectual Outcomes: Sex Differences in Response to Early Environmental Stimulation." *Sex Roles* 10:783–803.

Belsley, D. A., E. Kuh, and R. E. Welsch. 1980. *Regression Diagnostics: Identifying Influential Data and Sources of Collinearity.* New York: Wiley.

Behnke, A. 2008. *The Conquests of Genghis Khan.* Minneapolis, MN: Twenty-First Century Books.

Belsky, J. 1997. "Variation in Susceptibility to Environmental Influence: An Evolutionary Argument." *Psychological Inquiry* 8:182–6.

Bénabou, R. 1996. "Inequality and Growth." In *NBER Macroeconomics Annual 1996,* edited by B. S. Bernanke, J. J. Rotemberg, 11–74. Cambridge, MA: MIT Press.

Benedict, R. 1934. *Patterns of Culture.* New York: Houghton Mifflin.

Benson, D. S. 2006. *Six Emperors: Rise of the Mongolian Empire 1195 to 1295.* Mansfield, OH: Bookmasters.

Berg, A., J. D. Ostry, and J. Zettelmeyer. 2012. "What Makes Growth Sustained?" *Journal of Development Economics* 98:149–66.

Bernhardt, P. C., J. M. Dabbs, J. A. Fielden, and C. D. Lutter. 1998. "Testosterone Changes During Vicarious Experiences of Winning and Losing Among Fans at Sporting Events." *Physiology & Behavior* 65:59–62.

Best, S., and D. Kellner. 1999. "Rap, Black Rage, and Racial Difference." *Enculturation* 2:2, online at http://www.enculturation.net/2_2/best-kellner.html

Betzig, L. L. 1986. *Despotism and Differential Reproduction: A Darwinian View of History.* New York: Aldine.

Betzig, L. 2012. "Means, Variances, and Ranges in Reproductive Success: Comparative Evidence." *Evolution & Human Behavior* 33:309–17.

Betzig, L. 2014. "Eusociality in History." *Human Nature* 25:80–99.

Beyer, S., and E. Bowden. 1997. "Gender Differences in Self-perceptions: Convergent Evidence from Three Measures of Accuracy and Bias." *Personality & Social Psychology Bulletin* 23:157–72.

Bivens, J. 2012. "Inequality, Exhibit A: Walmart and the Wealth of American Families." *Economic Policy Institute Blog.* Downloaded http://www.epi.org/blog/inequality-exhibit-wal-mart-wealth-american/

Blanchflower, D. G., and A. J. Oswald. 1998. "What Makes an Entrepreneur?" *Journal of Labor Economics* 16:26–60.

Black, D. 1983. "Crime as Social Control." *American Sociological Review* 48:34–45.

Blau, J. R., and P. M. Blau. 1982. "The Cost of Inequality: Metropolitan Structure and Violent Crime." *American Sociological Review* 47:114–29.

Block, R. 1976. "Homicide in Chicago: A Nine-year Study (1965–1973)." *Journal of Criminal Law & Criminology* 66:496–510.

Blumstein, A., and R. Rosenfeld. 1998. "Explaining Recent Trends in U.S. Homicide Rates." *Journal of Criminal Law & Criminology* 88:1175–216.

Boas, F. 1887. "Museums of Ethnology and Their Classification." *Science* 9:587–9.

Bobo, L. 1991. "Social Responsibility, Individualism, and Redistributive Policies." *Sociological Forum* 6:71–92.

Bock, G., and J. Whelan, eds. 1991. *The Childhood Environment and Adult Disease.* Chichester: Wiley.

Bock, J. 2002. "Learning, Life History, and Productivity. Children's Lives in the Okavango Delta, Botswana." *Human Nature* 13:161–97.

Boehm, C. 1991. Comment on B. M. Knauft, "Violence and Sociality in Human Evolution." *Current Anthropology* 32:391–428.

Boehm, C. 1999. *Hierarchy in the Forest: The Evolution of Egalitarian Behavior.* Cambridge, MA: Harvard University Press.

Boehm, C. 2003. "Global Conflict Resolution: An Anthropological Diagnosis of Problems with World Governance." In *Evolutionary Psychology and Violence,* edited by R. W. Bloom, N. Dess, 203–37. Westport, CT: Praeger.

Boehm, C. 2012. *Moral Origins. The Evolution of Altruism, Virtue, and Shame.* New York: Basic Books.

Bolton, D., and A. Ockenfels. 2000. "ERC: A Theory of Equity, Reciprocity, and Competition." *American Economic Review* 82:166–93.

Bonica, A., N. McCarty, K. T. Poole, and H. Rosenthal. 2013. "Why Hasn't Democracy Slowed Rising Inequality." *Journal of Economic Perspectives* 27:103–24.

Booth, A., D. A. Granger, A. Mazur, and K. T. Kivlighan. 2006. "Testosterone and Social Behavior." *Social Forces* 85:179–204.

Booth, A., G. Shelley, A. Mazur, G. Tharp, and R. Kittok. 1989. "Testosterone, and Winning and Losing in Human Competition." *Hormones & Behavior* 23:556–71.

Booth, A., and P. Nolen. 2012. "Choosing to Compete: How Different are Girls and Boys?" *Journal of Economic Behavior & Organization* 81:542–55.

Borgerhoff Mulder, M., S. Bowles, T. Hertz, A. Bell, J. Beise, G. Clark, I. Fazzio, M. Gurven, K. Hill, P. L. Hooper, W. Irons, H. Kaplan, D. Leonetti, B. Low, F. Marlowe, R. McElreath, S. Naidu, D. Nolin, P. Piraino, R. Quinlan, E. Schniter, R. Sear, M. Shenk, E. A. Smith, C. von Rueden, and P. Wiessner. 2009. "Intergenerational Wealth Transmission and the Dynamics of Inequality in Small-scale Societies." *Science* 326:682–8.

Bourke, A. F. G. 2011. *Principles of Social Evolution*. Oxford: Oxford University Press.

Bowles, S. 2012. *The New Economics of Inequality and Redistribution*. New York: Cambridge University Press.

Bowles, S., and A. Jayadev. 2012. "Garrison America." *The Economists' Voice* 4(2) (2012).

Brands, H. W. 2006. *Andrew Jackson: His Life and Times*. New York: Anchor Books.

Branson, R. 1998. *Losing My Virginity*. New York: Crown.

Brown, D. 1991. *Human Universals*. New York: McGraw-Hill.

Burnham, T. C. 2007. "High-Testosterone Men Reject Ultimatum Game Offers." *Proceedings of the Royal Society B Biological Sciences* 274:2327–30.

Buser, T. 2012. "The Impact of the Menstrual Cycle and Hormonal Contraceptives on Competitiveness." *Journal of Economic Behavior & Organization* 83:1–10.

Buss, D. M. 1997. "Human Social Motivation in Evolutionary Perspective: Grounding Terror Management Theory." *Psychological Inquiry* 8:22–6.

Byrnes, J. P., D. C. Miller, and W. D. Schafer. 1999. "Gender Differences in Risk Taking: A Meta-analysis." *Psychological Bulletin* 125:367–83.

Cao, L., A. Adams, and V. J. Jensen. 1997. "A Test of the Black Subculture of Violence Thesis: A Research Note." *Criminology* 35:367–79.

Cárdenas, J. C., A. Dreber, E. von Essen, and E. Ranehill. 2012. "Gender Differences in Competitiveness and Risk-taking: Comparing Children in Colombia and Sweden." *Journal of Economic Behavior & Organization* 83:11–23.

Carré, J. M., J. A. Campbell, E. Lozoya, S. S. M. Goetz, and K. M. Welker. 2013. "Changes in Testosterone Mediate the Effect of Winning on Subsequent Aggressive Behaviour." *Psychoneuroendocrinology* 38:2034–41.

Carré, J. M., and N. A. Olmstead. 2015. "Social Neuroendocrinology of Human Aggression: Examining the Role of Competition-induced Testosterone Dynamics." *Neuroscience* 286:171–86.

Chagnon, N. A. 1987. *Yanomamö*. 5th ed. Orlando, FL: Harcourt Brace.

Chagnon, N. A. 1988. "Life Histories, Blood Revenge, and Warfare in a Tribal Population." *Science* 239:985–92.

Chagnon, N. A. 1992. *Yanomamö: The last days of Eden*. New York: Harcourt Brace.

Chamlin, and J. K. Cochran. 2005. "Ascribed Economic Inequality and Homicide Among Modern Societies. Toward the Development of a Cross-national Theory." *Homicide Studies* 9:3–29.

Charness, G., and U. Gneezy. 2012. "Strong Evidence for Gender Differences in Risk Taking." *Journal of Economic Behavior & Organization* 83:50–8.

Charness, G., and M. Rabin. 2002. "Understanding Social Preferences with Simple Tests." *Quarterly Journal of Economics* 117:817–70.

Chetty, R., N. Hendren, P. Kline, and E. Saez. 2014. "Where is the Land of Opportunity? The Geography of Intergenerational Mobility in the United States." *Quarterly Journal of Economics* 129:1553–623.

Chu, R., C. Rivera, and C. Loftin. 2000. "Herding and Homicide: An Examination of the Nisbett-Reaves Hypothesis." *Social Forces* 78:971–87.

Clark, A. E., and A. J. Oswald. 1996. "Satisfaction and Comparison Income." *Journal of Public Economics* 61:359–81.

Clarke, G. R. G. 1995. "More Evidence on Income Distribution and Growth." *Journal of Development Economics* 47:403–27.

Clutton-Brock, T. H., and A. C. J. Vincent. 1991. "Sexual Selection and the Potential Reproductive Rates of Males and Females." *Nature* 351:58–60.

Cohen, D., and Nisbett, R. E. 1994. Self-protection and the Culture of Honor: Explaining Southern Violence. *Personality & Social Psychology Bulletin* 20:551–67.

Cohen, D., R. E. Nisbett, B. Bowdle, and N. Schwarz. 1996. "Insult, Aggression, and the Southern Culture of Honor: "An Experimental Ethnography.""" *Journal of Personality & Social Psychology* 70:945–60.

Cohen, L. E., and K. C. Land. 1987. "Age Structure and Crime." *American Sociological Review* 52:170–183.

Cohen, L. E., and R. Machalek. 1988. "A General Theory of Expropriative Crime. An Evolutionary Ecological Approach." *American Journal of Sociology* 94:465–501.

Cohen, L. E., and R. Machalek. 1994. "The Normalcy of Crime. From Durkheim to Evolutionary Ecology." *Rationality & Society* 6:286–308.

Corak, M. 2013a. "Income Inequality, Equality of Opportunity, and Intergenerational Mobility." *Journal of Economic Perspectives* 27:79–102.

Corak, M. 2013b. "Inequality from Generation to Generation. The United States in Comparison." In *The Economics of Inequality, Poverty, and Discrimination in the 21st Century. Volume 1: Causes*, edited by R. S. Rycroft, 107–23 Santa Barbara, CA: ABC-CLIO, LLC.

Cornish, D. B., and R. V. Clarke. 1986. *The Reasoning Criminal: Rational Choice Perspectives on Offending*. Secaucus, NJ: Springer-Verlag.

Cortright, R. N., and T. R. Koves. 2000. "Sex Differences in Substrate Metabolism and Energy Homeostasis." *Canadian Journal of Applied Physiology* 25:288–311.

Cosmides, L., and J. Tooby. 1999. "Toward an Evolutionary Taxonomy of Treatable Conditions." *Journal of Abnormal Psychology* 108:453–64.

Courtwright, D. T. 1996. *Violent Land. Single Men and Social Disorder from the Frontier to the Inner City*. Cambridge, MA: Harvard University Press.

Crosby, F. J. 1976. "A Model of Egoistic Relative Deprivation." *Psychological Review* 83:85–113.

Croson, R., and U. Gneezy. 2009. "Gender Differences in Preferences." *Journal of Economic Literature* 47:448–74.

Dabbs, J. M., and Dabbs. 2000. *Heroes, Rogues, and Lovers: Testosterone and Behavior*. New York: McGraw-Hill.

Daly, M., and M. Wilson. 1982. "Homicide and Kinship." *American Anthropologist* 84:372–8.

Daly, M., and M. Wilson. 1988a. "Evolutionary Social Psychology and Family Homicide." *Science* 242:519–24.

Daly, M., and M. Wilson. 1988b. *Homicide*. Hawthorne, NY: Aldine de Gruyter.

Daly, M., and M. Wilson. 1990a. "Is Parent-offspring Conflict Sex-linked? Freudian and Darwinian Models." *Journal of Personality* 58:163–89.

Daly, M., and M. Wilson. 1990b. "Killing the Competition." *Human Nature* 1:81–107.

Daly, M., and M. Wilson. 1998. *The Truth About Cinderella: A Darwinian View of Parental Love.* London: Weidenfeld & Nicolson. vii + 68 pp.

Daly, M., and M. Wilson. 2001. "Risk Taking, Intrasexual Competition, and Homicide." *Nebraska Symposium on Motivation* 47:1–36.

Daly, M., and M. Wilson. 2005. "*Carpe diem*: Adaptation and Devaluing the Future." *Quarterly Review of Biology* 80:55–60.

Daly, M., and M. Wilson. 2008. "Is the "Cinderella Effect" Controversial? A Case Study of Evolution-minded Research and Critiques Thereof." In *Foundations of Evolutionary Psychology*, edited by C. B. Crawford, D. Krebs, 381–98. Mahwah, NJ: Erlbaum.

Daly, M., and M. Wilson. 2010. "Cultural Inertia, Economic Incentives, and the Persistence of "Southern Violence."" In *Evolution, Culture, and the Human Mind*, edited by M. Schaller, A. Norenzayan, S. Heine, T. Yamagishi, T. Kameda, 229–41. New York: Psychology Press.

Daly, M., M. Wilson, and S. Vasdev. 2001. "Income Inequality and Homicide Rates in Canada and the United States." *Canadian Journal of Criminology* 43:219–36.

Daly, M., M. Wilson, and S. J. Weghorst. 1982. "Male Sexual Jealousy." *Ethology & Sociobiology* 3:11–27.

Dawes, C. T., J. H. Fowler, J. Johnson, R. McElreath, and O. Smirnov. 2007. "Egalitarian Motives in Humans." *Nature* 446:794–6.

Dawkins, R. 1986. *The Blind Watchmaker.* New York: Norton.

Dawkins, R. 1996. *Climbing Mount Improbable.* New York: Norton.

Deaton, A., and D. Lubotsky. 2003. "Mortality, Inequality, and Race in American Cities and States." *Social Science & Medicine* 56:1139–53.

Deininger, K., and L. Squire. 1998. "New Ways of Looking at Old Issues: Inequality and Growth." *Journal of Development Economics* 57:259–87.

del Giudice, M. 2014. "Early Stress and Human Behavioral Development: Emerging Evolutionary Perspectives." *Journal of Developmental Origins of Health & Disease* 5:270–80.

Desmond, A., and J. Moore. 1991. *Darwin: The Life of a Tormented Evolutionist.* New York & London: W.W. Norton.

de Waal, F. B. M. 1989. *Peacemaking Among Primates.* Cambridge, MA: Harvard University Press.

Dickemann, M. 1979. "The Ecology of Mating Systems in Hypergynous Dowry Societies." *Social Science Information* 18:163–95.

Dollard, J., N. E. Miller, L. W. Doob, O. H. Mowrer, and R. R. Sears. 1939. *Frustration and Aggression.* New Haven, CT: Yale University Press.

Durkheim, E. 1895. *Les règles de la méthode sociologique.* [quoted from a 1958 translation by S. A. Solovay, and J. H. Mueller].*The Rules of Sociological Method*, edited by G. E. G. Catlin. Glencoe, IL: Free Press.

Duesenberry, J. S. 1949. *Income, Saving, and the Theory of Consumer Behavior.* Cambridge, MA: Harvard University Press.

Dykiert, D., G. Der, J. M. Starr, and J. J. Deary. 2012. "Sex Differences in Reaction Time. Mean and Intraindividual Variability Across the Life Span." *Developmental Psychology* 48:1262–76.

Easterlin, R. A. 1987. *Birth and Fortune. The Impact of Numbers on Personal Welfare.* 2nd ed. Chicago: University of Chicago Press.

Ebensperger, L. A. 1998. "Strategies and Counterstrategies to Infanticide in Mammals." *Biological Reviews* 73:321–346.

Eckberg, D. L. 1995. "Estimates of Early Twentieth-century U.S. Homicide Rates: An Econometric Forecasting Approach." *Demography* 32:1–16.

Eckel, C. C., and P. Grossman. 2001. "Chivalry and Solidarity in Ultimatum Games." *Economic Inquiry* 39:171–88.

Edwards, J. Ll. J. 1954. "Provocation and the Reasonable Man: Another View." *Criminal Law Review* 1954:898–906.

Eisner, M. 2011. "Killing Kings: Patterns of Regicide in Europe, AD 600–1800." *British Journal of Criminology* 51:556–77.

Ellis, L. 1995. "Dominance and Reproductive Success Among Nonhuman Animals: A Cross-species Comparison." *Ethology & Sociobiology* 16:257–333.

Enamorado, T., L. F. López-Calva, C. Rodríguez-Castelán, and H. Winkler. 2014. "Income Inequality and Violent Crime. Evidence from Mexico's drug war." *The World Bank, Latin American & Caribbean Region Poverty Reduction & Economic Management Unit,* Policy Research Working Paper 6935. Downloaded August 11, 2014 from https://openknowledge.worldbank.org/bitstream/handle/10986/18825/WPS6935.pdf?sequence=1

Erlanger, H. S. 1974. "The Empirical Status of the Subculture of Violence Thesis." *Social Problems* 22:280–92.

Ermer, E., L. Cosmides, and J. Tooby. 2008. "Relative Status Regulates Risky Decision Making About Resources in Men: Evidence for the Co-evolution of Motivation and Cognition." *Evolution & Human Behavior* 29:106–18.

Evans, D. S., and B. Jovanovic. 1989. "An Estimated Model of Entrepreneurial Choice Under Liquidity Constraints." *Journal of Political Economy* 97:808–27.

Fajnzylber, P., D. Lederman, and N. Loayza. 2002. "Inequality and Violent Crime." *Journal of Law & Economics* 45:1–40.

Farrington, D. P., and B. C. Welsh. 2007. *Saving Children from a Life of Crime. Early Risk Factors and Effective Interventions.* Oxford: Oxford University Press.

Festinger, L. 1954. "A Theory of Social Comparison Processes." *Human Relations* 7:117–40.

Festinger, L. 1957. *A Theory of Cognitive Dissonance.* Palo Alto, CA: Stanford University Press.

Flegg, A. T. 1982. "Inequality of Income, Illiteracy, and Medical Care as Determinants of Infant Mortality in Developing Countries." *Population Studies* 36:441–58.

Flinn, M. V., D. Ponzi, and M. P. Muehlenbein. 2012. "Hormonal Mechanisms for Regulation of Aggression in Human Coalitions." *Human Nature* 23:68–88.

Fong, C. 2001. "Social Preferences, Self-interest, and the Demand for Redistribution." *Journal of Public Economics* 82:225–46.

Forbes, K. 2000. "A Reassessment of the Relationship Between Inequality and Growth." *American Economic Review* 90:869–87.

Fox, S., and K. Hoelscher. 2012. "Political Order, Development and Social Violence." *Journal of Peace Studies* 49:431–44.

Frank, R. H. 1985. *Choosing the Right Pond: Human Behavior and the Quest for Status.* New York: Oxford University Press.

Frank, R. H. 1999. *Luxury Fever: Money and Happiness in an Era of Excess.* New York: Free Press.

Frank, R. H. 2009a. *The Economic Naturalist's Field Guide.* New York: Basic Books.

Frank, R. H. 2009b. "The Invisible Hand: Trumped by Darwin?" *New York Times, July 12, 2009.* Downloaded on July 8, 2013 from www.nytimes.com/2009/07/12/business/economy/12view.html; 2009b.

Frank, R. H., and P. J. Cook. 1995. *The Winner-Take-All Society: Why the Few at the Top Get So Much More Than the Rest of Us.* New York: Free Press.

Frankenhuis, W. E., C. and de Weerth. 2013. "Does Early-life Exposure to Stress Shape or Impair Cognition?" *Current Directions in Psychological Science* 22:407–12.

Frankenhuis, W. E., and K. Panchanathan. 2011. "Individual Differences in Developmental Plasticity May Result from Stochastic Sampling." *Perspectives on Psychological Science* 6:336–47.

Freud, S. 1925. "Some Psychical Consequences of the Anatomical Distinction Between the Sexes." In *The Standard Edition of the Complete Psychological Works of Sigmund Freud, Volume 19,* edited and translated by J. Strachey, 241–58. London: Hogarth.

Fry, D. P., ed. 2013. *War, Peace, and Human Nature. The Convergence of Evolutionary and Cultural Views.* New York: Oxford University Press.

Gangestad, S. G., M. W. Haselton, and D. M. Buss. 2006. "Evolutionary Foundations of Cultural Variation: Evoked Culture and Mate Preferences." *Psychological Inquiry* 17:75–95.

Garcia, S. M., H. Song, and A. Tesser. 2010. "Tainted Recommendations: The Social Comparison Bias." *Organizational Behavior & Human Decision Processes* 113:97–101.

Garcia, S. M., A. Tor, and R. D. Gonzalez. 2006. "Ranks and Rivals: A Theory of Competition." *Personality & Social Psychology Bulletin* 32:970–82.

Garcia-Gallego, A., N. Georgantzis, and A. Jaramillo-Gutiérrez. 2012. "Gender Differences in Ultimatum Games: Despite Rather Than Due to Risk Attitudes." *Journal of Economic Behavior & Organization* 83:42–49.

Gartner, R. 1990. "The Victims of Homicide: A Temporal and Cross-national Comparison." *American Sociological Review* 55:92–106.

Gartrell, C. D. 2002. "The Embeddedness of Social Comparison." In *Relative Deprivation: Specification, Development, and Integration,* edited by I. Walker, H. J. Smith, 164–84. Cambridge, UK: Cambridge University Press.

Gat, A. 2006. *War in Human Civilization.* New York: Oxford University Press.

Gavrilets, S. 2012. "On the Evolutionary Origins of the Egalitarian Syndrome." *Proceedings of the National Academy of Sciences, USA* 109:14069–074.

Gazzaniga, M. S. 2011. *Who's in Charge? Free Will and the Science of the Brain.* New York: HarperCollins.

Geary, D. C. 2010. *Male, Female: The Evolution of Human Sex Differences.* 2nd ed. Washington: American Psychological Association.

Gilens, M. 1999. *Why Americans Hate Welfare. Race, Media, and the Politics of Anti-Poverty Policy.* Chicago: University of Chicago Press.

Gilens, M. 2012. *Affluence and Influence. Economic Inequality and Political Power in America.* Princeton, NJ: Princeton University Press.

Gilens, M., and B. I. Page. 2014. "Testing Theories of American Politics: Elites, Interest Groups, and Average Citizens." *Perspectives on Politics* 12:564–81.

Gilligan, J. 1992. *Violence: Our Deadly Epidemic and Its Causes.* New York: Grosset/Putnam.

Giuliano, P., and A. Spilimbergo. 2014. "Growing up in a Recession." *Review of Economic Studies* 81:787–817.

Gladue, B., M. Boechler, and K. McCaul. 1989. "Hormonal Response to Competition in Human Males." *Aggressive Behavior* 15:409–22.

Glick, T. F., and D. Kohn, eds. 1996. *Darwin on Evolution. The Development of the Theory of Natural Selection.* Indianapolis, IN: Hackett.

Glowacki, L., and R. W. Wrangham. 2013. "The Role of Rewards in Motivating Participation in Simple Warfare." *Human Nature* 24:444–60.

Gneezy, U., K. L. Leonard, and J. A. List. 2009. "Gender Differences in Competition: Evidence from a Matrilineal and a Patriarchal Society." *Econometrica* 77:1637–64.

Gneezy, U., M. Niederle, and A. Rustichini. 2003. "Performance in Competitive Environments: Gender Differences." *Quarterly Journal of Economics* 118:1049–74.

Gneezy, U., and A. Rustichini. 2004. "Gender and Competition at a Young Age." *American Economic Review* 94:377–81.

Gonzalez-Bono, E., A. Salvador, M. A. Serrano, and J. Ricarte. 1999. "Testosterone, Cortisol, and Mood in a Sports Team Competition." *Hormones & Behavior* 35:55–62.

Gordon, D. M. 1994. "Bosses of Different Stripes: Monitoring and Supervision across the Advanced Economies." *American Economic Review* 84:375–79.

Gordon, D. M. 1996. *Fat and Mean: The Corporate Squeeze of Working Americans and the Myth of Managerial 'Downsizing.'* New York: Free Press.

Gordon, D. M. 1998. "Conflict and Cooperation: An Empirical Glimpse of the Imperatives of Efficiency and Redistribution." In , Recasting Egalitarianism, edited by S. Bowles, H. Gintis, E. O. Wright, 181–207. London: Verso.

Gove, W. R. 1985. "The Effect of Age and Gender on Deviant Behavior: A Biopsychosocial Perspective." In *Gender and The Life Course,* edited by A. S. Rossi, 115–44. New York: Aldine.

Gupta, N. D., A. Poulsen, and M. C. Villeval. 2013. "Gender Matching and Competitiveness: Experimental Evidence." *Economic Inquiry* 51:816–35.

Güth, W., R. Schmittberger, and B. Schwarze. 1982. "An Experimental Analysis of Ultimatum Bargaining." *Journal of Economic Behavior & Organization* 3:367–88.

Hakmiller, K. L. 1966. "Threat as a Determinant of Downward Comparisons." *Journal of Experimental Social Psychology* 2 (suppl 1):32–39.

Hanlon, G. 2013. "The Decline of Violence in the West: From Cultural to Post-cultural History." *English Historical Review* 128:367–400.

Hardy, I. C. W., and M. Briffa, eds. 2013. *Animal Contests.* Cambridge, UK: Cambridge University Press.

Harris, M. 1968. *The Rise of Anthropological Theory.* New York: T.Y. Crowell.

Hart, C. W. M., and A. R. Pilling. 1960. *The Tiwi of North Australia.* New York: Holt-Rinehart-Winston.

Hassett, J. M., E. R. Siebert, and K. Wallen. 2008. "Sex Differences in Rhesus Monkey Toy Preferences Parallel Those of Children." *Hormones & Behavior* 54:359–64.

Heider, F. 1958. *The Psychology of Interpersonal Relations.* New York: Wiley.

Henrich, J., Boyd, R., and P. J. Richerson. 2012. "The Puzzle of Monogamous Marriage." *Philosophical Transactions of the Royal Society B* 367:657–60.

Henrich, J., S. J. Heine, and A. Norenzayan. 2010. "The Weirdest People in the World?" *Behavioral & Brain Sciences* 33:61–135.

Herskovitz, M. J. 1958. "Some Further Comments on Cultural Relativism." *American Anthropologist* 60:266–73.

Herzer, D., and S. Vollmer. 2012. "Inequality and Growth: Evidence from Panel Cointegration." *Journal of Economic Inequality* 10:489–503.

Higgins, E. T. 1987. "Self-discrepancy: A Theory Relating Self and Affect." *Psychological Review* 94:319–40.

Hill, K., and A. M. Hurtado. 1996. *Ache Life History. The Ecology and Demography of a Foraging People.* Hawthorne, NY: Aldine de Gruyter.

Hills, J. 2004. *Inequality and the State.* Oxford: Oxford University Press.

Hines, M. 2010. "Sex-related Variation in Human Behavior and the Brain." *Trends in Cognitive Science* 14:448–56.

Hiraiwa-Hasegawa, M. 2005. "Homicide by Men in Japan, and its Relationship to Age, Resources and Risk Taking." *Evolution & Human Behavior* 26:332–43.

Hirschi, T., and M. Gottfredson. 1983. "Age and the Explanation of Crime." *American Journal of Sociology* 89:552–84.

Honneth, A. 2009. *Pathologies of Reason: On the Legacy of Critical Theory.* J. Ingram, trans. New York: Columbia University Press.

Howell, N. 1979. *Demography of the Dobe !Kung.* New York: Academic Press.

Howell, N. 2010. *Life Histories of the Dobe !Kung.* Berkeley: University of California Press.

Hrdy, S. B. 1974. "Male-male Competition and Infanticide Among the Langurs (*Prebytis entellus*) of Abu, Rajasthan." *Folia Primatologica* 22:19–58.

Hrdy, S. B. 1979. "Infanticide Among Animals: A Review, Classification and Examination of the Implications for the Reproductive Strategies of Females." *Ethology & Sociobiology* 1:13–40.

Huntingford, F. A. 1991. "War and Peace Revisited." In *The Tinbergen Legacy*, edited by M. S. Dawkins, T. R. Halliday, R. Dawkins, 40–50. London: Chapman & Hall.

Hutchinson, A. C. 2011. *Is Eating People Wrong? Great Legal Cases and How They Shaped the World.* New York: Cambridge University Press.

Isen, J. D., M. K. McGue, and W. G. Iacono. 2015. "Aggressive-antisocial Boys Develop into Physically Strong Young Men." *Psychological Science.* 26:444–55.

Jacobs, D. 1981. "Inequality and Economic Crime." *Sociology & Social Research* 66:12–28.

Jacobs, D., and A. M. Richardson. 2008. "Economic Inequality and Homicide in the Developed Nations from 1975 to 1995." *Homicide Studies* 12:28–45.

Jakobsson, N., M. Levin, and A. Kotsadam. 2013. "Gender and Overconfidence: Effects of Context, Gendered Stereotypes, and Peer Group." *Advances in Applied Sociology* 3:137–41.

Jarvie, I. C. 1975. "Cultural Relativism Again." *Philosophy of the Social Sciences* 5:343–53.

Jayadev, A., and S. Bowles. 2006. "Guard Labor." *Journal of Development Economics* 79:328–48.

Johnson, D. D. P., and J. H. Fowler. 2011. "The Evolution of Overconfidence." *Nature* 477:317–20.

Johnson, H. B. 2014. *The American Dream and the Power of Wealth. Choosing Schools and Inheriting Inequality in the Land of Opportunity.* 2nd ed. Florence, KY: Routledge.

Jones, A. F., and D. H. Weinberg. 2000. "The Changing Shape of the Nation's Income Distribution 1947–1998." *Current Population Reports P60-204.* U.S. Census Bureau.

Kaltenthaler, K., S. Ceccoli, and R. Gelleny. 2008. "Attitudes Toward Eliminating Income Inequality in Europe." *Euopean Union Politics* 9:217–41.

Kamas, L., and D. Preston. 2012. "The Importance of Being Confident: Gender, Career Choice, and Willingness to Compete." *Journal of Economic Behavior & Organization* 83:82–97.

Kaplan, H., K. Hill, J. Lancaster, and A. M. Hurtado. 2000. "A Theory of Human Life History Evolution: Diet, Intelligence, and Longevity." *Evolutionary Anthropology* 9:156–85.

Kawachi, I., B. P. Kennedy, K. Lochner, and D. Prothrow-Stith. 1997. "Social Capital, Income Inequality, and Mortality." *American Journal of Public Health* 87:1491–8.

Keeley, L. H. 1996. *War Before Civilization: The Myth of the Peaceful Savage.* Oxford: Oxford University Press.

Kehr, N., M. Daly, and M. Wilson. 1997. "Homicide in Canada: Perception and Reality." In *Lethal Violence: Proceedings of the 1995 Meeting of the Homicide Research Working Group,* edited by M. Riedel, J. Bouhanis, 89–96. Washington, DC: National Institute of Justice.

Kelley, J., and M. D. R. Evans. 1993. "The Legitimation of Inequality: Occupational Earnings in Nine Nations." *American Journal of Sociology* 99:75–125.

Kelly, M. 2000. "Inequality and Crime." *Review of Economics & Statistics* 82:530–39.

Kelly, R. L. 1995. *The Foraging Spectrum: Diversity in Hunter-Gatherer Lifeways.* Washington, DC: Smithsonian Institution.

Kempe, C. H., F. N. Silverman, B. F. Steele, W. Droegemuller, and H. K. Silver. 1962. "The Battered Child Syndrome." *Journal of the American Medical Association* 181:17–24.

Kiatpongsan, S., and M. I. Norton. 2014. "How Much (more) Should CEOs Make? A Universal Desire for More Equal Pay." *Perspectives on Psychological Science* 9:587–93.

Kingham, M., and H. Gordon. 2004. "Aspects of Morbid Jealousy." *Advances in Psychiatric Treatment* 10:207–15.

Kirkpatrick, L. A., and C. D. Navarette. 2006. "Reports of My Death Anxiety Have Been Greatly Exaggerated: A Critique of Terror Management Theory from an Evolutionary Perspective." *Psychological Inquiry* 17:288–98.

Kirkwood, T. B., and S. N. Austad. 2000. "Why Do We Age?" *Nature* 408:233–8.

Kluegel, J. R., and E. R. Smith. 1986. *Beliefs About Inequality: Americans' Views of What Is and What Ought To Be.* New York: Aldine de Gruyter.

Knauft, B. M. 1987. "Reconsidering Violence in Simple Human Societies. Homicide Among the Gebusi of New Guinea." *Current Anthropology* 28:457–500.

Kokko, H., and M. D. Jennions. 2008. "Parental Investment, Sexual Selection and Sex Ratios." *Journal of Evolutionary Biology* 21:919–48.

Krupp, D. B., L. A. Sewall, M. L. Lalumière, C. Sheriff, and G. T. Harris. 2013. "Psychopathy, Adaptation, and Disorder." *Frontiers in Psychology* 4:139. doi:10.3389/fpsyg.2013.00139

Kruuk, L. E. B., T. H. Clutton-Brock, S. D. Albon, J. M. Pemberton, and F. E. Guinness. 1999. "Population Density Affects Sex Ratio Variation in Red Deer." *Nature* 399:459–61.

Kuzawa, C. W., and Z. M. Thayer. 2011. "Timescales of Human Adaptation: The Role of Epigenetic Processes." *Epigenomics* 3:221–34.

Kuziemko, I., R. Buell, T. Reich, and M. I. Norton. 2014. ""Last-place Aversion": Evidence and Redistributive Implications." *Quarterly Journal of Economics* 129:105–49.

Kuziemko, I., and M. I. Norton. 2011. "The Last-Place Aversion Paradox" *Scientific American* http://www.scientificamerican.com/article/occupy-wall-street-psychology/

LaFree, G. 1999. "A Summary and Review of Cross-national Comparative Studies of Homicide." In *Homicide: A Sourcebook of Social Research*, edited by M. D. Smith, M. A. Zahn, 125–45. Thousand Oaks, CA: Sage.

Leary, M. R., and R. F. Baumeister. 2000. "The Nature and Function of Self-esteem: Sociometer Theory." *Advances in Experimental Social Psychology* 32:1–62.

Leary, M. R., and L. S. Schreindorfer. 1997. "Unresolved Issues with Terror Management Theory." *Psychological Inquiry* 8:26–29.

Leary, M. R., E. S. Tambor, S. K. Terdal, and D. L. Downs. 1995. "Self-esteem as an Interpersonal Monitor: The Sociometer Hypothesis." *Journal of Personality & Social Psychology* 68:518–30.

Lee, M. R., W. B. Bankston, T. C. Hayes, and S. A. Thomas. 2007. "Revisiting the Southern Culture of Violence." *Sociological Quarterly* 48:253–75.

Lemert, E. M. 1951. *Social Pathology: A Systematic Approach to the Theory of Sociopathic Behavior.* New York: McGraw-Hill.

Lentini, E., M. Kasahara, S. Arver., and I. Savic. 2013. "Sex Differences in the Human Brain and the Impact of Sex Chromosomes and Sex Hormones." *Cerebral Cortex* 23:2322–36.

Levitt, S. D. 1999. "The Limited Role of Changing Age Structure in Explaining Aggregate Crime Rates." *Criminology* 37:581–97.

Levitt, S. D. 2004. "Understanding Why Crime Fell in the 1990s: Four Factors that Explain the Decline and Six That Do Not." *Journal of Economic Perspectives* 18:163–90.

Lewis, O. 1961. *The Children of Sánchez: Autobiography of a Mexican Family.* New York: Random House.

Liem, M. C. A., and W. A. Pridemore, eds. 2012. *Handbook of European Homicide Research: Patterns, Explanations, and Country Studies.* New York: Springer.

Lindenfors, P., J. L. Gittleman, and K. E. Jones. 2007. "Sexual Size Dimorphism in Mammals." In *Sex, Size and Gender Roles: Evolutionary Studies of Sexual Size Dimorphism,* edited by D. J. Fairbairn, W. U. Blanckenhorn, T. Szekely, 19–26. Oxford: Oxford University Press.

Lindenfors, P., and B. S. Tullberg. 2011. "Evolutionary Aspects of Aggression: The Importance of Sexual Selection." In *Advances in Genetics, Volume 75: Aggression,* edited by R. Huber, D. L. Bannasch, P. Brennan, 7–22. Burlington, VT: Academic Press.

Lowie, R. H. 1917. *Culture and Ethnology.* New York: Basic Books.

Luckenbill, D. F. 1977. "Criminal Homicide as a Situated Transaction." *Social Problems* 25:176–86.

Luttmer, E. F. P. 2005. "Neighbors as Negatives: Relative Earnings and Well-being." *Quarterly Journal of Economics* 100:963–1002.

Lynch, J., G. Davey Smith, S. Harper, M. Hillemeier, N. Ross, G. Kaplan, and M. Wolfson. 2004. "Is Income Inequality a Determinant of Population Health? Part 1: A Systematic Review." *Millbank Quarterly* 82:5–99.

Lytton, H., and D. M. Romney. 1991. "Parents' Differential Socialization of Boys and Girls: A Meta-analysis." *Psychological Bulletin* 109:267–96.

Macfarlan, S. J., R. S. Walker, M. V. Flinn, and N. A. Chagnon. 2014. "Lethal Coalitionary Aggression and Long-term Alliance Formation Among Yanomamö Men." *Proceedings of the National Academy of Sciences* 111:16662–9.

Magee, S. P. 2013. "Lawyers as Spam: Congressional Capture Explains Why U.S. Lawyers Exceed the Optimum." In *The American Illness: Essays on the Rule of Law,* edited by F. H. Buckley, 100–17. New Haven, CT: Yale University Press.

Mallin, M. G. 1967. "In *Warm Blood: Some Historical and Procedural Aspects of Regina v. Dudley and Stephens." University of Chicago Law Review* 34:387–407.

Man, J. 2005. *Ghengis Khan: Life, Death, and Resurrection.* London: Bantom.

Marlowe, F. W. 2003. "The Mating System of Foragers in the Standard Cross-cultural Sample." *Cross-cultural Research* 37:282–306.

Marlowe, F. W. 2010. *The Hadza. Hunter-Gatherers of Tanzania.* Berkeley, CA: University of California Press.

Marmot, M. 2004. *Status Syndrome. How Your Social Standing Directly Affects Your Health.* London: Bloomsbury.

Marmot, M. G., G. Rose, M. Shipley, and P. J. Hamilton. 1978. "Employment Grade and Coronary Heart Disease in British Civil Servants." *Journal of Epidemiology & Community Health* 32:244–9.

Marvell, and C. Moody. 1996. "Specification Problems, Police Levels, and Crime Rates." *Criminology* 34:609–46.

Mazur, A. 2005. *Biosociology of Dominance and Deference*. Lanham, MD: Rowman,and Littlefield.

Mazur, A., A. Booth, and J. M. Dabbs. 1992. "Testosterone and Chess Competition." *Social Psychology Quarterly* 55:70–77.

McAlister, A. L. 2006. "Acceptance of Killing and Homicide Rates in Nineteen Nations." *European Journal of Public Health* 16:259–65.

Mehta, P. H., and R. A. Josephs. 2006. "Testosterone Change After Losing Predicts the Decision to Compete Again." *Hormones & Behavior* 50:684–92.

Mercy, J. A., and L. E. Saltzman. 1989. "Fatal Violence Among Spouses in the United States, 1975–1985." *American Journal of Public Health* 79:595–9.

Merton, R. 1938. "Social Structure and Anomie." *American Sociological Review* 3:672–82.

Messner, S. F. 1982. "Poverty, Inequality, and the Urban Homicide Rate: Some Unexpected Findings." *Criminology* 20:103–14.

Messner, S. F., L. E. Raffalovich, and P. Schrock. 2002. "Reassessing the Cross-national Relationship Between Income Inequality and Homicide Rates: Implications of Data Quality Control in the Measurement of Income Distribution." *Journal of Quantitative Criminology* 18:377–95.

Messner, S. F., L. E. Raffalovich, and G. M. Sutton. 2010. "Poverty, Infant Mortality, and Homicide Rates in Cross-national Perspective: Assessments of Criterion and Construct Validity." *Criminology* 48:509–37.

Milanovic, B. 2007. "Why We All Care About Inequality (But Some of Us Are Loathe to Admit It)." *Challenge* 50:109–20.

Mill, J. S. 1848. *Principles of Political Economy with Some of Their Applications to Social Philosophy*. London: John W. Parker.

Mishra, S., P. Barclay, and M. L. Lalumière. 2014. "Competitive Disadvantage Facilitates Risk-taking." *Evolution and Human Behavior* 35:126–32.

Mishra, S., L. S. Son Hing, and M. L. Lalumière. 2014. "Inequality and Risk-taking." *Evolutionary Psychology* 13: doi:10.1177/1474704915596295.

Mowat, R. R. 1966. *Morbid Jealousy and Murder*. London: Tavistock.

Mulvihill, D. J., M. M. Tumin, and L. A. Curtis. 1969. *Crimes of Violence*, Volume 11. Washington, DC: US Government Printing Office.

Murnighan, J. K., and M. S. Saxon. 1998. "Ultimatum Bargaining by Children and Adults." *Journal of Economic Psychology* 19:415–45.

Nadanovsky, P., and J. Cunha-Cruz. 2009. "The Relative Contribution of Income Inequality and Imprisonment to the Variation in Homicide Rates Among Developed (OECD), South and Central American countries." *Social Science & Medicine* 69:1343–50.

Neel, J. V., F. M. Salzano, P. C. Junquiero, F. Keiter, and D. Maybury-Lewis. 1964. "Studies on the Xavante Indians of the Brazilian Mato Grosso." *American Journal of Human Genetics* 16:52–140.

Nelson, R. J. 2011. *An Introduction to Behavioral Endocrinology*. 4th ed. Sunderland, MA: Sinauer.

Nelson, R. J., and B. C. Trainor. 2007. "Neural Mechanisms of Aggression." *Nature Reviews Neuroscience* 8:536–46.

Nesse, R. M., and G. C. Williams. 1994. *Why We Get Sick*. New York: Random House.

Neumayer, E. 2003. "Good Policy Can Lower Violent Crime: Evidence from a Cross-national Panel of Homicide Rates, 1980–97." *Journal of Peace Research* 40:619–40.

Niederle, M., and L. Vesterlund. 2007. "Do Women Shy Away from Competition? Do Men Compete Too Much?" *Quarterly Journal of Economics* 122:1067–101.

Niederle, M., and L. Vesterlund. 2011. "Gender and Competition." *Annual Review of Economics* 3:601–30.

Nielsen, F. 2004. "The Ecological-Evolutionary Typology of Human Societies and the Evolution of Social Inequality." *Sociological Theory* 22:292–314.

Nisbett, R. E. 1993. "Violence and U.S. Regional Culture." *American Psychologist* 48:441–9.

Nisbett, R. E., and D. Cohen. 1996. *Culture of Honor: The Psychology of Violence in the South*. Boulder, CO: Westview Press.

Nisbett, R. E., G. Polly, and S. Lang. 1995. "Homicide and U.S. Regional Culture." In *Interpersonal Violent Behaviors: Social and Cultural Aspects*, edited by R. B. Ruback, N. A. Weiner, 135–51. New York: Springer.

Nisbett, R. E., and T. D. Wilson. 1977. "Telling More Than We Can Know: Verbal Reports on Mental Processes." *Psychological Review* 84:231–59.

Nivette, A. E., and M. Eisner. 2013. "Do Legitimate Polities have Fewer Homicides? A Cross-national Analysis." *Homicide Studies* 17:3–26.

Norenzayan, A. 2006. "Evolution and Transmitted Culture." *Psychological Inquiry* 17:123–8.

Norton, M. I., and D. Ariely. 2011. "Building a Better America – One Wealth Quintile at a Time." *Current Perspectives on Psychological Science* 6:9–12.

Norton, M. I., D. T. Neal, C. L. Govan, D. Ariely, and E. Holland. 2014. "The Not-So-Common-Wealth of Australia: Evidence for a Cross-cultural Desire for a More Equal Distribution of Wealth." *Analyses of Social Issues & Public Policy* 14:339–51.

O'Brien, R. M. 2011. "The Age-Period-Cohort Conundrum as Two Fundamental Problems." *Quality & Quantity* 45:1429–44.

O'Brien, R. M., and J. Stockard. 2009. "Can Cohort Replacement Explain Changes in the Relationship Between Age and Homicide Offending?" *Journal of Quantitative Criminology* 25:79–101.

O'Brien, R. M., J. Stockard., and L. Isaaacson. 1999. "The Enduring Effects of Cohort Characteristics on Age-specific Homicide Rates, 1960–1995." *American Journal of Sociology* 104:1061–95.

Olson, J. M., C. P. Herman, and M. P. Zanna, eds. 1986. *Relative Deprivation and Social Comparison*. Hillsdale, NJ: Lawrence Erlbaum.

Omark, D. R., F. F. Strayer, and D. G. Freedman, eds. 1980. *Dominance Relations: An Ethological View of Human Conflict and Social Interaction*. New York: Garland.

Onon, V., ed. & trans. 1990. *The History and The Life of Chinggis Khan.* Leiden: Brill.

Orosy-Fildes, C., and R. W. Allan. 1989. "Psychology of Computer Use: XII. Videogame Play. Human Reaction Time to Visual Stimuli." *Perceptual & Motor Skills* 69:243–47.

Orwell, G. 1946. "Decline of the English murder." *Tribune (London)*, 15 February, 1946.

Otterbein, K. F. 2004. *How War Began.* College Station, TX: Texas A&M University Press.

Ostry, D. D., A. Berg, and C. G. Tsangarides. 2014. "Redistribution, Inequality, and Growth." *International Monetary Fund* Staff Discussion Note. Downloaded on November 25, 2014 from http://www.imf.org/external/pubs/ft/sdn/2014/sdn1402.pdf.

Ouimet, M. 2012. "A World of Homicides: The Effect of Economic Development, Income Inequality, and Excess Infant Mortality on the Homicide Rate for 165 Countries in 2010." *Homicide Studies* 16:238–58.

Palombit, R. A. 2012. "Infanticide: Male Strategies and Female Counterstrategies." In *The Evolution of Primate Societies*, edited by J. P. Mitani, J. Call, P. M. Kappeler, R. A. Palombit, J. B. Silk, 432–68. Chicago: University of Chicago Press.

Panchanathan, K., and W. E. Frankenhuis. 2016. "The Evolution of Sensitive Windows in a Model of Incremental Development." *Proceedings of the Royal Society B: Biological Sciences,* doi: 10.1098/rspb.2015.2439.

Paré, P.-P. 2014. "Indicators of Police Performance and Their Relationship with Homicide Rates Across 77 Nations." *International Criminal Justice Review* 24:254–70.

Peristiany, J. G., ed. 1965. *Honour and Shame: The Values of Mediterranean Society.* London: Weidenfeld & Nicolson.

Perotti, R. 1996. "Growth, Income Distribution, and Democracy: What the Data Say." *Journal of Economic Growth* 1:149–87. I

Persson, T., and G. Tabellini. 1994. "Is Inequality Harmful for Growth? Theory and Evidence." *American Economic Review* 84:600–21.

Pfaff, D. W., and Y. Christen, eds. 2013. *Multiple Origins of Sex Differences in Brain: Neuroendocrine Functions and Their Pathologies.* New York: Springer.

Pfennig, D. W., and J. P. Collins. 1993. "Kinship Affects Morphogenesis in Cannibalistic Salamanders." *Nature* 362:836–38.

Pfennig, D. W., J. P. Collins, and R. E. Ziemba. 1999. "A Test of Alternative Hypotheses for Kin Recognition in Cannibalistic Tiger Salamanders." *Behavioral Ecology* 10:436–43.

Pfennig, D. W., and P. W. Sherman. 1995. "Kin Recognition." *Scientific American* 272 (3): 98–103.

Phillips, J. A. 2006. "The Relationship Between Age Structure and Homicide Rates in the United States, 1970 to 1999." *Journal of Research in Crime & Delinquency* 43:230–60.

Piketty, T. 2014. *Capital in the Twenty-first Century.* Cambridge, MA: Harvard University Press.

Pinker, S. 2011. *The Better Angels of Our Nature. Why Violence has Declined.* New York: Viking.

Piquero, A., and P. Mazerolle, eds. 2001. *Life-course Criminology.* Belmont, CA: Wadsworth/Thomson.

Polo, M. 2005. *Travels in the Land of Kubilai Khan.* J. Minford, D. C. Lau, trans. London: Penguin.

Pongratz, J., K. Cakdeira, C. H. Reick, and M. Claussen. 2011. "Coupled Climate-Carbon Simulations indicate Minor Global Effects of Wars and Epidemics on Atmospheric CO_2 between AD 800 and 1850." *Holocene* 21:843–51.

Pridemore, W. A. 2006. "Demographic, Temporal, and Spatial Patterns of Homicide Rates in Russia." *European Sociological Review* 19:41–59.

Pridemore, W. A. 2008. "A First Test of the Poverty–Homicide Hypothesis at the Cross-national Level." *Criminology* 46:133–54.

Pridemore, W. A. 2011. "Poverty Matters. A Reassessment of the Inequality-Homicide Relationship in Cross-national Studies." *British Journal of Criminology* 51:739–72.

Prucha, F. P. 1984. *The Great Father: The United States Government and the American Indians.* Lincoln, NE: University of Nebraska Press.

Puzzanchera, C., G. Chamberlin, and W. Kang. 2014. "Easy Access to the FBI's Supplementary Homicide Reports: 1980–2012." (2014). Online at http://www.ojjdp.gov/ojstatbb/ezashr/

Rachels, J. 2003. *The Elements of Moral Philosophy.* 4th ed. New York: McGraw-Hill.

Raine, A. 2013. *The Anatomy of Violence.* New York: Pantheon Books.

Ram, R. 2007. "Roles of Income and Equality in Poverty Reduction: Recent Cross-country Evidence." *Journal of International Development* 19:919–26.

Ramseyer, J. M., and E. B. Rasmusen. 2010. "Comparative Litigation Rates. *The Harvard John M. Olin Discussion Paper Series # 681.*" (2010). Available at http://www.law.harvard.edu/programs/olin_center/

Raphael, S., and R. Winter-Ebmer. 2001. "Identifying the Effect of Unemployment on Crime." *Journal of Law & Economics* 44:259–83.

Ratchevsky, P. 1991. In *Ghengis Khan: His Life and Legacy*, edited and translated by T. N. Haining. Oxford: Blackwell.

Reza, A., J. A. Mercy, J. A., and E. Krug. 2001. "Epidemiology of Violent Deaths in the World." *Injury Prevention* 7:104–11.

Richerson, P. J., and R. Boyd. 2005. *Not by Genes Alone: How Culture Transformed Human Evolution.* Chicago: University of Chicago Press.

Riechert, S. E. 2013. "Maynard Smith & Parker's (1976) Rule Book for Animal Contests, Mostly." *Animal Behaviour* 86:3–9.

Robins, L. N. 1978. "Sturdy Childhood Predictors of Adult Antisocial Behaviour: Replications from Longitudinal Studies." *Psychological Medicine* 8:611–22.

Rogers, A. R. 1994. "Evolution of Time Preference by Natural Selection." *American Economic Review* 84:460–81.

Roodman, D. 2009. "A Note on the Theme of Too Many Instruments." *Oxford Bulletin of Economics & Statistics* 71:135–58.

Rosati, A. G., and B. Hare. 2012. "Decision Making Across Social Contexts: Competition Increases Preferences for Risk in Chimpanzees and Bonobos." *Animal Behaviour* 84:869–79.

Rose, M. R. 1991. *Evolutionary Biology of Aging*. New York: Oxford University Press.

Rosenfeld, R, and S. F. Messner. 1991. "The Social Sources of Homicide in Different Types of Societies." *Sociological Forum* 6:51–70.

Roth, R. 2009. *American Homicide*. Cambridge, MA: Harvard University Press.

Roth, R. 2011. "Biology and the Deep History of Homicide." *British Journal of Criminology* 51:535–55.

Rowlingson, K. 2011. *Does Income Inequality Cause Health and Social Problems?* York, UK: Joseph Rowntree Foundation. Available at www.jrf.org. uk/publications.

Runciman, W. G. 1998. "The Selectionist Paradigm and Its Implications for Sociology." *Sociology* 32:163–88.

Rupasingha, A., S. J. Goetz, and D. Freshwater. 2006. "The Production of Social Capital in US Counties." *Journal of Socio-economics* 25:83–101.

Rushforth, N. B., A. B. Ford, C. S. Hirsch, N. M. Rushforth, and L. Adelson. 1977. "Violent Death in a Metropolitan County. Changing Patterns in Homicide (1958–1974)." *New England Journal of Medicine* 297:531–38.

Russell, B. 1930. *The Conquest of Happiness*. London: Allen & Unwin.

Ruyle, E. E. 1973. "Slavery, Surplus, and Stratification on the Northwest Coast: The Ethnoenergetics of an Incipient Stratification System." *Current Anthropology* 14:603–31.

Salmon, C. A. 2003. "Birth Order and Relationships: Family, Friends and Sexual Partners." *Human Nature* 14:73–88.

Salmon, C. A., and M. Daly. 1998. "Birth Order and Familial Sentiment: Middleborns are Different. *Evolution & Human Behavior* 19:299–312.

Sanderson, S. K. 2001. "Explaining Monogamy and Polygyny in Human Societies: Comment on Kanazawa and Still." *Social Forces* 80:329–36.

Sefton, T. 2005. "Give and Take: Public Attitudes to Redistribution." In *British Social Attitudes 22nd Report*, edited by A. Park, 1–32. London: Sage.

Sell, A. 2011. "The Recalibrational Theory and Violent Anger." *Aggression & Violent Behavior* 16:381–9.

Siegel, A., and J. Victoroff. 2009. "Understanding Human Aggression: New Insights From Neuroscience." *International Journal of Law & Psychiatry* 32:209–15.

Silverman, I. W. 2006. "Sex Differences in Simple Visual Reaction Time: A Historical Meta-analysis." *Sex Roles* 54:57–68.

Smith, H. J., T. F. Pettigrew, G. M. Pippin, and S. Bialosiewicz. 2012. "Relative Deprivation: A Theoretical and Meta-analytic Review." *Personality & Social Psychology Bulletin* 16:203–32.

Solnick, S. J. 2001. "Gender Differences in the Ultimatum Game." *Economic Inquiry* 39:189–200.

Solomon, S., J. Greenberg, and T. Pyszczynski. 1991. "A Terror Management Theory of Social Behavior: The Psychological Functions of Self-esteem and Cultural Worldviews." *Advances in Experimental Social Psychology* 24:93–159.

Sorensen, T. 2008. *Counselor: A Life at the Edge of History.* New York: Harper Collins.

Starks, B. 2003. "The New Economy and the American Dream: Examining the Effect of Work Conditions on Beliefs About Economic Opportunity." *Sociological Quarterly* 44:205–25.

Steward, J. 1948. "Comments on the Statement of Human Rights." *American Anthropologist* 50:351–2.

Stiglitz, J. E. 2012. *The Price of Inequality.* New York: W.W. Norton.

Stone, A. A., J. S. Turkkan, C. A. Bachrach, J. B. Jobe, H. S. Kurtzman, and V. S. Cain, eds. 2000. *The Science of Self-report: Implications for Research and Practice.* Mahwah, NJ: Erlbaum.

Stouffer, S. A., E. A. Suchman, L. C. DeVinney, S. A. Starr, and R. M. Williams. 1949. *The American Soldier: Adjustment to Army Life.* Volume 1. Princeton, NJ: Princeton University Press.

Subramanian, S., and I. Kawachi. 2004. "Income Inequality and Health: What Have We Learned So Far?" *Epidemiological Review* 26:78–91.

Sulloway, F. J. 2007. "Birth Order." In *Evolutionary Family Psychology*, edited by C. A. Salmon, T. K. Shackelford, 162–82. Oxford: Oxford University Press.

Suls, J. M., and R. L. Miller, eds. 1977. *Social Comparison Processes: Theoretical and Empirical Perspectives.* Washington, DC: Hemisphere.

Suls, J. M., and L. Wheeler, eds. 2000. *Handbook of Social Comparison: Theory and Research.* Dordrecht: Kluwer.

Suls, J. M., and L. Wheeler, L. 2012. "Social Comparison Theory." In *Handbook of Theories of Social Psychology*, edited by P. A. M. van Lange, A. W. Kruglanski, E. T. Higgins, Volume 1, 460–82. Thousand Oaks, CA: Sage.

Tarnopolsky, M. A. 2008. "Sex Differences in Exercise Metabolism and the Role of 17-beta Estradiol." *Medicine & Science in Sports & Exercise* 40:648–54.

Thomas, J. R., and K. E. French. 1985. "Gender Differences Across Age in Motor Performance: A Meta-analysis." *Psychological Bulletin* 98:260–82.

Topçuoğlu, T., M. P. Eisner, and D. Ribeaud. 2014. *Sex Differences in the Effects of Parents' Use of Corporal Punishment on Children's Aggressive Behavior.* Zürich: Eidgenössische Technische Hochschule.

Townsend, P. 1979. *Poverty in the United Kingdom.* London: Penguin.

Trainor, B. C., and R. J. Nelson. 2012. "Neuroendocrinology of Aggression." In *Handbook of Neuroendocrinology*, edited by G. Fink, D. W. Pfaff, and J. E. Levine, 509–20. San Diego: Academic Press/Elsevier.

Trivers, R. L. 1971. "Parent-Offspring Conflict." *American Zoologist* 14:249–64.

Trivers, R. L. 1972. "Parental Investment and Sexual Selection." In *Sexual Selection and the Descent of Man, 1871–1971*, edited by B. Campbell, 136–79. Chicago: Aldine.

Trivers, R. L. 1985. *Social Evolution.* Menlo Park, CA: Benjamin/Cummings.

Trompf, G. W. 1990. *Cargo Cults and Millenarian Movements: Transoceanic Comparisons of New Religious Movements.* Berlin: Mouton de Gruyter.

Trussler, T. 2012. "Demographics and Homicide in Canada: A Fixed-effects Analysis of the Role of Young Males on Changing Homicide Rates." *Western Criminology Review* 13:53–67.

Tylor, E. B. 1871. *Primitive Culture*. London: John Murray.

United Nations Office on Drugs & Crime. 2013. *Global Study on Homicide 2013.* Online at http://www.unodc.org/documents/gsh/pdfs/2014_GLOBAL_HOMICIDE_BOOK_web.pdf

van Schaik, C. P., and C. H. Janson, eds. 2000. *Infanticide by Males and its Implications*. Cambridge, UK: Cambridge University Press.

Veblen, T. B. 1899. *The Theory of the Leisure Class*. London: Macmillan.

Verkko, V. 1951. *Homicides and Suicides in Finland and their Dependence on National Character*. Copenhagen: G.E.C. Gads Forlag.

Visser, J. 2006. "Union Membership Statistics in 24 Countries." *Monthly Labor Review* 129 (1):38–49.

Wakefield, J. C. 1992. "The Concept of Mental Disorder: On the Boundary Between Biological Facts and Social Values." *American Psychologist* 47:373–88.

Walberg, P., M. McKee, V. Shkolnikov, L. Chenet, and D. A. Leon. 1998. "Economic Change, Crime, and Mortality Crisis in Russia: Regional Analysis." *British Medical Journal* 317:312–18.

Waldmann, R. J. 1992. "Income Distribution and Infant Mortality." *Quarterly Journal of Economics* 107:1283–302.

Walker, R. S., and D. H. Bailey. 2013. "Body Counts in Lowland South American Violence." *Evolution & Human Behavior* 34:29–34.

Walker, R. S., K. R. Hill, M. V. Flinn, and R. M. Ellsworth. 2011. "Evolutionary History of Hunter-Gatherer Marriage Practices." *PloS One* 6 (4): e19066.

Walton, S., and J. Huey. 1992 *Made in America: My Story*. New York: Doubleday.

Wang, X. T., D. J. Kruger, and A. Wilke. 2009. "Life-history Variables and Risk-taking Propensity." *Evolution & Human Behavior* 30:77–84.

Wegner, D. M. 2002. *The Illusion of Conscious Will*. Cambridge, MA: MIT Press.

Welch, F. 1979. "Effects of Cohort Size on Earnings: The Baby Boom Babies' Financial Bust." *Journal of Political Economy* 87:S65–97.

Wiederman, M. W. 1997. "The Truth Must be in here Somewhere: Examining the Gender Discrepancy in Self-reported Lifetime Number of Sex Partners." *Journal of Sex Research* 34:375–86.

Wilkinson, R., and K. Pickett. 2009. *The Spirit Level. Why More Equal Societies Almost Always Do Better*. London: Penguin.

Williams, G. C. 1966. *Adaptation and Natural Selection*. Princeton, NJ: Princeton University Press.

Williams, J. K. 1980. *Dueling in the Old South. Vignettes of Social History*. College Station, TX: Texas A&M University Press.

Wilson, D. 2005. *Inventing Black-on-black Violence: Discourse, Space, and Representation*. Syracuse, NY: Syracuse University Press.

Wilson, M., and M. Daly. 1985. "Competitiveness, Risk-taking and Violence: The Young Male Syndrome." *Ethology & Sociobiology* 6:59–73.

Wilson, M., and M. Daly. 1994. "The Psychology of Parenting in Evolutionary Perspective and the Case of Human Filicide." In *Infanticide and Parental Care*, edited by S. Parmigiami, F. S. vomSaal, 73–104. Chur, Switzerland: Harwood Academic Publishers.

Wilson, M., and M. Daly. 1996. "Male Sexual Proprietariness and Violence Against Wives." *Current Directions in Psychological Science* 5:2–7.

Wilson, M., M. Daly, and N. Pound. 2010. "Sex Differences and Intrasexual Variation in Competitive Confrontation and Risk-taking: An Evolutionary Psychological Perspective." In *Hormones, Brain & Behavior*, 2nd ed., edited by D. W. Pfaff, A. P. Arnold, A. M. Etgen, S. E. Fahrbach, T. R. Rubin. New York: Elsevier.

Wilson, M. I., M. Daly, and S. J. Weghorst. 1980. "Household Composition and the Risk of Child Abuse and Neglect." *Journal of Biosocial Science* 12:333–40.

Wilson, M. I., M. Daly, and S. J. Weghorst. 1983. "Differential Maltreatment of Girls and Boys." *Victimology* 6:249–61.

Wilson, M. I., H. Johnson, and M. Daly. 1995. "Lethal and Nonlethal Violence Against Wives." *Canadian Journal of Criminology* 37:331–61.

Wilt, G. M. 1974. *Toward an Understanding of the Social Realities of Participating in Homicides*. Unpublished doctoral dissertation. Wayne State University.

Wingfield, J. C., R. E. Hegner, A. M. Dufty, and G. F. Ball. 1990. "The "Challenge Hypothesis": Theoretical Implications for Patterns of Testosterone Secretion, Mating Systems, and Breeding Strategies." *American Naturalist* 136:829–46.

Wolfgang, M. E. 1958. *Patterns in Criminal Homicide*. Philadelphia: University of Pennsylvania Press.

Wolfgang, M. E., and F. Ferracuti. 1967. *The Subculture of Violence: Towards an Integrated Theory in Criminology*. London: Tavistock.

Wrangham, R. W., M. L. Wilson, and M. N. Muller. 2006. "Comparative Rates of Violence in Chimpanzees and Humans." *Primates* 47:14–26.

Wright, R. 2004. *A Short History of Progress*. Toronto: House of Anansi.

Wroblewski, E. E., C. M. Murray, B. F. Keele, J. C. Schumacher-Stankey, B. H. Hahn, and A. E. Pusey. 2009. "Male Dominance Rank and Reproductive Success in Chimpanzees, *Pan troglodytes schweinfurthii*." *Animal Behaviour* 77:873–85.

Yam, P. 1996. "Catching a Coming Crime Wave. Profile: James Alan Fox." *Scientific American* 274 (6): 40–4.

Yamagishi, T., Y. Horita, H. Takagishi, M. Shinada, S. Tanida, and K. S. Cook. 2009. "The Private Rejection of Unfair Offers and Emotional Commitment." *Proceedings of the National Academy of Sciences, USA* 106:11520–3.

Zajonc, R. B. 1990. "Leon Festinger (1919–1989)." *American Psychologist* 45:6612.

Zak, P. J., R. Kurzban, S. Ahmadi, R. S. Swerdloff, J. Park, L. Efremidze, K. Redwine, K. Morgan, and W. Matzner. 2009. "Testosterone Administration Decreases Generosity in the Ultimatum Game." *PLoS ONE* 4 (12): e8330. doi:10.1371/journal.pone.0008330.

Zerjal, T., Y. Xue, G. Bertorelle and 20 co-authors. 2003. "The Genetic Legacy of the Mongols." *American Journal of Human Genetics* 72:717–21.

Zheng, H. 2012. "Do People Die From Inequality of a Decade Ago?" *Social Science & Medicine* 75:36–45.

Zilioli, S., and N. V. Watson. 2014. "Testosterone across Successive Competitions: Evidence for a Winner Effect in Humans?" *Psychoneuroendocrinology* 47:1–9.

Index

Ache, 205, 206
adaptation, 7, 15, 31, 34–7, 108, 117, 156, 199
Afghanistan, 20
age-crime curve, 53, 102–6, 157–63
Agnew, Robert, 88, 89
Alberta, 28
Alesina, Alberto, 175, 176, 185
Alexander, Richard D., 39, 47, 48
American Bar Association, 120, 121
American Dream, 172–9
Anderson, Elijah, 55, 128–30, 141
Angola, 20
antisocial personality, 154
Ariely, Dan, 166, 167, 169
Armenia, 92
Arrow, Kenneth, 192
Australia, 9, 169, 170, 177, 206
Azerbaijan, 92

baboon, 104
    Hamadryas (*Papio hamadryas*), 39
baby boom, 158, 159, 161. *See also* Cohort size
Bailey, Drew, 202–5
Bannon, James, 51, 52
Belsky, Jay, 154, 155
Bénabou, Roland, 185
Betzig. Laura, 95, 206
Bhutto, Benazir, 20
birth order, 160
Blanchflower, David, 191
Blau, Judith, 67, 68
Blau, Peter, 67, 68
Boas, Franz, 122, 123
Boehm, Christopher, 96, 197, 199, 208, 209
Borgerhoff Mulder, Monique, 203, 204

Boston. 141
Bowles, Samuel, 192–4
Boyd, Rob, 134, 135, 139
Brazil, 20, 117, 148, 204, 205
British Columbia, 28
Brooks, David, 172
Brown, H. Rap, 119
Burma, 20
Burnham, Terry, 115
Buser, Thomas, 111

Canada, 9, 27–9, 49, 50, 62, 64, 120–1, 145–7, 149, 176, 177, 182, 201
cannibalism, 61, 156
Carlin, George, 173
castration, 5, 115
Centers for Disease Control (USA), 8–9, 20–1
Chagnon, Napoleon, 96, 97, 204, 205
Charness, Gary, 109, 113, 114
Chicago, 120
China, 92, 95
Cinderella effect, 5–7, 14
code of the streets, 128, 129, 141
Cohen, Dov, 131–6, 138–41
cohort size, 158–63.
Colombia, 20, 21, 111, 143
competition, 1–3, 12, 17, 31, 33, 35, 38–57, 76, 87, 90, 92, 99–118, 129, 130, 137, 141, 147, 150, 156, 158, 159, 163–5, 168, 178, 189, 190, 197, 198, 205, 207, 209
cooperation, 43, 47, 48, 83, 96, 118, 132, 198, 199
correlation and causation, 2–3, 25–7, 148, 183, 185, 186, 207
Courtwright, David, 120, 208
crack cocaine, 147
Crick, Francis, 189

Crosby, Faye, 80, 87
cuckoldry, 43
culture
    cross-cultural diversity and universality,
    15, 16, 47, 55, 83, 84, 102, 107, 112,
    121–5
    definition. 121–3
    of honor, 3–4, 124, 125, 130–41
    of violence, 3–4, 15–7, 119–41
Cunha-Cruz, Joanna, 22, 72
Czech Republic *or* Czechoslovakia, 19

Daly, Martin, 4–9, 14–7, 24, 26, 28, 29,
    47, 49–52, 64, 99, 100, 102–4, 109, 110,
    130, 133, 136, 137, 139, 144, 149, 160,
    163, 211
Darwin, Charles, 31–9, 77, 122
Deaton, Angus, 137
Denmark, 175
Detroit, 51–3, 55, 99, 100, 106
del Giudice, Marco, 143, 160
Dickemann, Mildred, 95
dictator game, 112–4
dikdik (*Madoqua* sp.), 39
Duesenberry, James, 78, 79
Durkheim, Émile, 88, 101

egalitarianism, 3, 44, 46, 60, 97, 193, 194,
    197–201, 203–6, 209
Eisner, Manuel, 72, 97
El Salvador, 20
eland (*Taurotragus oryx*), 39
Elias, Norbert, 212
elk. *See* red deer
England. *See* Great Britain
Estonia, 56
Ethiopia 20
European Values Survey, 175
Evans, David, 191, 192

Ferracuti, Franco, 126–9
Festinger, Leon, 81–5, 87
Flegg, Anthony, 71
Forbes, Kristin, 186, 187
Fox, Jamie, 145
Fox, Sean, 72, 222
Frank, Robert, 76, 77, 79, 119
Frankenhuis, Willem, 153, 155, 157
Freud, Sigmund, 7

Gates, Bill, 190
Genghis Khan, 92–5

Georgia, 92
Germany, 19, 170
gibbon (*Hylobates* sp.), 39, 43
Gilens, Martin, 168, 171, 175
Gilligan, James, 101
Gini index. *See* Inequality
Giuliano, Paolo, 161
Glowacki, Luke, 201, 202
Gottfredson, Michael, 102, 193
Great Britain, 22, 111, 122, 132, 145–7,
    167, 169, 177, 179–81, 191, 192
    British Social Attitudes Survey, 167
Greece, 57
Greensboro (North Carolina), 194
Gross Domestic Product (GDP), 63, 66,
    181, 184, 189
guard labor, 193, 194
Güth, Werner, 113

Hadza, 205, 206
Hanlon, Gregory, 212
Hart, C.W.M., 206
Havel, Václav, 19
Heine, Steven, 83
Henrich, Joseph, 83, 84
Hiraiwa-Hasegawa, Mariko, 157, 158
Hirschi, Travis, 102, 193
Hislop, Robert, 52
Hobbes, Thomas, 198
Hoelscher, Kristian, 72
homicide
    as an "assay" of relationship-specific
        conflict, 14
    book (Daly & Wilson, 1988), 16–17, 130
    definition, 9–12
    intentional, 10
    rates, 1–4, 8, 9, 11–7, 19–29, 49–51,
        55–7, 61–4, 67–72, 87, 90, 102–4, 119,
        129, 130, 135–8, 141, 143–51, 157–9,
        162, 163, 199–202, 204–8, 210, 212
    scenarios, 8, 9, 14, 16, 48, 51–5,
        99–102, 106, 131–2
    unlawful, 10
Homo economicus, 75, 76
Horatio Alger Association, 174, 177
Howell, Nancy, 44–6, 205, 206
hunter-gatherers, 43–7, 96, 112, 157,
    198, 200–9
Hrdy, Sarah, 5

Iceland, 56, 57
Indian Removal Act of 1830 (USA), 120

terror management theory, 85, 86
testosterone, 115–118, 131
Thompson, Nicholas, 121
Tiger salamander (*Ambystoma tigrinum*), 156
Tiwi, 206
Toronto, 51, 120
Toronto *Globe & Mail*, 182, 183
Townsend, Peter, 65
Trivers, Robert, 7
trust, 181, 192, 193, 210
Tsimane, 204
Tylor, Edward, 122

Uganda, 20
Ukraine, 92
ultimatum game, 112–5
unemployment, 22, 23, 53, 65, 103, 104, 144, 149, 158, 194
United Kingdom. *See* Great Britain
United Nations, 9–12, 65
    Demographic Yearbook, 21, 28, 143
    Development Agency, 185
    Global Study on Homicide, 9, 12, 102, 103
    Office on Drugs and Crime (UNODC), 9–11, 51, 102, 103
United States of America (USA), 3–4, 6, 9, 20–9, 50–6, 62–9, 71, 79, 80, 100, 108, 117, 119–21, 125–41, 143–9, 152, 158, 159, 161–3, 165–79, 184, 188, 189, 192–195, 210
    Census Bureau, 64, 66, 67, 69, 147
    Federal Bureau of Investigation (FBI), 50, 51, 69, 137, 146, 147
    National Health Interview Survey, 152
Uzbekistan, 92

Veblen, Thorstein, 77–9
Venezuela, 97, 204

Vesterlund, Lise, 110, 111
Vidal, Gore, 75

Waldmann, Robert, 71
Wales. *See* Great Britain
Wałęsa, Lech, 2–1
Walker, Rob, 47, 202, 204, 205
Wall Street Journal, 181
Wallace, Alfred Russell, 32
Walton, Sam, 190
warfare, 10–2, 20, 27, 47, 48, 92, 93, 117, 198, 199, 201, 202, 205, 207
Watson, James, 189
Weber, Max, 88
Weghorst, Suzanne, 5–6
Welch, Finis, 159
Wente, Margaret, 182
Whitehall Studies, 179–81
Wilkinson, Richard, 180–4
William the Conqueror, 49
Williams, George C., 31, 37
Wilson, Margo, 4–9, 15–7, 24, 26, 37, 49, 51–7, 64, 89, 99, 100, 102–4, 106, 109, 110, 130, 133, 136, 137, 144, 163, 211
Wilt Swanson, Marie, 52, 53
Wolfgang, Marvin, 54, 55, 126–129
Wolof, 200
World Bank, 11, 72, 73, 184, 185
World Health Organization (WHO), 9–12, 20–1, 146
World Values Survey, 175
Wrangham, Richard, 201, 202

Xavante, 205

Yanomamö, 96, 97, 204, 205

Zak, Paul, 115
Zerjal, Tatiana, 93, 94
Zheng, Hui, 151–3

CPSIA information can be obtained
at www.ICGtesting.com
Printed in the USA
BVOW09s0522300617

488184BV00008B/70/P